WELLINGTON
RANKIN

His Family, Life and Times

WELLINGTON RANKIN

His Family, Life and Times

Montana Attorney • Politician
Cattleman • Land Baron

Volney Steele

Bridger Creek Historical Press
an imprint of Champions Publishing

Bozeman, Montana

Cover photo: Montana Historical Society, Helena. Photograph digitally tinted.

Publisher's Cataloging-in-Publication
(Provided by Quality Books, Inc.)

Steele, Volney.
    Wellington Rankin : his family, life and times :
    Montana attorney, politician, cattleman, land baron / by
    Volney Steele. -- 1st ed.
      p. cm.
    Includes bibliographical references and index.
    ISBN 1-888550-10-4

    1. Rankin, Wellington Duncan, 1884-1966. 2. Rankin
family. 3. Montana--Biography. I. Title.

F735.2.R36S74 2002   978.6'032'092
                   QB133-620

Published by   Bridger Creek Historical Press
                An imprint of Champions Publishing
                1627 W. Main #148
                Bozeman, MT 59715
                (406) 585-0237

ISBN: 1-888550-10-4
Printed in Canada

Quantity discounts are available on bulk purchases of this book for educational purposes or fund-raising. For information, please contact the publisher.

FORWARD

To say that Wellington Rankin presents an enigma is to belabor the obvious. Possessing perhaps Montana's most adept political mind–ever–the man failed to be elected time and time again. Awash in property and wealth, he reached his peak as a courtroom attorney who defended the downtrodden. A horseman of real repute, he proved unable or unwilling to sustain a quality ranching operation.

One can argue that Wellington, throughout his life, paid a heavy price for being Jeannette's brother. Indeed, she cast a deep shadow, and it frequently enveloped him. Yet Wellington's relationship with her was one of care, concern, and commitment; further, he held the family purse strings!

The Wellington-Jeannette relationship long has needed solid research and analysis–and Dr. Steele's work offers strong foundation for that process. Vol Steele has survived the exhaustive process of interviewing Wellington's friends, his enemies, and his family. The results reveal some real surprises.

Is there a home-grown Montanan alive who does not have a "Wellington Rankin story"? This volume sorts through the stories, sifts fact from fiction, and launches the unraveling of a persistent enigma. Good work!

Dave Walter
Research Historian
Montana Historical Society
Helena, Montana

Acknowledgements

The completion of this biography has taken many years. Any success that the work achieves is directly proportional to those people who helped me. I want to thank especially the folks who were willing to be interviewed, among them a diminishing number of friends and family and acquaintances of Wellington D. Rankin. Charles Rankin (no relation), the former editor of *Montana, The Magazine of Western History* and other reviewers sanctioned by the Montana Historical Society, led me to avenues of research that I would not have otherwise discovered. Dave Walter, historical researcher for the Montana Historical Society was always willing and happy to discuss my book, and made many good suggestions to further the study. He also helped me by reading and critiquing some of my early efforts. I am especially indebted to Mr. Dennis Williams, Toston area rancher and historian, who encouraged me, and scrutinized for me some of the more complicated land acquisitions. Michael Dougherty and his associates of Champions Publishing made the prolonged and un-exciting, frustrating process of publication almost pleasant. His fathomless energy, patience, and attention to detail was indispensable.

Volney Steele, August 2002

TABLE OF CONTENTS

PREFACE

Igraduated from medical school in 1945 and followed that with several years in the U.S Navy, a general practice in Meeker, Colorado, and some years of post-graduate training in the field of Pathology. I left a satisfactory practice in Little Rock, Arkansas to make the journey to Montana. I was restless. I needed the outdoors–the hunting, the fishing, the horses, and the skiing. Most of all, I needed freedom from a decadent south where racial prejudice flared. The lure of the West was overwhelming.

I drove into Bozeman, Montana shortly after New Year's Day in January 1959. We arrived in a blizzard. My wife and I, our four children, and flotsam sufficient to suggest a shipwreck, were compressed into our five-year-old Plymouth station wagon, which had recently been outfitted with vulcanized "corn cob" snow tires. This was the end of the line and the place where I planned to continue my medical practice

Our exhausting weeklong journey from the South, (much of which included following the tail lights of a snow plow through a large part of Wyoming) ended on Bozeman's Main Street. Here, through the blowing snow and partially obscured car windows, we read the local Chamber of Commerce sign: WELCOME TO BOZEMAN. 14,500 WONDERFUL PEOPLE AND A COUPLE OF OLD SORE-HEADS. Bozeman, a college town in Montana's Gallatin Valley, would be my home to this day, most of a half century. I left a degree of financial security, family, friends, and the safety of sanctuary among professional colleagues to start over, to live and work and practice with people who shared my vision.

Few were new to the country then. I was, and as a newcomer I was fascinated with Montana stories and characters. In the collection of yarns that caught my ear, one man stood out: Wellington Duncan Rankin. A Rankin story, I soon learned, was a topic guaranteed to get a response. Rankin tales were repeated over and over, with frequent embellishments.

Wellington Rankin

Favored with power, wealth, prestige, and an expansive ego, attorney Rankin's life inspired myths. People who didn't know him talked as if they did. At any time in history he would have been an outstanding persona. From bar stools and front rooms throughout Montana, self-appointed experts pontificated about Rankin's law practice, business exploits, wealth, and land holdings. Most of all, they spoke of his neglect of livestock and hiring practices on his ranch fiefdom. Folks said you could drive through Broadwater County and recognize Rankin land by its rundown buildings, gaunt cattle, ambiguous fences, and weed-infested pastures. Whether praising Rankin or vilifying him, all the storytellers agreed that Rankin was the best trial lawyer in Montana, without peer. "If you ever get in trouble, get Rankin," they said. "He'll get you off."

Rankin as a politician had friends in high places. As a powerful Montana Republican, Rankin knew President Teddy Roosevelt personally. He knew and corresponded with President "Ike" Eisenhower. He was a close associate of many of Montana's political leaders, such as Senators Thomas J. Walsh and Burton K. Wheeler.

His authority as an attorney and politician helped forge, mold, and cast our state. He was anti-corporation and represented the working man. A Robin Hood to some, Rankin's law practice frequently defended the poor. He found time to represent helpless women and children. To others he was notorious for allegedly not paying his bills. His caustic personality rankled some. A few enemies labeled him disloyal since he was the brother of Congresswoman Jeannette Rankin, who voted against the United States entering World Wars I and II (one of fifty "no" votes in 1916; the sole negative vote in 1940). Some Montanans saw this genetic connection to his sister as somehow unpatriotic.

After I retired from medical practice in 1986, with spare time and a consuming taste for Montana history, I wanted to write his biography. My goal was to portray him from all sides. I began my research into his interesting and dynamic life by interviewing people who knew him personally—a rapidly diminishing group. I wanted to show both his noble and less noble facets. I explored old newspapers where much of his public career was chronicled. Luckily I uncovered one scratchy taped interview taken with the man himself. In the sources at my disposal, Rankin was reflected in flawed and distant mirrors. What was his true self? What impact did he leave on Montana?

Another historian who attempted to discover the true Rankin said:

> "[The] stories [about Wellington Rankin] may all be false, but, even if they are, they are a significant part of Montana history by the mere fact that they were inspired by an actual historical figure whom people felt compelled to transform into legend. It is important...that the mythical Rankin be distinguished from the historical Rankin and

Preface

that these two characters, the myth and the man, be dealt
with as a whole."[1]

In the 1960s, Montanans were less sophisticated than those who
came later, and few appreciated or understood the abstract. I attended an
art show at the Montana State College Student Union in Bozeman where
paintings and sculpture were proudly displayed. A goodly number of
local citizens attended. Many came to show support for the college.
Others came because Montana's long winter nights offered little to do.
One of the works presented was exceptionally abstruse; a canvas covered with variegated colors and designs. A local rancher looked at the
painting for a long time. He then turned to the painter who stood near
his work and said, "I'd like to ask you a question."

The proud young artist said, "Of course. How can I help you?"

Still looking at the masterpiece, the confused observer asked, "How
do you know when a picture like this is done?"

I ask myself the same question.

INTRODUCTION

"When you had Rankin on your side, you had somebody"

Wellington Duncan Rankin was a native Montanan: a handsome, physically strong man. He was as comfortable in the saddle at roundup as he was in Theodore Roosevelt's fashionable Oyster Bay, New York, drawing room. He stood tall on the Montana landscape for more than a half a century, during an era when Montanans preferred masculine leaders and rugged men who radiated self-confidence. Rankin was endowed with all of these attributes.

He was a power broker in Montana politics from 1912, when he ran unsuccessfully on the Bull Moose ticket for the House of Representatives, until his death in 1966. He shared the political stage with some of the states most illustrious leaders: men such as United States Senators Thomas J. Walsh, Burton K. Wheeler, and James Murray; Congressmen Lee Metcalf and Mike Mansfield; Governors Sam C. Ford and Joseph M. Dixon; as well as his sister Jeannette–the nation's first, and Montana's only, congresswoman.

Rankin amassed millions during his lifetime. He became one of the state's leading, attorneys. As a dynamic trial lawyer, he simply domineered courtrooms, and could hold a jury's attention with theatrics, logic, and bursts of temper. He was a rancher and politician. He made shrewd investments in land, cattle, property, mining interests, and oil. He owned a hotel and an office building in downtown Helena. At one time Rankin controlled a million acres of Montana land and ran more than 25,000 head of cattle.

Despite his pioneer family heritage, and his prominence in the public eye, no biography has been written about him. No in-depth study of his role in Montana history has been conducted, and only a faint paper trail marks his path. Rankin was notorious in his failure to keep personal records. He kept no diary, business journals, or logs. One rancher who knew him well suggested that, in this regard, Rankin was a little smarter

4

Introduction

than Richard Nixon.[1] Verifiable facts about Rankin are hard to come by, and most cannot be proved or disproved by documents.

A researcher must follow Rankin's tracks in much the same way a deer hunter tracks his prey: by looking for a bruised leaf, a cracked branch, or a place where the bark has been scraped from a tree by his massive antlers. A likeness of the man, created some thirty-five years after his death, can be impressionistic at best. It must be fashioned from newspaper clippings, court reports, miscellaneous records, and recollections from the fading memories of those who knew him directly or indirectly. The result resembles an artist's collage, fragments of data pasted on pages. The few people still alive who remember Rankin fall mainly into one of two categories: those who despised him, and those who revered him. The former despoil his memory, while the latter protect him.

Rankin grew up in a prominent, Missoula family during the last decades of the nineteenth century, at the end of the territorial frontier period and the beginning of statehood in 1889, and during the ebbing Victorian era at the turn of the century.

His father, John, was an intelligent, self-made, and hard-working man. He was a successful builder, a businessman and an early entrepreneur, who migrated west in 1869 with scant formal education. John was a strong, forceful influence on his family and especially his son. His death in 1904, while Rankin was in college at Harvard, struck young Rankin hard. He had lost the stable, masculine role model that guided his younger years.

Women surrounded the young Rankin, and he was adored as the only son. In this feminine social ambience, it is fair to assume that young Rankin was spoiled by the adulation of his sisters. The younger ones looked up to him as a father figure, especially after their father's death. This stimulation in his early life undoubtedly strengthened his masculinity.

Wellington's mother and five sisters were exceptional women.[2] His mother, Olive Pickering Rankin, was a school teacher who came west to the Montana Territory to teach. Like most pretty young teachers, she was soon snapped up as a wife. Within a year of her arrival, she had married Missoula's most eligible bachelor—John Rankin. Her teaching career was a challenge and short-lived. Her calling as a homemaker was equally challenging. Her life now intertwined with the handsome John Rankin, Olive accepted the Presbyterian religion as her own when she married into this Scottish family that had long held this religious tradition.

Seven children came in rapid succession. She taught them the Golden Rule and the Ten Commandments. Olive was strong in her beliefs and instilled in her brood a sense of righteousness, responsibility, and independence. The family was not "fundamentalist" in their practice of Christianity. While neither John nor Olive attended church regularly, the children attended Sunday school in the Presbyterian Church faithfully.[3]

Three of the five Rankin daughters–Jeannette, Harriet, and Edna–cast themselves as independent thinkers. All three were women ahead of their time. Each was active in the early twentieth-century women's movement.

Jeannette, the oldest, was a strong advocate for women and children's rights and worked with the underprivileged. She became a forceful national voice for suffrage and peace. She was elected congresswoman from Montana in 1916, the first woman in the country to hold a national office. This honor came from a remote and rural state in a male dominated community.

Harriet served as Dean of Women at Montana State College (Missoula) from 1920-1935. "Hattie," as she was called by friends and family, worked for Jeannette in Washington D. C. in 1918 after the death of her husband, Oscar Sedman. During World War II she joined the Red Cross and lived in London throughout the war. Most Americans in Europe who were not in the service came home. She stayed and survived the dangerous German buzz-bombs.

Edna, the youngest of all, was arguably the most independent of the three. She graduated from law school at Montana State College as the university's first woman graduate admitted to the Montana Bar. She had little interest in the practice of law, and soon after her graduation in 1915, she assisted Jeannette in her first campaign for congress. She married John McKinnon of New York, a marriage that produced two children but did not survive the depression. Later, During the mid-1930s Edna joined a small courageous group of men and women who promoted birth control nationally and internationally. This organization promoted diaphragms and spermicidal jellies from street corners and any other available podium. They were part of a movement that was very unpopular in most places and especially in a conservative Montana. She was subjected to ridicule, even from her brother. Nevertheless, this became her life's work.[4]

Mary and Grace, the other two sisters, were attractive and popular young women who chose well-circumscribed married lives. Grace became Mrs. Thomas Kinney of Pierce, Idaho. Mary married Herbert Bragg and lived in Los Angeles.[5] According to Wellington, Mary was the prettiest of the sisters. At the university, she was "Queen of the May."[6]

Wellington Rankin was raised in a household of independent women whose needs were provided by a loving, hard-working father. Wellington believed that women should be protected, if not placed on a pedestal. He supported most women's causes or at least was less antagonistic towards them than most of his contemporaries during the early decades of the twentieth century. He lovingly offered his moral, financial, and physical support to his sisters They accepted it, and used him to try out their ideas.

Introduction

The Rankin house was a forum for Wellington and his sisters as they debated the philosophies and issues of their day. John and Olive tolerated and even encouraged (oftentimes heated) arguments on topics that may not have been fare heard in other homes. As the six children grew to adulthood, loud and boisterous arguments rattled the china and chandeliers. Discussions often approached the point of near physical violence between the older siblings. But nevertheless, there was a bond of love and affection between them that was stronger than any cause they may have debated.

The Rankin home was always open to their friends for visits and parties. And the Rankin brood was encouraged to invite their friends. The Rankin household was the site of many spontaneous get-togethers and parties.

When his father died, Wellington assumed the responsibility of managing the family assets. It was still a time when women were not expected to take on such burdens. There is some evidence that Jeannette, the oldest child, resented not being given the charge. Nonetheless, her brother managed the affairs so well that there continued to be money available to support his mother during her long life and to educate his sisters in some of America's finest educational institutions.

Rankin graduated from Harvard Law School in 1910 and returned to Montana where he opened a practice in Helena. In time he became an icon of Montana's legal profession. His peers considered him the finest trial lawyer of his time; his contemporaries said that he could simply dominate a courtroom.[7] Some asserted that when you had Rankin on your side in a court of law, "you had somebody." Because of this reputation, Rankin, the lawyer, was in great demand.

The young Wellington Rankin was propelled into the political arena by his success as a young lawyer and influential people who respected him. Associates like Thomas J. Walsh (an attorney who would become a Montana senator), and family acquaintances like Joseph M. Dixon (publisher and attorney who would become a governor of Montana) contributed to this shift toward politics. With these kind of friends and a law degree, it was preordained that Wellington would enter politics.

Two years after returning to Montana, he challenged the state's political hierarchy. He offered himself as the Bull Moose Party's candidate for a seat in the House of Representatives. Rankin was soundly defeated.

This was only the first of many defeats Rankin suffered. He ran for office nine times, losing all but one election. In 1920, he was elected attorney general. Although he could not win elections for himself, his presence in the races made his opponents work harder. His political success was most evident behind the scenes. He was a staunch Republican who received and maintained the respect of leaders of both parties. In 1924, Governor Dixon appointed him to the position of Associate Justice of the Supreme Court of Montana. In 1925, President Calvin Coolidge appointed him U. S. Attorney for Montana. He was re-appointed to this position in 1930 by President Herbert Hoover. Though appointed by Republican leaders, he had to have the support of Democrats such as Thomas Walsh, Burton K. Wheeler, and James Murray as well. For many years Rankin directed the state Republican Party where he managed campaigns, brokered campaign issues, and influenced political appointments.

Rankin's greatest ambition was to be elected to national office. He especially coveted a seat in the United States Senate. This prize remained forever beyond his reach. He ran and lost five times for the Senate. The campaigns for the Senate, in 1942 against the powerful Democrat James Murray and against Lee Metcalf for congressman in 1952, were both narrow losses. Rankin was handily defeated on two occasions for governor. His defeats were seldom predictable, despite having powerful and relentless enemies in the state.

The Anaconda Copper Mining Company, his long time nemesis, controlled most of Montana's newspapers at the time. They viciously attacked Rankin at every opportunity. His prominent sister, Jeannette, had caused the Rankin name to be forever linked with pacifism and feminine rights, unpopular beliefs to many Montana voters. His personality also worked against him. Along his political journey he was sometimes abrasive. A few contemporaries accused him of being arrogant, patronizing, and condescending.

All of this may have affected his campaigns, but there were probably other reasons for his defeats. The time he had available for politics was limited. Rankin was a busy man with a full-time practice of law and numerous court cases throughout the state. Over time, as he accumulated business property, ranches, and cattle, management occupied much of his energy. Most of his opponents were full-time politicians and could devote more time to campaigns.

Wellington Rankin was a proud man and undoubtedly felt frustration and disappointment with his record. Whatever his feelings, they were never revealed to the outside world. He did not dwell on defeat nor wallow in disappointment; rather, he turned his experiences to advantage. He honed and sharpened his political skills. The man who twice propelled his controversial sister, Jeannette, into Congress, learned well the political byways of his state. With a superior knowledge of the workings of Montana, Rankin became chairman of the Montana Republicans in 1939. During the 1940s and 1950s, he was a power not only within the local party, but at the national level as well.

Rankin had a sense of humor and used it to best advantage in court. However, he was sensitive about some things. Rankin's best friend, Judge Lester Loble of Helena, recalled a time when he and Rankin were pallbearers at Senator Thomas J. Walsh's funeral. While carrying the famous man's casket, the judge said to Rankin intending humor, "Hang on tight, Wellington, this may be as close as you ever get to the U.S. Senate." As a politician whose greatest ambition was to be elected to this important national office, Rankin found little humor in the quip.[8]

Rankin continued to pursue the acquisition of land. He drove hard bargains. He was inordinately prosperous, and by the mid-1950s his large ranch holdings were scattered along the banks of the Missouri River: from the foothills of the Crazy and the Bear's Paw mountains; to the flat, windswept, arid lands of the central and eastern part of the state. He was the largest individual landowner in the United States at this time, and he stocked his spacious ranch holdings with thousands of cattle.

Many who criticized Rankin for his business dealings and land management practices knew little about his other sides. Some knew him only as one of the finest trial lawyers Montana ever had. Some knew him as a political power who dominated Montana's Republican Party. Others saw him as a charismatic, sympathetic friend-in-need to the underdog.[9]

Judge Loble said the following at a memorial service for Rankin held on February 21, 1967, before the Montana Supreme Court:

> It is difficult to think of him as dead—he seemed indestructible… Among the lowly and poor, those upon whom society had turned its back, poor and abused, he was at his best… A legend, a never to be forgotten character, one of Montana's great jury lawyers… He knew no fear and it is such men who shape the destinies of nations. He amassed a fortune. In the making of his fortune never for a moment did he abandon his extensive law practice, or refuse to come to the defense of the defenseless.[10]

Gretchen G. Billings, editor of *The People's Voice*, a liberal Montana newspaper, wrote after Wellington's death; "W.D. was a most outrageous man… he was a law unto himself." Further she wrote, "Mr. Rankin would probably have been delighted with this statement… he made no bones about his satisfaction in 'outraging people.'" Billings also said, "his biography must not be written in words like 'mild' or 'subtle.'" In her opinion, Montana history must record his fights for the underdog and his early years as counsel for the defense of injured working men.[11]

The *Great Falls Tribune* described him as "the kind of guy everybody hated until they needed him."[12]

Rankin's net of acquaintances was widespread. Montana's famous actor, Gary Cooper, knew and respected Wellington. His father, Charles Cooper, was a Helena judge and one of Rankin's friends. The actor gave Rankin credit for starting him on a career in Hollywood. Cooper said in an interview after he became successful:

> In retrospect, I realize that I was merely following the best advice I ever got about acting. I heard it, surprisingly enough, not in Hollywood, but from a lawyer friend of my father's in Montana, several years before I ever arrived in Los Angeles. An excellent trial lawyer, his name was Wellington Rankin.... We were sitting around one evening discussing Rudolph Valentino. Those were the days when Valentino was an idol. Mr. Rankin allowed that I should go to Hollywood and get into the movies. He marshaled his arguments like a trial lawyer, "Look at this fellow Valentino. After all what does he do? Look how this fellow puts over an idea. He thinks of it so strongly that it becomes obvious to the audience. When he looks at a girl you know he's thinking of taking the clothes off her.... when he walks up and kisses her, he is halfway beyond that kiss already."[13]

In a letter to Wellington, Cooper said:

> I shall never forget the boxing lessons you used to give me in your office at the most unorthodox hours, and I also hold you partially responsible for my good fortune in Hollywood because you were the first to put the bee in my head about becoming an actor.[14]

A nameless sage said that those who make history have no time to write about it. Rankin hadn't the time nor the inclination to save and develop biographical information. One might suspect that, as an attorney, he may have avoided personal records because they might incriminate. This was not his style. He was not the kind of man who would worry about incriminating himself. He simply cared little for records in and of themselves. For instance, he repeatedly refused to respond to Harvard alumni inquiries when, in the 1930 Harvard anniversary report, most of his classmates wrote elaborate, boring, and self-promoting summaries of their lives. Rankin's entry said, "Nothing has been heard from Rankin since 1910."[15] This characteristic of avoiding record keeping seems to be a family trait. Few of Jeannette Rankin's papers can be found either. Is it possible that many were destroyed?

Wellington Rankin is a more colorful westerner than any fiction writer could invent. The same can be said about his family. The historical facts we know about are the stuff of novelists and Hollywood.

If we are to tell the true story of the West, the focus must be on the frontier family. According to Elliot West in, "Stegner, Storytelling, and

Introduction

Western Identity," writers need to reconstruct western family stories to understand the nature of the characters. He says that Wallace Stegner, the great western storyteller, "...made the family what it ought to be in our stories and what it always has been in western history–a central part of people's lives, a powerful shaping force...and the main emotional arena in which a western identity has developed."[16]

A Rankin family portrait, circa 1896–1898, pictures a handsome and somber assembly. The family is posed around a table with a framed photograph, of deceased second daughter Philena, placed next to an open book, presumably the Bible. Viewing the portrait we are witness to the end of one century and the beginning of another–the passing of the Victorian era. With death as the centerpiece, what brave thoughts and wishes were in the minds of the Rankin family on this occasion as they gathered? It is not our privilege to know this, but by scraping together as much information about the family as possible, we may better understand one short segment of Montana history.

This biography attempts to paint a picture of a western man, a Montanan, from the scant information provided by news items and imperfect memories. More solid information may be stored in some obscure location: an attic, storage room, or some musty museum collection or library. If found, a clearer picture will emerge some day. This is important since Wellington Duncan Rankin had a complex relationship with the events of his time, his place, and in the history of Montana. In the meantime we must be grateful for what we have: an incomplete composite of one of the great figures of Montana's twentieth century.

1
THE RANKINS OF MONTANA

"Once you take them on you have to take on the whole damn bunch"[1]

The parents of Wellington Rankin and his five sisters were pioneers. John Rankin and Olive Pickering came to the Montana Territory from entirely different backgrounds, but with one thing in common, they had the spirit of adventure in their souls.

John Rankin

The Rankin family patriarch, John, was born in Canada at Apin, Ontario in 1841. His parents had emigrated from Scotland forty years earlier. He was the fourth born in a family of twelve. John left home with only three years of primitive education in a school built of logs. He was fourteen, a peppery Scotch Canadian, and penniless. He went south to Shelby, Michigan to work for his oldest brother. There he worked as a carpenter and learned the trade over the next fourteen years. It was a craft that not only supported him in Michigan, but gave him the financial security he needed to travel west. He knew that his building skills would be welcomed anywhere.

John and his younger brother, Duncan, left Michigan for the Montana Territory in 1869.[2] The Civil War was over. Tales of adventure and riches beckoned young ambitious men to this exciting destination. Travel to the west was easier said than done. Any route to the thinly populated Territory of Montana was grueling, dangerous, time consuming, and expensive. An early writer remarked, "Montana has always been far off–in miles, in time, and facilities for getting there… it is almost an outside world."[3]

In 1869, wayfarers could choose from several modes of transportation. Overland travelers, by wagon or horseback, followed old and clearly marked trails established by Indians, explorers, fur traders, and thousands of immigrants heading west. The final destination, the Bozeman Trail, was through Sioux country and very dangerous. Most people contemplating the trip chose between riverboat or railway, the two commercial methods of travel.

The most popular of these was via the Missouri River. Boats of all descriptions had plied this great highway of muddy, unpredictable water since the Lewis and Clark expedition of 1804-06. After these legendary explorers returned to the East, the river was used extensively, first by fur traders and later by hundreds of gold-seekers.

Fort Benton was a former trading post on the banks of the upper Missouri River established in 1850. After 1862 it became a busy transportation and distribution center—truly Montana Territory's inland "seaport." Its location was also handy for overland travelers and freight wagons that came by way of the Fisk Trail, which extended west from Fargo, Dakota, through Fort Union to connect with the Mullen Road. The big gold discoveries in Montana at Bannock and Alder Gulch in 1862 and 1863 had transformed this cluster of houses on the banks of the upper Missouri River into a bustling and vigorous hub of military and business activity.

River traffic expanded rapidly. As technology advanced and steamboats replaced more primitive craft, the Chippewa, in 1860, became the first powered vessel to make it all the way to Fort Benton. Until replaced by railways, river traffic was a profitable business, hauling supplies and people and bringing back pelts of fur and gold. In some cases, the profit from one round trip to Fort Benton exceeded the cost of the boat.

In 1864 there were thirty to forty steamboats chugging up and down the river between Fort Benton and Fort Union at the mouth of the Yellowstone. Cargo arriving at Fort Benton was shipped by freight wagon to destinations in Montana, Idaho, and even Canada. In 1867, 960 people, more than a million dollars worth of gold dust and ore, furs, and other goods were moved to and from Fort Benton by river. In its heyday, the port at Fort Benton employed approximately 2,500 men and 3,000 freight teams with an estimated 20,000 oxen and mules available for use.

By 1869 the railroad route was beginning to replace the waterway and would eventually displace boat traffic entirely. River transportation, however, was cheaper and thought to be more reliable, even though a steamboat cabin from St. Louis to Fort Benton cost three hundred dollars. Captain John Mullen in 1865 quoted the price of passage from St. Louis by steamer to Fort Benton at one hundred to two hundred dollars and from ten to twelve cents per pound for freight.[4] Young strong men like John Rankin and his brother could defray much of the cost by hiring on as laborers on one of the boats.[5]

John Rankin and his brother were hired as crewmen and headed upstream. We do not know where they boarded, but more than likely they found their way from Michigan to St. Louis at the mouth of the Mississippi River, where most riverboats were provisioned for the roughly 3,000 mile trip to Fort Benton. It is possible that they traveled overland to St. Louis, or they could have joined steamboat passengers at Clinton, Indiana and followed the Wabash River to Terre Haute, and from there by railroad to St. Louis.⁶ We do not know the name or type of boat they boarded or who the other passengers were. Both Wellington and Jeannette Rankin, when interviewed many years later, said that it was a Missouri River "flatboat."⁷ It was most likely a steamboat. Whatever kind of boat they boarded, it was undoubtedly loaded to the gunnels with cargo and passengers with their belongings. If it was powered by steam, John and Duncan may have paid their way by sawing wood from trees along the bank; it required many cords of wood a day to fire the boilers and keep a riverboat's paddle wheels turning.⁸

Nursing a boat of any kind upstream was exhausting work. If John's trip was like other recorded experiences, sometimes the water rushed swiftly along and other times it was sluggish and indolent. Frequently, brute human force was required to keep the boat moving upstream. There was a lot of danger to a vessel, its passengers, and crew from lightning, prairie winds, snags and sweeps, Indian attacks, and disease, especially from drinking the filthy Missouri River water.⁹

Thus, the two voyagers saved money for future investments by paying the price of passage in time, sweat, and labor. Theirs was a particularly slow trip. For two and a half months of grueling work in the spring of 1869, they poled and pulled, and perhaps winched from a "dead man" on shore, against the temperamental current.¹⁰ Finally, their boat ground to a halt on Cow Island, many miles from the docks at Fort Benton. Low water often stranded vessels here. Carrying their carpenter's tools and meager gear, the two Canadians joined other crew and passengers and walked the forty-mile path to Fort Benton, the end of their river journey. As the two brothers and their companions walked to Fort Benton they were no doubt aware of danger from Indian attack.

While on the river, passengers and crew kept up with current events up and downstream as they exchanged greetings with other boats they passed. For some time the relationship between white people and the Native American tribes in the area around Fort Benton was strained. The so-called "Indian Removal" to reservations was in full swing in Montana. White people were suspicious and afraid of Indians and the Indians distrusted the white man's motives. Both societies were justified in their apprehensions.

During 1869-1870, the region around Fort Benton, the hub of the Territory's commercial activity, was under siege. In the early summer, a group of Crows attacked a small wagon train and killed two white men just a few miles from the fort. This naturally alarmed the surrounding white community. Hysterical citizens in downtown Fort Benton, seeking revenge, shot and killed two innocent Indians-a young Blood and a young Piegan. It so happened that the Piegan was the brother of an important Indian leader, Mountain Chief. The Piegans of course were infuriated. The Blackfeet, Blood, and River Crow joined the enraged tribe on the warpath. Bands of as many as twenty angry Indians carried on a ferocious crusade to seek vengeance. During the period of January through October 1869, fifty-six white people were killed and at least one thousand horses stolen.[11]

John and his brother walked into this milieu apparently without fear. Like many other newcomers, they only had a vague sense of life in this frontier territory.

What the Rankins knew about the region when they purchased a team of oxen in Fort Benton and started their drive south is unclear. John probably did not pull an empty wagon. No doubt, he paid for this part of the trip by hauling supplies from the boat docks to the miners at Helena. He planned that his skill as a carpenter would be needed to rebuild Helena after the devastating fire of February 1869 gutted part of the town. However, he arrived too late. By the time he and his brother entered the gold camp, most of the reconstruction of fire damage was completed.

Fires often plagued the growing city known better at the time by its mining camp moniker, the "Last Chance Gulch." Since this was the first of six fires over a five-year period in the crowded and close-packed community of Helena, John might well have waited to keep his skill with hammer and saw productive. But he and his brother were restless and anxious to make a fortune, and they moved on to other ventures.

In Helena, John and Duncan were known as "the Canada Boys." The two young men built a stamp mill at Unionville, four miles up Last Chance Gulch. This was no small undertaking and suggests that the brothers had money saved from their years of labor in Michigan. It also implies that they had the engineering ability required to build and operate a business of this kind. During most of 1869, they crushed ore others dug.

This partnership and the enterprise didn't last and the two brothers parted company. In later years Wellington Rankin recalled that his father was "a young man interested in getting ahead."[12] This implied that, Duncan, was less ambitious than his older brother. Wellington later hinted at the division between them, saying, "Uncle Duncan was a kind of noisy fellow and a big fellow that talked too much…bigger than my father, he [John] was always watching him [Duncan] for fear he was going to get into some trouble or something because he talked too damn much… I never liked him."[13]

John turned away in search of his own venue. Crushing rock was a monotonous way to make a living and sibling strains probably developed that led to the separation. John never discussed this enterprise with his children. The "Canada boys" had traveled together a long way. Their journey together was over and another phase of John's life was beginning.

Wellington Rankin

The entrepreneurial spirit of the time, and the belief in the white man's manifest destiny, drove John Rankin as it did most of the western emigrants of his day. He and others like him were driven by the knowledge that the riches in land and minerals of the West were for the taking. It was the place to be.

It is doubtful that John gave much thought to the plight of the Native Americans and their claim to the land. Immigrants like John were preoccupied with their pursuits and had little time to contemplate the plight of the Indians. At this time in Montana history few people saw the Indians as more than an impediment to "progress." The Indian "problem" was being "resolved," and there were great things happening. A man with the "right stuff" might find prosperity.

Although present day historians mark the end of Montana's "Gold Rush" at 1870, a large percentage of the population was still involved in the acquisition and processing of the precious metal. Paula Petrik, in *No Step Backward*, tells us that in 1870, thirty-seven per cent of Helena's population was still actively involved in gold mining.[14] There was still opportunity for someone with ambition to make a fortune in gold.

The West was the place to be if one had the entrepreneurial spirit, and John Rankin would prove that he had "it." Americans were moving westward and John wanted to be there to meet them. The Northern Pacific Railroad line was being lured into the Territory by a right-of-way and the promise of millions of acres of Montana's finest timberlands along with unknown quantities of natural resources.[15] Most people on the Montana frontier watched these developments knowing that their financial destiny depended on the railroad. This link to the "outside" promised countless blessings.

The young carpenter left Helena and traveled 165 miles across the continental divide in the fall of 1870 to the Cedar Creek Mining Camp near the town of Superior. He most likely crossed the divide at the Mullen Pass west of Helena, and then followed the Clark Fork and Little Blackfoot rivers. John Mullen established a trail here in 1860. The young Rankin planned to stake his claim at Cedar Creek and prospect for gold.

John had a knack for being in the right place at the right time. The "color" at Cedar Creek was discovered in 1869, about the time John arrived at Fort Benton. To illustrate how quickly news of gold strikes spread, this settlement of a few people had already boomed in population to 1,486 within a year of the strike. This was a rich find and eventually produced a million dollars worth of gold. About 3,000 men toiled here for several years until the gold dust was exhausted. Undoubtedly John earned his share-money that he would use to stake future projects.

Although boom and bust towns like Cedar Creek had gold, they lacked other goods. In *Patterns of Montana Towns*, John Alwin describes early mining villages as, "…ganglia for the evolving frontier regions."16 Missoula and the surrounding Bitterroot valley was just such an emerging nerve center, providing the goods and services that nearby mining camps needed to survive. A place that needed men like John. When the metal at Cedar Creek waned, John put his roots down in Missoula, an established and growing community.

Missoula had changed dramatically by 1869 when John Rankin arrived. It was a small place with fewer than three thousand residents. This represented about fifteen percent of the 20,000 population of the Territory.[17] There were about fifty buildings in the town that included a flourmill, two stores, two large hotels, two blacksmith shops, two livery stables, a billiard room, a sawmill, a post office and several saloons. The place was growing and John saw opportunity for a builder.

This was the "wild" west after all. When storekeeper Christopher P. Higgins began the settlement in 1858 at Hell Gate Ronde, east of present day Missoula, he opened his store with $4166.01 worth of clothes, soap, candles, hardware, tools, and other goods. He sold overcoats for $45, and whiskey for $8 per gallon to the fifty-four residents of the place. Within two years, fourteen of the fifty-four residents died, and none of natural causes. When one of the citizens, Big Nick, shot his friend Overlander over an Indian woman, the Coroner's verdict was, "Damned good shootin.'"[18]

Rankin visualized the Bitterroot Valley to the south as providing space for the growth of the fledgling city. It was a large open space circled by mountains and forests. There was abundant water and rich and fertile soil, and all at a relatively low altitude. The valley was well situated for farming at a time when the territory desperately needed locally grown produce. Its reputation as a productive valley with water for the irrigation of fruit trees and fine grain crops spread. H. G. Merriam in *The Golden Valley* provides us a poetic description of the Bitterroot Valley with a geological twist, "A great Bowl, basin of a prehistoric lake, drained and carved by a Monstrous, overpowering mass of Glacial ice from the North, With Space..."[19]

John Rankin's carpenter tools and his engineering expertise were immediately employed. By the year 1872, at thirty-two years of age and just two years after arriving in Missoula, he was one of the community's most successful men.

He had constructed several buildings in Missoula from sawed lumber, among them a protestant church that served as a place of worship for Missoula's Presbyterians, Episcopalians, and Methodists.[20]

One of his projects was of great importance to the economy and good will of the Missoula community. At the time, there was no ford across the Clark Fork River which bordered the town and restricted development. A seasonal ferry had functioned intermittently since 1863. The river was treacherous during the winter freeze and impossible to cross during the spring run off. A bridge over the Clark's Fork was imperative and Rankin responded to the challenge.

The first bridge built over the river in 1869 by William Stevens washed away in 1871. Another builder started the bridge at Higgins Street but relinquished his contract to Rankin.[21] In 1873, Rankin finished the project.[22] A few years later he constructed a 250-foot-span bridge over the Clark Fork five miles south of town named the Blockhouse Bridge. These bridges were a testament to Rankin's engineering competence.[23]

As John Rankin's construction business prospered, he began investing in property. The Rankin family ranch, where the family spent much of its time, was a 1,480-acre spread bordered by forests and hills some six miles north of the town. The rich fields were irrigated by water from Grant Creek, which meandered through the property. At that time only a few families lived in the area, but during the last decades of the nineteenth century the population grew and the resulting community thrived.

The creek, ranch, and its surrounding environ were later named after Captain Richard Grant, one of the engineers of the Mullan Road, and the ranch's first owner.[24] The ranch was a place of historical significance. Lewis and Clark recorded a rest camp near here in their journals on July 3, 1806. Indians camped and traded here. Early Mormons also used the place to trade with the Indians before the area was settled.

When John purchased the Grant Creek ranch, he acquired a water-powered sawmill that was already on the property.[25] The town of Missoula was growing and his lumber business flourished. The mill supplied most of the lumber used in building the U.S. Army's base at Fort Missoula in 1877.

In the summer of 1877, fear and panic swept Missoula. After a series of confrontations with white settlers and the military in Idaho, the Nez Perce decided to flee their reservation located on Idaho's Clearwater River, and travel down Lolo Creek into Montana's Bitterroot Valley in a desperate attempt to reach Canada. This was the beginning of "the war few wanted and everybody lost."[26]

White settlers and local Indian people in the Bitterroot had lived together for years without conflict. The local Flatheads were peaceful, and the Nez Perce who had traversed the area for more than forty years to hunt buffalo were not belligerent. But a year earlier, Lt. Colonel George Armstrong Custer and the Seventh Regiment of cavalry had been killed at the Little Big Horn by the combined forces of the Sioux, Cheyenne, and other belligerent tribes. White people throughout the Territory were afraid. Therefore, with the Nez Perce on the "warpath" and headed over the Lolo Trail toward Missoula, there was alarm.

Territorial Governor B. F. Potts asked for civilian volunteers to support Captain Charles C. Rawn's limited forces stationed at the still unfinished Fort Missoula.[27] John Rankin was among the two hundred civilians who responded to the Governor's call. He joined Volunteer Company #6 and served for about two weeks under Captain Rawn.

The regular soldiers and the volunteers erected breastworks and entrenched themselves in order to halt the flight of the hostile Indians. The soldiers chose the narrowest point of the trail along Lolo Creek, twelve miles from Missoula, to stand their ground. Here the soldiers and volunteers huddled in anticipation of a bloody confrontation. Their purpose as Captain Rawn said, was "to compel the Indians to surrender their arms and ammunition, and to dispute their passage by force of arms."[28]

Things turned out a little differently than expected. On July 28, 1877, Chiefs Joseph, Looking Glass and White Bird, exhibited superior military logic. They guided their large entourage–women, children, warriors, horses, and camp paraphernalia–silently at night along a narrow game trail around the impenetrable pass and breastworks.

A potentially bloody battle was avoided. The episode was later labeled "Fort Fizzle," humiliating both the soldiers and the civilians who participated.[29] The *Helena Independent*, not known to harbor a great deal of sympathy for the Native Americans, said later, "… it was the boldest, most fearless, audacious and confident tactical movement we have known…"[30]

John, according to his family, was particularly embarrassed by his part in the fiasco of "Fort Fizzle." The fact of John Rankin's involvement was more important than the result; it characterized him, to his children, as a true pioneer.[31]

By 1878 John Rankin was a wealthy man by local standards. In this same year, John Rankin was elected county commissioner as a Republican.[32] This was the extent of his political career. John didn't like politics and he was probably relieved to end his term.

Joseph M. Dixon was the Bitterroot county attorney at the time. He would later own the local newspaper, The *Missoulian*, serve as U.S. Senator from Montana, and also as governor of the state. During Dixon's term as county attorney, John Rankin and the other commissioners were upset at Dixon's frequent absences from his office. Rankin threatened to employ a new statute to force Dixon from the position. An irate Dixon told Rankin that, "he [Rankin] did not know any more law than a jaybird." Later the commissioners said that they had only meant to give Dixon a "good scare."[33] In later years, when Wellington became attorney general of Montana in Dixon's administration, the two men battled throughout their terms.[34]

In 1891, John erected a three story brick building on Front Street. This eighty-six by ninety foot structure he called the Rankin Block. Within this building, there was space for stores and a sixty-five room hotel that he would manage himself.[35]

All this was accomplished by a man who had only three years of formal education, and one that was very elementary by any standard of the times. Though his education was limited, John knew and appreciated the value of learning. He was intelligent and he thirsted for knowledge. Accordingly, he studied calculus and other subjects at night to aid him in his engineering and construction work. Education became almost a fetish with him and later, as we will see, he made certain that all of his children appreciated the importance of scholarship. He helped to locate the state university at Missoula in 1896 and subsequently his children became graduates of the university.[36]

His military stint aside, John Rankin was known as an aggressive individual though he had did not believe in settling disputes with guns. According to his children, he was a tolerant, understanding, and humanitarian person. Jeannette Rankin, in an interview many years later, claimed that he "abhorred mistreating the Indians."[37]

John wasn't a complete pacifist however. He was known to use his fists to settle more than one argument. Wellington states during an interview, "I think my aggressiveness comes from my father... he would fight at the drop of a hat. He was a powerful man. You couldn't argue long... A man of big hands and he would start swinging. I have seen him fight, and [he] enjoyed fighting."[38]

John Rankin was unscathed during his time in the military, but a civilian accident almost took his life. During the construction of a stone building in Missoula, he met with an unusual accident that could have been fatal. During a nearby political meeting, participants decided to fire an old cannon. One can only imagine that the cannon wasn't the only thing that was "loaded." Whiskey was almost certainly involved. The men crammed the gun with powder and used a gunny sack as a wad. Rankin had just come around the corner of his building when the gun was fired. The load struck him in the head. He was unconscious for ten days and afterward never completely regained his hearing nor the vision in his right eye.[39]

Obviously frontier communities were dangerous places, but this was a time of change. The frontier created its own society and the mix of people varied widely from place to place. Montana mining camps like Helena, formed with impermanence in mind, were populated by a far different kind of people than those who came to an agricultural town like Missoula. Farm towns attracted families and the family brought a sense of stability. Permanence brought churches and schools. In 1870 when John Rankin came into the valley, some of this feeling of constancy already existed. The sense of security on the west side of the continental divide and especially the Bitterroot Valley was due in large part to the early settlement by the Jesuits. The presence of the church and women "civilized" the area.[40]

Olive Rankin

Olive Pickering who became Mrs. John Rankin, was reported to be

John Rankin's House in Missoula immediately after construction was finished in 1883. Photo: Montana Historical Society, Helena.

the second school "marm " to teach in Missoula.[41] She was born in New Hampshire in 1854. Olive was an educated well-bred easterner who was disillusioned with the prospects offered to women in the 1870s in New England. Her old line New England family dated back to a land grant by the King of England in 1692. Olive left the safety and comfort of her New Hampshire home and farm to become a schoolteacher in the west. She arrived in Missoula nine years after John.[42]

Young Olive Pickering was teaching school in New Hampshire in 1878, when her uncle, William Berry, on an infrequent visit east, kindled her desire to go to Montana. Her interest grew when she learned that a schoolteacher was needed in Missoula.[43] Uncle Bill, a veteran of the California gold rush in 1849 and the Montana gold rush in the 1860s, and now Missoula's elected sheriff, had a lot of stories to tell. These tales captured the young woman's imagination.[44] Olive became so enamored with the West and the idea of starting a new life that she begged her parents' permission to go.

Her mother and father relented, but with the condition that Olive's older sister, Mandana, accompany her. At first Mandana refused. After much begging and many tears she relented. Moreover, since Uncle Bill was visiting in New Hampshire at the time, he would travel with the girls as well.[45]

Olive's determination to head west demonstrated a great deal of boldness. Few women were so adventurous. She left her family, friends, teaching position, and the comforts of the Eastern Seaboard to find a new life. One can only speculate about the extensive preparations of a wardrobe, and packing, and the last-minute family warnings and lectures endured before the day of departure. Other young women have left accounts of this painful, sad and solemn time. Tragically, the separation was often permanent.[46]

In 1878, travelers going from the east coast to Montana took the Union Pacific as far as Corinne, Utah, in relative luxury. The rest of the trip north to Missoula by way of Virginia City and Helena was by stagecoach. Early roads were rutted and rough, and little more than trails. On the route north through Virginia City and Butte there were dangerous mountain passes. Travel was subject to weather and could be extremely uncomfortable.

Many travelers of that period describe harrowing experiences. Granville Stuart, an early cattleman and hardy Montana westerner, tells of a trip through Idaho loaded with passengers into a freight wagon. "With four little rats of mules to draw it... they 'stalled' in every low place..." Also his connecting stagecoach to Red Rock (near Dillon), Montana descended with its wheels "double roughlocked." Stuart wrote, "The narrow road would round sides of precipices, where trees grew hundreds of feet below us..."

Riding in the rough carriage day after day was bad enough, but the overnight accommodations could be primitive. Early travelers along the route to Virginia City complained a great deal about some of the overnight stations, especially one known by the descriptive term, "Dirty Woman's Ranch."[47]

Regardless of the discomfort, Olive viewed the trip as high adventure. Her sister Mandana saw it differently. On one steep hill, Olive recalled, the stage driver tied a log to the back of their wagon to act as a brake. The rig skidded its way down the steep grade, and Olive said later, "I laughed, and Mannie [Mandana] prayed."[48] During parts of the journey the women were urged to keep out of sight and stay quiet as they passed through Indian territory.

During their seven-day stage trip, one night was spent in the boisterous, rowdy, "wide open" mining camp of Butte. Her more conservative older sister kept the adventurous Olive confined and protected in the stage office. She was not allowed to see the sights, much to her regret.[49]

The trip on to Missoula was uneventful. Mandana within a few months returned to her home in New Hampshire and her fiancé. Olive would not see New England again for 35 years.[50]

Montana was still a frontier with living pioneer characters. This was demonstrated daily to Olive during the early part of her life in Missoula. She discovered that her Uncle Bill wasn't the only storyteller in the town. During her short teaching career, she boarded with a pioneer family, the Dickinsons. Mr. W.H.H. Dickinson was a storekeeper and his wife was the former schoolteacher, Emma Slack. Young Olive was surprised and somewhat taken aback to see that he wore what he said was an Indian

The John and Olive Rankin family. Left to right front row: John, Mary, Edna, Grace, and Olive. Left to right back row: Jeannette, Harriett, Phila (in photograph), and Wellington. Photo: Montana Historical Society, Helena.

scalp on his belt. She also noted that he had a strange bald spot on his head, and was told that this was the result of an attempted scalping.[51]

At this time in history, women had limited outlets. Teaching gave them status wherever they went. Most women who entered the profession found many frustrations with the life, but it offered the best career for a single woman. Young women, therefore, were willing to work for less. The short terms and rapid turnover did not discourage them from applying for jobs. Teachers' credentials were variable and, quite often, young women who entered the profession had hardly mastered the subjects they were called upon to teach.

Olive was under no illusions as to her own qualifications. She told her children that, "I was young and good looking and dressed well, and the school board probably knew that I needed a job, so they always gave me one."[52] When Olive was asked if she could teach algebra, she said she thought she could teach "as much as is needed."[53] She knew little algebra, but planned to learn and stay ahead of the class.

Teachers came west with different motivations. Some were crusaders who felt an obligation to carry education and culture west in an attempt to civilize the rowdy. A few looked upon themselves as missionaries. Others had no such ulterior motives and came west to find a husband. As one young woman confided to a friend, "I cannot say that teaching is perfectly congenial to my taste…. I think there is nothing so nice as housekeeping…. [I] think teaching is second best."[54]

Western communities, even more stable ones like Missoula, had an abundance of bachelors. Once they had acquired enough wealth to feel permanent, many sought a wife. In 1868, the white population in Missoula County was 2,544. Two thousand forty six of these were male.[55] Eligible women were scarce. Lonely men like John Rankin sized up every new woman that came into the community. Olive came to teach children, but like many other attractive young women who came west, her teaching career was cut short by marriage. John had found his bride.

Once the red-bearded John Rankin entered her life the result was inevitable, and the school board probably began looking for another teacher. While John was "sparking" Olive, he often drove by the schoolhouse in his buggy with a fine span of horses. She couldn't ignore this handsome man with the long, curly, brown hair and a red beard. His daily visits to the schoolhouse delighted her pupils, and undoubtedly her as well. The courtship would have blossomed into marriage quickly had Olive not insisted on completing her one-year teaching contract.

The young twenty-year-old schoolteacher married the thirty-nine-year-old Rankin in August 1879. The marriage ended Olive's teaching career. It appears that she was pleased with her success in finding such a fine partner for life–a self-made, hard working, and successful man. Both John and Olive were in the right place at the right time.

As was typical of the time, Olive gave birth in rapid succession to seven children. The first four (Jeannette, Philena, Harriet, and Wellington, the only boy) were born during John and Olive's first four years of marriage when they lived on their Grant Creek ranch. The other three (Grace, Mary, and Edna) were born after the Rankins moved into the house in Missoula. Jeannette was born June 11, 1880 and was destined to become one of the most famous women of her century. Wellington made his appearance on September 16, 1884, the same year that Helena, the city where he spent most of his adult life, became the capital of the Montana Territory. It was also the year that the last of the free roaming buffalo were killed in Eastern Montana.

Born on the ranch, the first four Rankin children spent their early years learning chores. Like all other frontier ranch kids involved with livestock and gardening, they developed skills necessary for frontier survival. So many families moved into Grant Creek that a school was built and the Rankin children began their education during the summers.

In 1884, Rankin constructed a large home for Mr. Fred Kennett. The next year he constructed his own house. It was said that these were among the first "good" residences built in the town of Missoula.[56] The family house was located in town on 134 Madison Street. Shaped like a Maltese Cross, the three-story brick house had the first hot and cold running water in Missoula. It also had a large, zinc bathtub, a forced-air furnace, and a kitchen bin that could hold two hundred pounds of flour for Olive's bread making. A Burmese-style cupola with a glass walk-around adorned the roof. The house was meant to be a home, but it was

Wellington Rankin, "The Boy," at age five or six. Photo: Montana Historical Society, Helena.

also a symbol of the family's prosperity.

Guests came and went amid much family activity. A piano and most family time were centered in a large hall where Olive spent her days. The kitchen and the dining room were also places where the family met. These locations came alive as "a stage for lively family discussions about politics, religion, and controversial subjects...which often led to family quarrels."[57]

Olive Rankin abdicated much of her family responsibility during the later years of her life, and passed the maternal responsibilities to Jeannette. She was described as, "A large woman of regal bearing, dressed for company in purple velvet…she was treated like royalty…She sat in her chair and let others take care of her."[58] At times she seemed spiritless and one close family friend subsequently suggested that she may have had a thyroid deficiency. There is an implication in Jeannette's interviews and Edna's statements that their mother's lack of drive disappointed them. This was not Wellington's feeling. He attributed most of his good qualities to his mother, of whom he was extremely fond.

Olive lived nearly ninety-three years and died in 1947.[59] She was, Wellington said, "a very positive woman in her convictions and her judgments." He told an interviewer, "I think I get my better judgment from my mother."[60]

Wellington went on to say, "People always had to come to her, but she was very much loved …[she] had more friends than the girls had. Almost never went to a party [but was] not shy on her ideas. …strong convictions, but not at all the type like Jeannette. She was slow to move, was cool and calm."[61]

Wellington, "The Boy," was his mother's favorite and was often protected by her when he crossed his older sisters. Like adolescent boys, he was mischievous. According to one story, his pranks disrupted his sister Jeannette's eighteenth birthday. John had constructed a dance floor with elaborate decorations in the yard for the celebration. Lanterns were hung, and music played. Many friends came, some from long distances. During this genteel party, Wellington and some impish friends greased a pig and turned it free among the dancing guests. While this riotous activity disturbed the peace, the boys unhitched the guests' horses from their buggies and surreys and switched them around. Since many of the animals and buggies were rented from livery stables in Missoula, this led to more confusion. Jeannette was furious. And it was only due to her mother's intervention that Wellington kept his scalp.[62]

Wellington Rankin's relationship with his sisters is important to the overall story of his life. His desire for power and control began when he assumed the role as the head of the household upon his father's death. All the Rankin women were independent thinkers even though they depended on their brother for guidance and financial support. To some degree this independence proved a political liability to him in later years.

Jeannette Rankin

There was little in Jeannette's youthful temperament to suggest that Olive and John Rankin's first born would be sent to the United States Congress in 1916 and again in 1940. She was an indifferent student. One teacher said, "Few courses seemed to fire her imagination or exercise the muscles of her mind."[63] She became bored with school but continued because the family expected her to. She may have seen college as a way out. During her senior year in 1902 at the university in Missoula, she

Jeannette Rankin. Photo: Montana Historical Society, Helena.

wrote in her diary, "Go! Go! Go! It makes no difference where, just so you go! Go! Go!"[64]

She was the first woman in the country elected to a national office, and she was picked for this position in a state with a strong male dominated culture. She must have received many votes from miners, farmers, and cowboys. Most women voted for her as they exercised their first democratic opportunity in Montana's polls. This was an opportunity that was in large part the result of Jeannette Rankin's leadership in the state's campaign for a woman's right to vote. Jeannette said many times, "The first time I voted, I voted for myself."

During her youth, she doctored animals on the ranch and could run her father's sawmill. For much of her early life Jeannette was called upon to direct the Rankin household. Her mother willingly relinquished her position to Jeannette even before John died. Jeannette took care of her younger sisters. She nursed her father when he became fatally ill with Rocky Mountain Spotted Fever. All this she did in addition to her pursuit of an education, virtues that were seldom seen in young women of the time.

Jeannette's sisters recalled her dictatorial manner as a foster parent. She controlled their lives, sewed their clothes, and on one occasion arranged for a doctor to come to the Rankin home to take out their tonsils. She gave her younger sisters no warning. Edna, the youngest, said later in an interview, "She [Jeannette] just told me I was going to have my tonsils out and I had nothing to say about it at all."[65]

Throughout their early life, Wellington and Jeannette had a normal sibling relationship but they debated issues that regularly resulted in anger. This intellectual rivalry did not push them apart, rather, it honed their skills in debate and bound them closer together in an attachment that held throughout their lives. Wellington later said in reference to Jeannette:

> ...as a little kid ...[Jeannette] led the fight, fought with the kids and anybody else to fight for our side. She always had a certain amount of leadership. A lot of feeling about things. She had an imagination. I remember that as a little girl she would sit reading Bible stories ...the tears streaming down her cheeks.[66]

Immediately following her graduation from the university, Jeannette was in limbo. Few occupations were open to young women during this time. Marriage, teaching school, or becoming an "old maid" were the main choices. She chose teaching and for a short time taught at Grant School (the country school she herself attended near her father's ranch north of Missoula). She also taught at Whitehall, Montana for a short time.

Jeannette received plenty of proposals from local swains, but none were accepted. She had a core of privacy and wanted to control her own destiny. Some have suggested that she never found a man that equaled her brother Wellington. Even though he was four years younger than her, he was a "man's man" and had already demonstrated admirable signs of strength and leadership. She was not sexless. One of her colleagues who knew her well commented on her "passionate nature," and said that even in her fifties there was a sense of "banked fires."[67]

Jeannette and her brother Wellington, both with strong personalities, developed an interesting relationship through the years. There was conflict but it was productive for them both. One of Jeannette's biographers said, "This epic rivalry persisted beneath an exterior of love and companionship. She was the philosopher—he the realist. He was a master in the strategy of law, real estate, and money—she was the master of ideas and people. Wellington could be staid and severe in public and frequently embarrassed Jeannette with cold humor and observations about her morals. He thought she talked too much and made promises she couldn't keep. He was critical of her lifestyle. This peculiar conflict between brother and sister had a profound influence on Jeannette's life."[68]

In 1904, after her father's death, and during a visit to her seriously ill brother at Harvard, Jeannette saw the tenements of Boston and got a firsthand look at what she described as "squalor and deprivation."[69] This experience was one of the major turning points of her career. Now she had her "cause." With this as an incentive, she enrolled at the University of Washington in Seattle to study social work. She now had a purpose that she viewed as worthy of her intelligence and energy. Her mission was not a simple one. She needed money, experience, power, and a place to work in order to bring about any meaningful reform.

At this time, the "settlement house" was private charity's answer to the problems confronting millions of immigrants in the overcrowded slums of New York, Chicago, and San Francisco. These were places where the foreign born could learn English, were taught the customs of the country, were helped to find places to live, were assisted in looking for work, and were offered some health care. However, the cause that most motivated Jeannette was the health and welfare of children. Throughout her long career of service to the underprivileged, the rights of children predominated.

Her experience assisting the less fortunate began in 1907 when she worked in a settlement house in San Francisco. Not only did she see first hand the atrocious conditions under which many people had to live, but also she was amazed and enlightened at the dedication of those who worked with the poor. It was here that her ambition to make a contribution in this largely unknown and unappreciated field of social welfare was molded.

At the age of twenty-eight she enrolled in the New York School of Philanthropy. While there, Jeannette was influenced by such outstanding liberals as attorney Louis D. Brandeis, later associate justice of the Supreme Court, Booker T. Washington, the ex-slave, educator, and proponent of Negroes' rights.[70]

Her life focus was now established. Jeannette readily saw that social reforms would be slow to come unless women were given the opportunity to vote. She said later, "I saw, that if we were to have decent laws for children, sanitary jails, and safe food supplies, women would have to vote."[71]

While doing settlement-house work in San Francisco, Washington State, and New York City, Jeannette absorbed much of the developing political Progressive platform. She was not alone. Evolution from the status quo was sweeping the country. Workers were demanding better hours and wages with some success, Congress passed a pure food and drug act, and some states ordered compulsory vaccination.[72] Progressive ideals included one that the three eldest Rankin sisters and their brother would strive for: woman suffrage. Many years later, in an interview given at the age of ninety-two, Jeannette said about that period of her life:

> "I began to read why the men didn't want the women to vote, the horrible things they said about women. I was telling Wellington about it, who was at Harvard, about this woman suffrage, and one day he said, 'Well, why don't you do something, that's more important than what you're doing.'"[73]

With support from Wellington, the most influential man in her life, Jeannette was soon a major player in the state of Washington's successful bid for a woman's right to vote. It was here that she began to appreciate the partisan value of grassroots support in public issues. She retained this appreciation throughout her burgeoning political career. Through the efforts of Jeannette and of all of those who vigorously sought suffrage in Washington State, the issue passed by popular vote in 1910.

She had arrived in the State of Washington a year earlier to work with the Children's Home Societies of Spokane and Seattle. She found this effort frustrating. Answering a newspaper ad for help with the Suffragists' movement, Jeannette joined the Washington suffragists as a volunteer without pay. It was in this position that she honed her skills as a campaigner for causes.

Moving from town to town, holding meetings and speaking wherever she was able, her enthusiasm was contagious and her methods effective in gaining support for the cause. In the final analysis, the successful crusade of the Washington suffragists broke the deadlock against women's emancipation in the country as a whole, and set an example for other states to follow.

Jeannette Rankin's work in that great contest did not go unnoticed. She was soon hired to work in New York organizing suffrage clubs and speaking on street corners or anywhere else people would listen. Always in her presentations, whether formal or informal, standing on a crate in the poorer section of a city or at the podium of a lecture hall, Jeannette invariably made the following point: that her efforts were not just for her, but for the six million women and their children who deserved a better life. She fervently believed that enfranchised women could accomplish this end. After her work in New York, she crusaded for the same goals in Ohio, Massachusetts, and Florida.

Moving from place to place and seldom sleeping in the same bed two nights in a row was a difficult life. The work was demanding and frustrating, and unfortunately, often discouraging. Jeannette stayed with the national suffrage movement for five years. During this period she made at least a dozen trips across the continent by train, drove great distances by car on rough roads, planned and marched in parades, and lobbied and addressed legislatures in several states. For all of this effort she was paid very little and had to scrape to subsist. Even though she was an experienced crusader, she had few successes and many failures. Nonetheless, she gained a great deal of knowledge about the needs of her country, and the name of Jeannette Rankin became permanently engraved on the minds of the American people as a leading suffragette of the time.[74]

Suffrage had seen some success in the western part of the country, but the national movement to allow women the vote was still considered radical. Some saw it as extremism. Even President Grover Cleveland reflected the predominant masculine position when he said, "Sensible and responsible women do not want to vote. The relative positions to be assumed by men and women in the working out of our civilization were assigned long ago by a higher intelligence than ours."[75]

There was a well-financed and powerful National Anti-Suffrage Association that preached that if suffrage passed, women and children would be forced into the streets to be "political" to the detriment of American home life. The enemies of suffrage used religious and moral arguments to get public support.

In fact, much of the opposition and financial muscle toward suffrage came from liquor wholesalers and bar owners. They feared, and rightfully so, that the Women's Christian Temperance Union, an organization that supported women's right to vote, might curtail their business and push through a prohibition measure. In Montana, the Anaconda Copper Mining Company also challenged the enfranchisement of women because of the industrial reforms they expected women would support. Again, they were right in their assessment.[76]

Many people criticized suffragists for attempting to disrupt the sanctity of the home. Replying to charges that a woman's place is in the home, Jeannette repeatedly said, "It is beautiful and right that a mother should nurse her child through typhoid fever, but it is also beautiful and right that she should have a voice in regulating the milk supply from which the typhoid resulted."[77]

Radical positions were not exclusively those of the anti-suffrage movement. Lida Stokes Adams, a prominent suffragist, best illustrates an extreme feminist position. She felt so strongly about women's rights that she said after the sinking of the Titanic in reference to the masculine chivalry demonstrated at this disaster, "…the women should have insisted that the boats be filled with an equal number of men."[78]

Life was seldom easy for Jeannette. By coincidence, she was in Congress when both World Wars were declared. Her vote against the United States entry into both conflicts was extremely controversial. She encountered tremendous pugnacity and outright hatred from many quarters. Many people never forgave her.

Jeannette Rankin learned to live with hostility. Much of the hostility was directed at her because she was a pacifist. As Kevin Giles said in Flight of the Dove, "She lived in an era when dissent was considered disloyal and when patriotism was believed to be synonymous with the glory of war."[79]

Many years later, her biographer, Norma Smith, would say about her, "…she would not be defeated. She worked until she was nearly 93 years old, through wars, depressions, ridicule, calumny, fatigue, many outright failures, and a few successes, for a better life for humanity. Jeanette Rankin was a determined woman."[80]

Jeannette also had a serious health problem. During most of her adult years she suffered from a condition known as tic douloureux or trigeminal neuralgia–an intermittent, excruciating, sharp and sometimes almost intolerable torture in the right side of her face. The condition is characterized by trigger zones in the skin that when touched result in an electric-like, shattering and almost intolerable pain. Treatment today requires brain surgery, but only medication for pain was available to her. Very few of her close associates knew about this awful condition and she went through most of her life, and a lot of it in the public eye, never knowing when she would be struck again. Later, when surgical techniques became available to treat the condition, she refused it because she was afraid a complication from the surgery might affect her speech–her main instrument in communication. At the age of eighty-nine Jeannette had surgeons sever her right fifth cranial nerve, and the pain was finally gone. She was left however with a partially paralyzed sagging face and slurring of her speech.[81]

Jeannette was a Rankin through and through. A proud Scotswoman who, according to her niece, was "a free thinker, never thought anything was beyond her comprehension, and had the courage to stand up for her principles."[82] She was able to stand up, in part, because of her family, especially her brother Wellington, who was a major political, moral, and financial influence in her life.

Philena and Harriet Rankin

The second child, Philena, was born in 1882. She died at the age of nine from what was assumed in retrospect to be a ruptured appendix.

Harriet was born next, in 1883. She married Oscar Sedman, a mining engineer, and the son of a well-known pioneer family of Virginia City, Montana. Oscar died along with thousands of others in the influenza epidemic of 1918. Harriet's career included the position of Dean of Women at the University of Montana from 1920-1935. Hattie, as friends and family called her, worked for Jeannette after the death of her husband. During World War II she joined the Red Cross and lived in London throughout the war.

The last three children in the family were born in the town of Missoula. These in order were Grace, Mary and Edna. All three girls were popular, attractive, outgoing, and vivacious.

Grace and Mary Rankin

Grace and Mary seemed especially content to marry and live less intense and controversial lives, unlike their siblings Wellington, Jeannette, and Edna. Grace was considered by some to be the most beautiful of all the Rankin girls. She became Mrs. Thomas Kinney, and her husband was a forest ranger at Pierce, Idaho.

Mary was, according to her brother, "...a very pretty woman...very wonderful woman–the only one of the girls that I could make any claims of any beauty. She was queen of the May at the University..."[85] She taught English at Montana State University and later in the school system of California. Mary married Herbert Bragg and lived in Los Angeles.

Edna Rankin

As a young father figure Wellington certainly applied his patriarchal views to his younger sister Edna.

Edna, born in 1883, was the youngest of Wellington's sisters. She was a humorist, and at an early age she developed talent as a mimic. Her sense of comedy was an asset in her life.[84] Arguably, she was the most independent Rankin. She had all the attributes of her other sisters but had a restlessness that was unique to her.

John Rankin died while Edna was quite young. During her formative years Wellington functioned as her father figure. He accepted patrimony naturally. While her mother and Jeannette provided a feminine view, Wellington was the one Edna turned to for advice and guidance–even though he was only a few years older than her.

Edna was a pretty girl who blossomed in the years following her father's death. She grew into a popular, attractive young woman who loved stylish clothes and dancing. A luminary on the Missoula social scene, she had many suitors and might have married young had not Wellington had other plans for her, which Edna didn't mind following. She cared greatly for her older siblings, and was influenced by the political and social issues espoused by the two eldest.

Edna was a Rankin, and for Rankins education came first. Wellington saw to it that she began college at nearby Montana State University in Missoula. He then sent her east, first to the University of Wisconsin and then, like her sisters, to study at Wellesley, and "reap the benefit of the older environment of which their mother is a native."[85] Edna graduated in 1913, about the time Wellington began his private law practice in Helena.

While in the East, Edna stayed involved politically with Jeannette's campaign for women suffrage. Her role there was a supportive, if not a traditional one. In the National American Woman Suffrage Association's gathering in Washington in March 1913, she and other Montana women dressed as Indians standing out among the five thousand people marching on Congress. When the woman slated for the role of Sacajawea did not show at the rally, Edna was drafted for the part. She was a fair-haired, blue-eyed "Indian" maiden dressed in white buckskin.[86] The women were spat upon and insulted as they marched along Pennsylvania Avenue. The march proved to be both exciting and somewhat dangerous.

Edna had hopes for public service and a desire to pursue Progressive ideals so it seemed natural that her future might lie in the legal profession. Wellington may have even had visions of her as a partner in his law firm. As the elder brother acting in his father's stead, he was adamant that Edna attend law school at the University of Montana. Edna was eager to end the formal education process, but Wellington insisted.

A decision coerced upon her independent spirit was painful although she acquiesced. In addition, the societal attitude toward women in higher education at the time was skeptical and somewhat hostile. This posture was difficult to challenge as is evident during Edna's legal training. She was once slated to receive a scholarship but it was given to a man instead.

One professor was particularly antagonistic and assigned Edna the rape cases to discuss. In this Victorian age, "nice" girls did not publicly speak of things such as rape. She accepted the challenge. This certainly contributed to her ability to bypass false modesty in her future endeavors.[87] In spite of the difficulties, or perhaps to prove a point, Edna was the first woman graduate of Montana University Law School to be admitted to the Montana Bar.

Law school prepared Edna Rankin for what was to come in her future. Wellington convinced her to study public speaking and the art of communication, as well as, legal subjects. These skills were of inestimable value to her later in her life when she spoke to hostile audiences or in uncomfortable settings.

Wellington had won the battle but lost the war. After graduation his sister never practiced law. She worked in his office in Helena, but the relationship between the two was strained.

Wellington's hopes for his sister's law career did not stop her from developing a personal life. She married Jack McKinnon and bore two children. The marriage didn't survive the Great Depression and the sudden death of their seven-year-old son. The younger child, Dorothy, remained with her mother after the breakup of the marriage.

Edna's courage and determination were equal to that of her sister Jeannette. Just as Jeannette found her cause in social work in Georgia, Edna found a calling that she felt could improve the world. In 1936, while employed in Washington, D.C., Edna developed an overwhelming concern for the many women who she felt were forced by the standards of the times into unwanted pregnancies. She saw the tragedy of children brought into a world where they were not wanted–where disease, hunger, and abuse made their lives miserable. Biographer Wilma Dykeman described her feelings accurately in her book about Edna Rankin McKinnon in later years entitled, *Too Many People, Too Little Love.*

Working for the cause of birth control was not a socially accepted endeavor at the time. Edna's mentors in this unpopular field were Margaret Higgins Sanger and Dr. Clarence Gamble. They had organized a group called the Pathfinders, which disseminated information about contraception. Sanger, a nurse, had invented the term "birth control" and since 1912 had labored to establish clinics to educate women in what was eventually called family planning.

In 1929, Sanger founded what later became the Planned Parenthood Federation. Her efforts resulted in her being imprisoned eight times. Obscenity rules, such as the Comstock Law, "even banned discussion of the topic, mailing of information about it, or importation of contraceptive devices..."[88] Of course these stringent rules were invoked to keep information about birth issues silent. Even after such laws were no longer on the books, the attitude toward the subject of women and their personal problems were taboo. As late as 1948 Edna was not allowed to use the term "birth control" in a radio interview.[89]

Dr. Gamble, heir to the Proctor & Gamble fortune, had attended Harvard Medical School. Soon afterward, he discovered that he preferred fighting overpopulation. He referred to his stance as "anti-storkism" over more traditional avenues of medicine. He became Sanger's disciple, and Edna Rankin McKinnon's friend. Although there was little money available, he used his own funds to keep Edna actively involved and at the forefront of their battle to help women escape the bonds of undesired pregnancies.

Edna became a Sanger disciple and, with the blessing of the national organization Sanger had founded, returned to Montana to travel and lecture on population control. She drove back and forth and around the state over poor and often hazardous roads. She spoke at public meetings and at both organized and unorganized assemblies. She even preached in the streets.

Because of, "poverty, poor roads, a lack of trained physicians, isolation, extreme weather, or simply their own choice, women in the Rocky Mountain West often did not have qualified medical care and turned to each other for aid in giving birth, as a source for contraceptive information, and for help in aborting unwanted children."[90]

Infant mortality was high in the United States in the 1930s, but only a few people, like Edna, felt a need for family planning. Catholics and Protestants alike rebelled against the sexual implications, which rubbed against church doctrine like sandpaper. Most Americans valued large families and viewed any move in the direction of limiting them as a threat to privacy.

Hostile and almost always ignorant of family planning issues, her audience was repeatedly shocked with details previously screened from the public arena. Topics like birth control, feminine hygiene, contraceptive devices, anatomical terms, and mannequin demonstrations made them uncomfortable. Edna's efforts, and those of other Sanger disciples were considered abrasive and many of the women they hoped to educate and help resented them. Those who welcomed the speakers were not able to defend them for fear of public shame.

Edna's experience was similar to that of Jeannette's during her quest for the woman's vote and world peace. Both contended with the attitude of men–especially rural men. She later recalled, "We struggled against the machismo [that] Jeannette encountered, 'I'm a man because I can kill,' and also the one I encountered, 'I'm a man because I can sire twenty children.'"[91]

Wellington, shared the same views as most men did at the time. Edna, who saw her brother as a Progressive, underestimated his response to her newfound crusade. In contrast to Rankin's more liberal stance toward the women's vote, he was chagrined when Edna became active in the education of women about birth control. He was as shocked as other people of the time when confronted with "female" problems. He also worried about the potential disgrace to the family name and the possible damage to his political aspirations. When Edna tried to get him to understand that her work was a worthy cause, he said, "That may be, but it is not going to be your life's work."

"And why shouldn't it be? It's important," she argued.

"Sewers are important but you don't have to dig them," he replied.[92]

If Edna were able to say to him, as she told others later, that her effort was for the sake of humanity, it would not have convinced her brother, the former Progressive. Who knows what forces were stirring his reactions to her crusade? Was it the influence of the strict Victorian age that had just passed? Some religious belief hitherto repressed? Was it more likely that his astute ability to fathom changing social and political standards, and his sister's involvement in such a liberal pursuit, would affect his conservative political ambitions adversely?

The latter sounds most plausible. He still smarted from Jeannette's strong stands against war, painful recollections that were regurgitated by his enemies each time he entered the political arena in the state.[95] In his early fifties, Wellington was a prominent lawyer and well-known politician, but like many others, Wellington was no longer progressive. He had imperceptibly shifted sides and at mid-career aspired to the leadership of the Republican Party in Montana and the nation. He reflected the contemporary male view, and coupled this scorn with an active concern for Edna's reputation and that of the Rankin family's–to say nothing of the harm such gutter work could have to his political ambitions.

Wellington's attitude was typical in his time. The American Medical Association (AMA) was consistently conservative, but it reluctantly joined in the effort (albeit languidly) to educate women in birth control the same year that Edna began her work in 1937. In Montana, there was a distinct reluctance on the part of the Public Health Department, practicing physicians, and institutions to openly discuss the problems. They reacted to the pressures of conservatives and religious fundamentalists.[94] As a burgeoning politician in a conservative state, her brother was under great pressure to keep his growing power. Wellington's antagonism toward Edna's work comes as no surprise.

Unfortunately, by trying to preserve the family reputation, Wellington also broke the Rankins apart. Edna felt that she could not continue to work in Montana without her brother's blessing. His influence and prestige within the family was unquestioned. Disillusioned, she left Montana and worked for the same cause in Tennessee.

There and in other Southern states, she battled the same ignorance and intolerance she had encountered in Montana. In the South, she sharpened her ability to deal with uneducated or arrogant audiences. Her skills in debating and speaking came together with her sense of humor and common wisdom. In her wake, she left informed followers from all social strata. Child welfare clinics and centers for birth control sprang up behind her.

From then on, Edna followed a career of service to women that would take her around the country and the world. During her long career, she worked in thirty-two states and numerous foreign countries, including Kuala Lumpur, Singapore, Japan, Malaya, Nigeria, and even the Islamic stronghold Saudi Arabia. Her last venture was in Ethiopia.

In many ways, her exile from Wellington's reach and Montana conservatism may have been to her advantage. Edna still had the support of her mother, Olive, and her sister, Jeannette. She also maintained friendly, yet distant, contact with Wellington by mail. If she was gone from his sight, she was not forgotten. At one point in the late 1940s or early 1950s, he managed to put his personal aversion to her occupation aside and buy her a car. She acknowledged it gratefully as a grand present, writing to him, "I wish you could know what joy and what a sense of release it has given me. Each person I take in it sends you messages of thanks."[95]

Like her brother, Edna overcame most barriers and learned to accept defeat. Her humor and talent for comedy helped as she became inured to rejection and ridicule. Proudly she wrote, "Every single child born on this earth should be wanted and cherished.... Everywhere I went I looked for the children first.... One person...can make a difference in this part of the world."[96]

One contemporary said:

> Edna was fearless... She'd go anywhere, meet anyone, venture anything—and always beautifully dressed, in command of the situation. She wasn't my style...I can't imagine a woman alone going to all those places—on that sort of work! Of course, she was from Montana. And I've always lived here in Boston.[97]

By 1963, Edna Rankin McKinnon had embraced another cause: Christian Science. Like Wellington, she had long believed in the Church of Christ Scientist and its teachings–particularly its beliefs in terms of healing. Edna was no longer of the best health, and years of travel had worn on her. Visiting Djakarta, Indonesia, in 1963, she was able to observe the influence of a Christian Science missionary and healer, Adele Blok, and she wrote to her family about her experiences there:

> I felt I gained much through my friendship with her.... There were a number of occasions when I needed help, both emotional and physical, because that whole situation is frustrating to say the least, and on one occasion when I returned from Bali, I lost my voice and even the ability to breath[e], to the point that I thought I was passing on. She worked steadily until 3 A.M., at which time I said to myself that I could lie down and still breath[e]. The next morning I was well....[98]

In a note addressed just to Wellington, she added:

> I wish you could know and talk with Miss Blok. She has had wonderful grounding with Mr. [Paul Stark] Seeley and she knows how to give it to others. She is doing a fine job with the Church and has encouraged many Indonesians to study C.S.... I send much love...[99]

If she could not discuss matters of family planning with her brother, she nevertheless found other ways to make contact. Her enthusiasm for Christian Science must have pleased Wellington because it was his accepted religion, too.

Sadly, Edna never did get the moral support from her brother that she craved. His seeming lack of acceptance of her lifestyle and ambitions troubled her greatly. Edna spoke later of a recurring dream about Wellington concerning his sometimes lack of acceptance of her lifestyle and ambitions. According to the fantasy, her brother was in a fort, behind a stockade, and calling for help. Edna struggled in vain to reach him, but was never able to break through the walls.[100]

• • •

As the only boy, Wellington had paternal feelings toward his sisters, even the older ones. In return, all of the Rankin women mothered him and catered to him. The "high strung" family had frequent disputes.[101] Tempers could flare and physical expressions were frequent when frustrations reached a peak. They were a strong brood, and bonded even though they bickered among themselves. They always stood together against outsiders.

Winfield Page, a Republican politician from Missoula who was eventually defeated by Jeannette and Wellington in congressional elections, spoke of the Rankins in an interview in 1980. He recalled, "Once you take them on you have to take on the whole bunch. The Rankins are aggressive and they are formidable, the whole bunch."[102]

2
EDUCATION

"The cowards never started and the weak died on the way."

People who immigrated west were unique. The simple fact that they came set them apart. Of the thousands of Americans and Europeans who might have braved the hardships, only a small percentage actually did. It was an opportunity, but it was a gamble. Only a few found the fortune in land or opportunity they sought. Only a select group that was willing to adjust to a new, a diverse, and arduous environment. As Elliott West says in *Growing Up with the Country*, "With its image of splendid possibilities, it drew outsiders to it, thereby creating frontier society in the first place ...Emigration was a sifting. It made for a society heavily weighted with persons of a particular bent."[1] As someone said, "The cowards never started and the weak died on the way."[2]

The traditional myth of Western settlement is one of masculine motivation toward conquest, profit, and town building. This was a lot of the story. However, it was a more complex issue than this. Pioneer parents were driven to produce the kind of life they left behind, and family and education of children were at the top of the list. As one pioneer mother said, "...man alone never settled a country, never built an empire, never even stayed 'put' unless accompanied by wife and children..."[3] And children became the center of the family's existence. They were the future and western people knew it.

Youth was part of the optimism so characteristic of the West. If the pioneer immigrants were unique, their children were distinctive as well. Their work and play, and the austere lifestyle and environment, and the security of their identity as a part of a family resulted in attitudes and behavior long recognized as "Western." These include optimism, individualism, a cooperative spirit, a work ethic that accepted long hours, determination, pragmatism, and impatience with arbitrariness. Some of the traits were not as commendable. Western children too readily accepted violence. They were also handed down an exploitive frame of mind that eventually played havoc with the environment.[4]

As soon as it was financially feasible, an educational system, however primitive, was devised wherever groups of immigrants settled. From place to place there was great variety in the quality of education. However, most Western people, no matter how diverse their origins, viewed this as common ground upon which they could base their social order and community progress.

They weren't all so altruistic however. Times were tough, money was scarce, and some frontier men and women were reluctant to spend their hard earned savings on education. Some families only allowed their children to attend school for a few years or until they were old enough and physically able to help on the farm or ranch. Mostly for economic reasons some places in the West were slow to see education as important. And there were some families who simply didn't believe in "book larnin'." As late as the 1880s only 40 percent of eligible children attended school.[5]

This certainly was not the case with the Rankins. This frontier family considered knowledge an absolute requirement. Moreover, they were financially able to assure that their children received the best instruction. In retrospect, frontier families invested more in the local school than many of their descendants do today. With limited funds, they constructed the building, located a teacher, took part in activities, and used the place for town meetings, social gatherings, and for voting. All this effort on the part of adults communicated the value of education and community endeavor to frontier children.

The Grant Creek School

The three oldest Rankin children, including Wellington, began their education in the one-room school on Grant Creek, built sometime before 1880.[6] A former student described it as:

> ...a one-room school with a porch which was used as a cloakroom and for wood storage. There were no plants in the school as the temperature often dropped below freezing during the night.... A picture of George Washington and the U.S. flag were the only permanent decorations.... There was no well or indoor plumbing.... The school boasted both girls' and boys' outhouses ...boys to the north and girls to the south.[7]

A student in the rural west had to have a strong desire for an education. As someone said in reference to children of the frontier, "... learning is a personal matter like dying and that each one in the last analysis has to do it for himself."[8]

The accomplishments of many of those who attended a country

school are impressive. Their successes form a record that repudiates the short school terms, often only three months per year. There was a rapid turnover of sometimes poorly prepared teachers. Many schools were inadequately constructed and some had sod roofs. They were often inefficiently heated and uncomfortable. Most schools had outdoor privies; at others, the children used nearby woods when necessary. A small school was lucky if it had a few books and a blackboard. Teachers learned to "make-do" and used everything available, from Bibles to printed labels to educate their charges. Religious teaching, discipline, and lessons in the morality of the times were a subtle part of their daily exercises. For instance, the popular McGuffey's Reader contained reading exercises that were prescriptive. Years after leaving school, graduates could remember stories and poems memorized from their reader, such as "Up, Up Lucy, Why Do You Lie in Bed," or "Try, Try, Again." Reading and writing were the most important subjects, but grammar, history, and geography followed closely. There was little or no science.[9]

The class size and closeness that also allowed independent growth and study had no small affect on Wellington Rankin's life. Like many others who began their education in a country school, he was proud of this beginning. His class was tiny, and mostly composed of himself and a few of his sisters. It was an atmosphere of camaraderie and belonging. Thousands of young men and women in rural America were educated in country schools where they were molded, shaped, and their rough edges sanded smooth.

Ask anyone who attended a country school to reminisce, and you will hear a narration laced with nostalgia. Primarily, it was a memorable period. It was more like family than school. Lifetime friendships were formed.

While as many as eight grade levels were represented in one class, a skillful teacher made the system work by shifting focus from one level of instruction to another throughout the day. While the instructor taught one level, the others studied and worked on assignments. Veterans of this kind of schooling, with few exceptions, have little doubt about the quality of education they received. Invariably the women (and a few men) who taught them, guided them through the pangs of puberty, cleaned their crusty noses, instructed them in the fine art of interaction, and gave them lessons in personal hygiene, are forever alive in their memories.

Like family, the older children helped the teacher care for the younger ones. They saw to it that dirty hands, after a trip to the outhouse or before lunch, were washed in a basin with water from a bucket that simmered on the wood stove at the end of the room. Elder students also helped supervise the younger students during recess when games of Fox and Geese, Red Rover-Red Rover, or Hide and Seek relieved the strain of study.[10]

Amazingly some of the teachers stayed on year after year for little pay until they became an institution themselves.[11] Former students remember most of these dedicated instructors as caring, sensitive, and kind individuals. They were a tough breed. To prepare their group for the good life, they had to take charge and maintain discipline. Sometimes even capital punishment was given. They were admired for this toughness.

The students graduated by these teachers were not restricted to a country life. Many like the Rankins of Missoula, successfully challenged higher institutions of learning and found lives as professionals. Many graduates of country schools boast of their classes' high achievement statistics. One rancher from a remote area in Montana bragged humorously that 20 percent of his class became doctors—there were only five students. The physician from that class specialized in orthopedics and earned a national reputation. The other classmates became ranchers or married ranchers, and lived long productive lives.[12]

Using the same logic Wellington Rankin could have spoken about the high percentage of political achievers attending the one-room school at Grant Creek, since he and his sister Jeannette were enrolled at the same time, and his sister Harriet was destined to be Dean of Women at Montana State University.

Here is an appraisal of students who graduated from a one-room rural school in Nebraska in the 1890s, "...eleven graduated from college, and three from a conservatory of music, twelve became teachers, one an attorney, one an engineer, one a noted eye specialist, one a prominent artist and two were widely known musicians. Several were successful farmers, and not one seems ever to have been involved in crime."[13]

Some fortunate children, like those of the Rankin family, received home schooling as well. Olive's training as a teacher helped her supplement her children's desire for knowledge. Though less formally educated than his wife, John Rankin was a living example of the importance of education. He was self-educated and successful and his obsession for education for his children had a positive effect on them all. The desire to get an education and the support of parents in doing so was not the rule on the frontier. The Rankins were exceptional people with exceptional ambition.

Speaking primarily about Jeannette Rankin, a woman of strong purpose, but equally applicable to the other children of the family, and especially Wellington, Linda Peavy and Ursula Smith said in their book, *Pioneer Women*, "...Might some of that courage and determination have come from growing up as the daughter of Olive Pickering Rankin...?"[14] No doubt, and her influence, especially on the older children, persisted throughout all their long lives. In later interviews, Wellington always referred to his mother as, "A woman of conviction."[15]

Harriet Rankin and other contemporaries said that the quick-minded Wellington could understand the lessons and get "everything" without studying. This ability to comprehend faster than most of his class-mates was seen as remarkable by his family and close associates in view of a head injury he suffered at the age of six that nearly terminated his life. Struck in the head by a piece of cordwood as it was thrown from a wagon, Wellington remained unconscious for a long period and developed what a local physician called "brain fever." After his consciousness returned he suffered from amnesia. According to his family, he didn't recognize his parents and had to learn to walk and talk again. Only a few years later, he excelled in his studies and his superior intellect was apparent. A less successful student in his class said, "I wish I'd been hit on the head with a piece of cordwood."[16]

The University

In 1903 Wellington Rankin earned a Bachelor of Science degree from the University of Montana in Missoula.[17] By this time, the town of Missoula had grown to a population of about five thousand. The University was in its tenth year, and it was only six years since the cornerstone of Main Mall was laid.

Getting the legislature to select Missoula as the place for the University had not been easy. It was a matter of politics. Politically powerful people with money from Great Falls were also trying to get the institution. However, fifty Missoula citizens went to Helena to lobby in 1893, and came back with the prize. This successful political effort didn't come without a price. According to one source, it took five gallons of whiskey, one case of beer, two dozen Appolinaris,[18] one case of wine, three hundred and fifty cigars, and one corkscrew, to win over the legislature. The Missoula elite who handed out the cigars and poured the whiskey also agreed to support Helena over Anaconda as the State Capital.

The Grand Opening of the foundling educational institution on September 11, 1895 was a spectacular affair. The hundreds who attended were entertained by the musical renditions of the Mandolin, Banjo, and Guitar Club.

The first university President was Oscar J. Craig from Purdue University in Indiana. He was a former professor of History and Political Science, a good organizer and worker. He opened the university with only five faculty members. There were a number of required courses, but Latin and Greek, studies that some teachers believed were synonymous with education, were taught but not required. The requirements to graduate were 32 credits and a thesis. Wellington D. Rankin's thesis in 1903 had the imposing title of, "The History of the Creeds."[19]

By the time Wellington graduated, the faculty numbered thirteen. Most of them had masters' degrees. The professors worked hard for salaries that varied from $1,000 to $2,000 per year. Sometimes they

Wellington Rankin at age nineteen. Photo taken at Harvard or Cambridge. Photo: Montana Historical Society, Helena.

taught as many as twenty classes a week. The quality of the education that a student received was apparently good. Several early graduates were accepted elsewhere for graduate school, Also, two men were granted Rhodes Scholarships (one in 1904 and the other in 1907) and Wellington had no trouble getting accepted for further study at Harvard University.[20]

Harvard

As the other Rankin siblings did afterward, Wellington went east to continue his education. Some of the Rankin women went to Wellesley. Wellington chose Harvard. This great school, steeped in tradition, was one of the oldest institutions for higher learning in the country. It was a natural choice for a Rankin son.

In Boston he rubbed shoulders with some of the elite scion of northeastern families. There were several Adams, an Alden, a Tilden and some Putnams in his class. Some of these New England young men may have been distantly related to Rankin. After all his mother, Olive, was a New England Pickering. Although, a novelty among the mainly New York and northeastern-bred Harvard men, Wellington was not the only westerner in his class. He had two peers from Arizona, one from Colorado, and another from Wyoming.

In addition, Wellington had another Montanan close by. His room-mate and closest friend at Harvard was Ellis Sedman from Virginia City. Ellis was a well-known "Grizzly" football star and slightly older than Wellington. He came from a prominent mining and ranching family. The Sedmans gained their wealth by controlling the water supply to some of Alder Gulch's largest stamp mills. They also raised horses on the famous Snowcrest Ranch in the Ruby Valley.[21]

According to Virginia Ronhovde, Wellington's niece, Ellis Sedman was known as a sympathetic individual, the "kind of person that you would go to if you were in trouble."[22] Ellis and Wellington, two enter-prising Montanans, hired a cook and provided a boarding house for other Harvard students. Their companionship probably eased the tran-sition for one another into this eastern aristocratic college. What fol-lowed was probably the lowest point in young Wellington's life.

John Rankin, Wellington's adored father, died unexpectedly in 1904 while his son was attending school in Boston. He was a hale and hearty sixty-three years old when a tick bite followed by Rocky Mountain spot-ted fever struck him down.[23] Wellington became the titular head of the household as the surviving male.

John Rankin's sudden death loaded his twenty-year-old son with immense burdens. He was a student engrossed in higher education and now a decision maker for a large family of women. He was forced to handle the sale of the estate's livestock, dispose of the estate's property, and manage his father's extensive investments. Since Olive Rankin had no experience with financial matters, and because the protocol of the time obliged a male son to resolve estate issues, Wellington was selected to sort through the dilemma. He had to deal with his own grief as well. He was overwhelmed.

The Rankins continued to live comfortably after John's death, thanks to the patriarch's resourcefulness and to Wellington's ability to manage. However, this effort took its toll on young Wellington. After settling as much of the business in Missoula as he could, he returned to Boston to continue his undergraduate education.

His youth and the added stress of distance engulfed him. Away from home and mostly surrounded by strangers, Wellington suffered what was then called a "nervous breakdown"–a total mental collapse. In retrospect the illness may have been an acute depression. Ellis returned to their room after a short absence and found his friend and roommate sitting at his desk, "unaware of his surroundings." The episode was no minor psychological ailment. Wellington was seriously ill–so serious that Jeannette took the long train trip from Missoula to Boston to be with her brother. Because of the history of his head injury as a child, there was a great concern that this event was somehow related and his so-called "brain fever" had recurred.

Psychiatric illnesses were not well understood or classified at that time. Quite possibly, Wellington feared a consequence of his childhood brain injury for much of his life. His sudden collapse on this occasion, one over which he had no control, influenced him for many years. Close friends and relatives say that forever after he empathized with people suffering from mental illness.

There is no evidence that Rankin had much affinity for any particular religion up until this time, but this would change during his stay at Harvard. Ellis Sedman was a practicing Christian Scientist. As Wellington's closest friend at Harvard, his influence on the young Rankin crossed into the religious realm.

The Church of Christ Scientist, founded by Mary Baker Eddy in 1866, was based on biblical readings as they pertained to healing. Its founder taught that man was created in God's image, and thus inherited unlimited energies and capacities for benefiting humanity and curing illness. Although ridiculed by the press and pulpit, the leader, as she called herself, touched a large segment of the population during the later stages of the eighteenth and early nineteenth centuries. Her tenets that, "There is no death" "God is the healer," "no such person as the devil," "heaven and hell are not places," "there is no life in matter," appealed to many in spite of such vitriolic and prolific critics as Mark Twain. He denounced her as "a charlatan, a crook," and a woman who regarded herself as "a second Virgin-mother."[24]

Independent thinkers like Rankin must have been particularly attracted to a religion that was based on the principle of "understanding" and not simply "belief." The popularity of this religious and healing movement tempted many who were disenchanted with the medical profession as it existed at that time. "The sick like drowning men," Mary Baker Eddy said prophetically, "catch whatever drifts toward them."[25]

Wellington credited Ellis and his faith in Christian Science for his eventual complete recovery from the "nervous breakdown." According to Virginia Ronhovde, he said that Ellis and his doctrine had saved him. "He could have gone off the deep end," she related. "Well, he not only didn't go off the deep end, he got so much better that he graduated on time from Harvard Law."

Wellington became a lifetime member of Mary Baker Eddy's

Christian Science movement.[26] Three of his sisters, Hattie, Mary, and Edna, influenced by this important family incident, and by his leadership, also joined the Christian Scientist Church. Jeannette never accepted it.[27]

As it turned out Jeannette's trip "back east" became a six-month vacation. Her brother recovered and she and another young woman from Missoula who had accompanied her on the trip were able to see the sights in Boston. As an extra treat, Montana Congressman Joseph M. Dixon, also a Missoulian, arranged for Jeannette, Wellington and their friends from Harvard, to attend the inaugural ball in Washington D. C. for President Theodore Roosevelt. Friends also invited Jeannette and Wellington to stay in New York for a few days in the Waldorf Astoria. But as Norma Smith says in her, as yet unpublished manuscript, *Fighting Pacifist, Jeannette Rankin and Her Times*, "…Jeannette saw some sights that tourists were not expected to notice: the sufferings of the slum dwellers in Boston and New York."

Both Jeannette and her brother were shocked at the poverty and terrible living conditions in the poor sections. This was the first time either had seen such "grinding" misery. Wellington, although impressed, was less so than his sister, which is made evident in her future effort.[28]

Wellington's competent management of his family's affairs, assured that there was adequate money for tuition and travel for all the Rankin children. This was a degree of affluence only available to a few frontier families. With his father gone, Wellington learned more about livestock, farming, and business management; knowledge that he would retain and use in the future as he pursued a career in the law, ranching and politics. His sisters became accomplished cooks and homemakers and students, and they looked to their brother as the ostensible head of the household, and he played the part well. Jeannette, who was more independent than her sisters, may have been an exception to this but she admired and respected her brother as did the rest.

When it came to family discussions and arguments, no one was excluded, from the youngest to the oldest. Olive, although she abandoned most of the responsibility of running the house and younger children to Jeannette, and the family business to Wellington, was nevertheless a forceful intelligence in family discussions and arguments. Wellington was reported to have said about his mother, "So often we argue–she is usually right."[29]

As the head of the family he was not always obeyed, and was often disconcerted by the aggressive, independent, uncompromising and non-Victorian pursuits of his sisters–especially Jeannette and Edna. But they always supported him and looked to him for encouragement and advice–and for financial support. Wellington doled out family funds, and established accounts and income sources for his sisters and his mother.

Oxford

Even with the added responsibility Wellington assumed after his father's death, he continued his education. In 1905 he earned a Bachelor of Arts from Harvard and went abroad for a year to study literature and philosophy at Oxford University. Although some sources say he went abroad as Montana's first Rhodes Scholar, the merit is only legend. During his political career this myth was used for him and against him. Those who opposed him suggested this made him an elitist. Those who supported him used it to emphasis his excellent education. There is no evidence that he used it either way.

Little is known about this period of his life except that he participated in boxing and competed in rowing contests. After study in England, he traveled in Europe. None of his friends or acquaintances felt that he was impressed favorably by the Old World. He commented many years later that he remembered Venice primarily for its dirty canals. This was a normal response from a young Montanan accustomed to the free flowing, clear and unpolluted streams of his boyhood.[30]

We know little about young Wellington's time at Oxford or his trips to Europe. He was financially able to "get away." He probably needed some time to himself without family pressures, time to collect his thoughts and plan for the future. After Oxford, Rankin returned to Harvard to study law.[31]

Harvard Law

There is no way to know why Wellington Rankin chose the law as a career. Certainly family friends, attorneys, college professors, and others must have influenced him about the advantages of this professional avenue. Leaders of the legal field, before and during Rankin's time, were writing such lofty comments as, "The lawyers best deserve to be called the leading class," or law journals were telling their readers as early as 1870 that, "in every age of civilized man, the lawyers have been an important instrument in the work of refining and elevating the race." Some even went so far as to say that of all the professions, law was to become, "...the most obvious vehicle both for claimed respectability and for upward mobility."[32] All these were words that may have motivated and fueled the ambitions of a young, aggressive, and intelligent man at the turn of the century–especially a self-confident westerner like Wellington Rankin.

Rankin chose Harvard Law School. He was armed with an S.B. from the University of Montana and an A.B. from Harvard. This fine 90-year-old liberal institution was one of the few law colleges that required a baccalaureate degree for admission. When Rankin matriculated in 1906, it is doubtful that he was much concerned about the history of the place.

He probably knew that it was the most prestigious and elite school in the country. He may have known also that Harvard was the creative leader in the field of law and that many other schools in the United States emulated its curriculum and form of teaching.

At Harvard, students faced three years of study. Modern legal historians agree that the idea of learning law, the Harvard way, by "case study," has dominated American legal education for the last 110 years.[33] This was a program that absorbed the Socratic system of recitation and quiz, and question and answer.

If he didn't know at the time that Harvard exams were notoriously difficult and that sometimes one-third of a class failed, he likely found out soon after enrolling. Although a student's admission required an undergraduate degree, there was otherwise little selectivity. The school's professors, beginning the first school year and continuing into the final stretch, undertook by severe testing the surgical and impersonal elimination of laggards. Wellington's graduating class of 1909 consisted of about one-half of those who started. Harvard Law School was an exhausting struggle for survival and a shocking experience for those who failed.[34]

One of Wellington's classmates who later taught at the university for over fifty years said in a letter to his father in 1906, "…as I settle down and the novelty wears off, I have nearly gotten over the stage where I dream law every night as I did at first."[35]

During the last of the nineteenth century and early part of the twentieth, the study of law was in a transitional phase. Schools had to keep abreast of technical, political, international and social changes. America was no longer isolationist. The Spanish American War of 1899-1900 changed that forever. An aura of progressivism prevailed, and labor and its unions were pushing with some success for improved wage and hour legislation. Farmers were organizing and the Granger movement challenged the power of the railroads. The Pure Food and Drug Act was passed by Congress in 1905.[36]

James Barr Ames was the Dean of Harvard Law School from 1895-1910. He and the former Dean, Christopher Columbus Langdell, saw the law as a science with principles and doctrines to be applied to the "ever-tangled skein" of human affairs. Together they molded the Harvard curriculum.[37]

Their theories were not without powerful critics. The American Bar Association and a few disgruntled Harvard alumni, saw Harvard Law as a school that was preparing its students primarily for litigation. The ABA lobbied the university to include more courses in social science. Roscoe Pound, who would replace Ames in 1910, criticized the Harvard system for its lack of courses in sociology, economics, and philosophy. Pound would inject all of these into the school's curriculum when he was later in charge.

Education

Pound was a reformer and his articulate arguments had a lasting effect on the administration of justice in the United States. During his long career at Harvard (1910-1947) Pound influenced law toward a practical and pragmatic approach. His way of thinking emphasized the dependency of legal rules on the changing social conditions and is still adhered to daily in the courts of America. Case law has stood the test of time for ninety years. All this came after Wellington Rankin graduated.[38]

Rankin did absorb the "case" approach to the practice of law. The strict confidence in common law of the nineteenth century was fading away and was replaced by precedents rather than principles. Lawyers tried to discover the "underlying theory of law," and looked, "for cases 'on all fours,'" whose facts duplicated the ones from the case at hand.[39] According to Louise Rankin Galt, an attorney and Wellington's wife in later years, the attorney Rankin was very successful in using case law. He would instruct his associates in regard to a case as follows: "Well, there should be a case on such and such a point...this is bound to be the law, there's bound to be something on it, now get out to the law library and find it. Generally he was right. Just from his reasonings, not from the study, because he wouldn't open a law book and study anything unless you brought something to him..."[41]

The idea of "pure" and "scientific" law was also challenged by none other than Harvard University's most distinguished alumnus, associate Justice Oliver Wendell Holmes, Jr., who talked about the, "necessary instability and inconsistency of any given state of the law."[42]

One vitriolic critic said that a Harvard-trained lawyer will, "...argue any side of any controversy," or is, "...unable to advise a client when he is safe from litigation..." ...or is, "...a mere hired gladiator."[43] Rankin graduated in the class of 1909 and filled at least one of these predictions. He certainly became a "gladiator" in the courts and political arenas of his home state.

Western states like Montana were affected by the legacy of their territorial governments. Patronage, factionalism, and boosterism had inspired the leadership in Montana courts. These three "horsemen" had resulted in corrupt combinations of business and government that encouraged the flow of federal dollars into elite frontier pockets. There was little criticism (except from those who were cheated) because nearly every citizen in one way or another benefited.

Private individuals and corporations illegally trespassed federal lands and forests for profit. Those who were contracted to supply them embezzled from Federal army posts and Indian reservations. As writer William Kittredge later analyzed the law of the early West, "The Law does not always command much respect even from those who bring it. People seeking frontiers are often people seeking escape from law ..."[44]

The Montana legal and political environment was corrupt enough to provide a good target for a young idealist like Wellington Rankin. It was a good place for a potential reformer to incubate. It was also, as one historian said, recognizably full of "unusual opportunities."[45] Rankin was uniquely prepared to partake of as many of these "unusual opportunities" as possible: in his personal life, in the field of law, in the political arena, and in the pursuit of wealth.

3
THE YOUNG ATTORNEY

Young attorney Wellington Rankin was ready in every way to become a leader when he came to Helena in 1909. Many people at this time in history held a prestigious law degree from Harvard in awe. He had something else that guaranteed a degree of insurance–he was financially secure. This was a time when education was available only to those who could afford it.

As sociologist Charles Horton Cooley wrote shortly after the turn of the century, "…money was the only way to education, to choice of occupation, to books, leisure and variety of intercourse, it was essential to the intellectual life; there was no belonging to the cultured class without it." It was an age too when ambitious, educated, young men like Wellington sought an opening, and they were bound to get it. Their aim as Cooley stated is, "not to raise the lower class, but to get out of it." The rising young man "…strikes out for wealth, power or fame."[1] Attorney Rankin was on his way up.

Rankin was well-built but not tall. Unless photographs lie, the youthful attorney was athletic, handsome, always immaculately dressed and a Beau Brummel type. As a young attorney and "man about Helena," he had his suits made to order by "Nifty Bill," a tailor in Helena. He always dressed in "uniform" with suit and tie. A contemporary said, "He couldn't pass a mirror without admiring himself."[2]

He was a boxer and a horseman. One source says, the best "Indian-wrestler" in Montana. His fits of temper were legendary. One newsman later described him as "impatient, with a hair-trigger temper, displayed at times to telephone operators and other underlings. Conversely, he could be charming, disarming and downright friendly."[3]

One critical historian describes the youthful Rankin as follows:

> Handsome, brilliant and dynamic, Rankin could also be
> magnetic and pleasant when he desired, but he was a vic-

tim of his own qualities. He was overweeningly ambitious, intensely selfish, erratic, mercurial, vituperative, and temperamentally undisciplined. He was almost incapable of liking anyone whom he could not dominate.[4]

In a frontier state where individuality and masculinity counted for a lot, such striking characteristics were an asset, if only partially true. Rankin found almost immediate attention in his home state.

He started his practice with the reputable law firm of Nolan & Walsh. Cornelius B. Nolan and Thomas J. Walsh were heavy hitters in Montana law and politics. Colonel Nolan, a member of the state legislature, was a military man and pioneer who had emigrated from Ireland to New York and Pennsylvania in 1873. He was a power in the Democratic Party and a distinguished attorney. Nolan studied law at Saint Louis Law School before he came to Montana. He was respected for many reasons but especially because his honesty had been tried by fire. As Attorney General for Montana from 1897–1901, he had the onerous duty of prosecuting those who bribed legislators to elect copper king W. A. Clark into the U.S. Senate. In pursuit of these scoundrels he was himself faced with bribes, which he refused. Cornelius B. Nolan had earned a reputation of honesty.

Thomas J. Walsh was a Democrat and a nationally known attorney at the time Rankin worked for him. He was also from an Irish immigrant family, and had obtained his education in Wisconsin. He practiced law a short time in South Dakota and came to Helena in 1890. Defeated twice for public office to Congress, he was finally elected in 1912 to the U.S. Senate when he beat Joseph A. Dixon. For the next twenty years he represented Montana in the Senate. Walsh would later be chairman of the Democratic National Convention and gain fame for his role in the discovery and prosecution of those politicians involved in the notorious Teapot Dome affair. In 1933, he was appointed by President Franklin Roosevelt to be the Attorney General of the United States. He died suddenly before he could assume this important post.

Senator Walsh could best be described as dignified. He was not flamboyant, nor a back-slapper. Unlike many other politicians of the time, he neither smoked nor drank. The public saw him as able and industrious. He was not a great speaker, but could get his point across forcefully. Walsh was a progressive and his honesty and integrity were seldom challenged.

Jerre C. Murphy, in his 1912 book, *The Comical History of Montana*, describes some of the political leaders in Montana at the time as worthy of irony, if not humor. From the information available today, Nolan and Walsh, can be excluded from the following Murphy pronouncement:

...there was pride; there was incentive to effort and

Wellington Rankin. Photo courtesy Montana Historical Society

reward for achievement.... the man who not only believed that a horse thief should be hung but who had assisted in hanging him was quite likely to be a man of integrity in ordinary business dealings.[5]

The fact that Rankin was considered suitable to join such luminaries as Nolan and Walsh is evidence of his talent, family background, and Harvard degree. He was charismatic, handsome, intelligent, and favored with other attributes that foretold a brilliant future. As a young

Republican, albeit one with progressive values, he was an odd partner for the pair of Democrats.

Rankin worked for the prestigious Nolan & Walsh for only two years before he opened his own office. His short stay with them suggests something else about his character. He would not, and could not, be dominated. Rankin was totally independent. Regardless, the mutual respect between Wellington and his partners continued throughout all their lives.

The Mining Culture

"The thicker the fumes the greater our financial vitality."[6]

To truly trace Wellington Rankin through the maze of Montana politics and his legal profession from the early decades of the twentieth century until the end of his career, it is essential to have a firm understanding of the influence of the mining industry in the State of Montana.

Mining, especially copper mining, dominated the history and life of Montana throughout the later part of the nineteenth century and most of the twentieth century. Thousands of foreign-born miners responded to the industries' need for laborers. Political influence, especially by the Butte copper mining companies, had long been a factor in the state capitol. Harsh working conditions and environmental abuses were flaunted rather than corrected, and the mine owners had the strength and political clout to get away with what they would.

William A. Clark, copper millionaire and president of the Montana Constitutional Convention of 1889, had the audacity to say in a speech concerning the environment and mining-caused air pollution:

> "I must say that the ladies are very fond of this smoky city, as it [Butte] is sometimes called, because there is just enough arsenic there to give them a beautiful complexion, and that is the reason the ladies of Butte are renowned wherever they go for their beautiful complexions.... I say it would be a great deal better for other cities in the territory if they had more smoke and less diphtheria and other diseases. It has been believed by all the physicians of Butte that the smoke that sometimes prevails there is a disinfectant and destroys the microbes that constitute the germs of disease....it would be a great advantage for other cities to have a little more smoke and business activity and less disease."[7]

T. J. Walsh's office in the Penwell Block in 1911. Wellington Rankin is on the left and Thomas Walsh is on the right. Photo: Montana Historical Society, Helena.

The wealth derived from copper spoke louder than reason. Plants, animals, and humans were crippled or dying from exposure to arsenic and other substances being spewed into the atmosphere when this statement was made. Few of Montana's leaders cared.

The saga of the so-called copper kings reads like the opening to a fairy tale: "Once upon a time there were three kings. Their names were William A. Clark, Marcus Daly, and F. Augustus Heinze. They ruled the entire kingdom of Montana."

Clark was a "tight white starched little man, proud and pinch-fisted....a Presbyterian and a patriot. ...He had no humor and no vices. He was intelligent, efficient, ruthless." Penniless at the age of twenty-four, he came to Montana Territory. There, in 1863, his industriousness made him rich. He bought a silver mine, built a stamp mill and, later, a smelter for copper. He bought and sold more mines and leases, and made millions in the process.[8]

Clark's biggest competitor, Marcus Daly, was a miner with experience on the famous Comstock lode in Nevada. He arrived in the Butte area a few years after Clark. He was hailed as a "miner's miner." An Irish Catholic opposed to Clark's Protestant favoritism, Daly sought the help of George Hearst and Henry H. Rogers of Comstock Mine fame and purchased the Anaconda Mine for $30,000. This partially played-out silver property was immediately discovered to have a seam of copper fifty feet wide, and thus was ranked "the richest copper mine in the world." While

Clark smarted, Daly sold it to the Standard Oil Company for more than $24 million. Before the ink was dry on the transaction the mine was capitalized at $75 million.[9]

The copper "wars" began soon thereafter. Historian David Emmons writes that Clark and Daly fought over more than money. Theirs was a religious conflict between the Catholic Daly and Presbyterian Clark and their followers.[10] According to Clark, Daly was uncouth and had made his discovery of the Anaconda by accident. He did everything he could to belittle him. Daly, in turn, spent a lot of money and untold effort to influence and stifle Clark's overt political ambitions; in this he was only partially successful.

In 1889, Clark chaired Montana's Constitutional Convention. He was instrumental in getting Helena crowned as Montana's capital, and was eventually seated as U.S. Senator from Montana in what has been called the most corrupt election in the state's history. Confirming votes were sold at upwards of $10,000 each.[11]

When Rankin came home in 1909, the fall-out from the "War of the Copper Kings" still soured the atmosphere. The young Rankin's first associate in law practice, Cornelius Nolan, was Montana Attorney General from 1897 to 1901. During his term he prosecuted attorney John Ball Wellcome, William A. Clark's chief agent, for bribing legislators on behalf of Clark's first bid for the U.S. Senate.[12] During the two years that Rankin was associated in law practice with Nolan he no doubt learned of the nefarious behavior and schemes of the various state corporations. This probably contributed to Rankin's anti-corporation attitudes throughout his lifetime.

The third copper king was F. Augustus Heinze. He was German-Irish and described by some as handsome and ostentatious. As a young, ambitious miner (some say mining engineer), in his twenties, he found his way to Butte in 1889. Heinze purchased the Rarus Mine with money raised through complicated schemes. This mine adjoined other rich properties belonging to the Boston and Montana Company, his former employer. Heinze was able to tap into these mines underground, keeping "the Company" and especially Daly at bay in the courts. In 1906, when he had reached the end of his legal rope, he sold out to the Standard Oil Company for millions. He used this fortune to develop a competing syndicate to rival the Amalgamated. However, Heinze faced bankruptcy within a year.

He and an associate banker attempted to corner United Copper. In this and other endeavors they had used their banks as reservoirs. On the sixteenth day of October in 1907, astute depositors, perhaps on cue, withdrew their money from these banks and left Heinze and his banking partners unable to meet their obligations. They were ruined and the financial world was near panic. J. Pierpont Morgan used his influence and money to shore-up the Trust Company of America and the panic dissolved.[13] During his feeding frenzy Heinze had developed a taste for liquor and died of cirrhosis of the liver in 1914.[14]

There were a number of reasons why Montana's politics was in limbo when Wellington Rankin returned to Montana in 1909. Daly was dead; Clark was serving, without distinction, his bribed seat in the U.S. Senate; and F. Augustus Heinze was well on his way toward losing his fortune and destroying his liver on Wall Street. The copper interests, which consolidated and evolved into the Anaconda Copper Mining Company (ACMC), aptly named after a snake, still held the state in its grasp. The powerful affiliations it and its subsidiaries had with smaller corporations and cattle and sheep moguls dictated the political climate.

Montana politics was in a state of foment. The State of Montana had been a territory for twenty-five years, from 1864-1889. The political lega-cy of that period lingered into the twentieth century. Always supervised by outside officials, those locally elected officials developed a resentment for the federal government, while at the same time clamoring for more federal assistance.

Shortly after he arrived in Helena, Rankin found his political beliefs at odds with the old Republican guard. A Republican since birth, he was now a young Turk. He was idealistic and ebullient with progressive ideas that gnawed at the roots of some of the older conservative attorneys and politicians. Like other bright, college graduates, Rankin wanted to make his mark, which meant he must rebel against the status quo. The status quo was mostly a hang-over from the territorial times, and the evolving transient population and economy. The mainstream Republican was captive to great industrial power, and this was especially true here in Montana where mining interests held sway.

Rankin entered this scene at a time of change. Jerre Murphy's net-work of frontier individualists had already been altered as Montana's population center shifted east. As the western mining towns grew, so did small agricultural settlements on the state's central and eastern plains. Thousands of homesteaders were settling in the prairie country and foothills. The dryland migration began in the 1860s as a few immigrants took advantage of the 160-acre tracts offered by the federal government. It boomed with the help of promoters, railroad press agents, and land speculators, especially after the Homestead Act increased land allotments to 320 acres in 1909.

When Rankin returned to his home state, tarpaper-covered lean-tos and dugouts of dryland farmers were popping up in eastern Montana. This homestead push continued steadily until 1920, increasing Montana's population to 548,889 by the end of that year.

The flood of immigrants during the last decades of the nineteenth century into Montana left a residue that was not unique in the West. By 1900, 20-30 per cent of the population were foreign born and this diver-sity would be an important ingredient to the political future of the State.[15]

The influx included Germans, Canadians, English, Irish, and Norwegians. Many of the newcomers were from the central and north-central United States, where liberal ideas had already begun to take hold.

Montana was known as "Cattle Country," and truly it was for a while, until the sheep industry replaced cattle as the leading agricultural activity by 1900. The cattlemen who had driven off the bison, and who had unsuccessfully resisted the homesteader's fences, and who nearly to a man believed that sheep ruined the range for cattle and that these inferior animals were raised by inferior men, (namely Hispanics, Basques, and Mormons), were now being usurped themselves. Now at the turn of the century, Montana was the leading sheep-raising state in the country.[16]

The period from 1900 to 1920 was good for Montana farmers. These were the "wet" years when the usually arid plains were blessed with moisture and produced bumper crops. And many homesteaders who had come before and many who followed, were happy and prosperous.

It was not destined to last. The drought returned, and by the 1920s, the bumper crops produced by the rains and virgin soil of the plains were no more. By this time farming had become mechanized and many farmers were left with debt, machinery and the memory of better times.[17] As usual, much of the agricultural adversity was blamed on the government and many who toiled for a living in the soil became radical in their politics.

The Progressive Movement

Out west not just cattle needed a brand. Each political party, political event, politician, voter, or even the man or woman on the street was stamped and belonged to one faction or another. In Montana these designations played a role during the inchoative period of political and economic development after statehood in 1889. This is not to say that this form of tagging makes it any easier to understand the vagaries of the economic and political climate during the first few decades after statehood. It doesn't. A student of this so-called Progressive period out west will find it hard, if not impossible, to categorize and make comparisons with our more modem definitions.

Throughout the twentieth century the words progressive, liberal, and conservative found their way into common usage. Used as weapons in a derogatory sense, the very term, liberal or conservative, was often employed to ridicule or chastise one sect by another. The liberal or conservative was progressive, if, he or she favored gradual improvement of society; women's vote, improved public health, or strict child labor laws, to name a few. Obviously in any culture this is a broad definition and can include a multitude of problems that deserve "fixing." In 1912 Theodore Roosevelt's Bull Moose Party considered itself Progressive. It was a splinter group from the mainstream Republican Party that was disenchanted with over-powering corporate influence. It was short-lived and by the time of the first World War it was no longer popular with the politicians or the public.

The true liberal is a "Pollyanna" figure; a party or person who sees a "goodness and light", and accepts without question the essential decency of man. This is of course the "ideal." It was an oversimplification, but the Liberal was usually open-minded, perhaps even broad-minded in contrast to those elements of conservatism that were almost engraved in stone–tenets based on the preservation of established dictates, social stability and reliance on "the established." In other words a staunch conservative doesn't believe in "rocking the boat," or perhaps better, he or she believes that, "If it ain't broke don't fix it." By simply standing by old policies, however, the conservative can do damage. For example, in the field of protection of the environment, the conservative is usually less concerned than the liberal. Someone, obviously prejudiced, said in this regard, "To compare a conservationist to a conservative is similar to comparing cosmology to cosmotology." In contrast a liberal may be so radical and aggressive that he or she becomes dangerous. The radical, motivated and determined, may spew out ideas and philosophies that border on anarchy or Socialism or Communism.

These are the extremes of both camps, but by and large the population is more middle of the road and leans more or less perceptively in one direction or another. Depending on many factors, among which is the economic status of the time, there is a constant shifting of the political sands. Few people hold to extreme views in either direction throughout a lifetime.

If we look at liberal as "left," and conservative as "right," it is easier to understand. Most see the Republican as more conservative and the Democrat as liberal. This also is an over-simplification. Keep in mind that there were varying degrees of shading and overlapping that made classification difficult to impossible. There were liberals with just a tint of conservative in them. The opposite was also true. New people were coming west and there was a continual change in voter population and political philosophy. Add this to a "boom and bust" economic structure and the classification becomes even more difficult. For these reasons and others, politicians and political leaders could and did change horses in the middle of the stream. Nevertheless and to confuse the picture more, even when the public figure rode a different horse the brand didn't always change.

To recognize the political stripes of institutions or people during the Progressive period of the west is difficult. There are no hard and fast rules or yardsticks to measure with. The following story gives emphasis to the dilemma. Someone was asked to describe and define modern day pornography. The answer was, "I will know it when I see it." Readers will, be able to look beyond the labels and see the characters and organizations for what they were. They will "know" it when they "see" it.

Progressive Politics in Montana

During the early 20th Century, especially in eastern urban centers of the United States, accepted social codes and injustices were being challenged. The "progressives" who wanted change, such as Jane Addams of Hull House in Chicago, tried to right some of the country's social ills: political corruption, exploitation of women and children, lack of women's rights, legal and illegal traffic in alcohol, abuse of workers by employers, and others.

The progressives were middle-class citizens, not radicals. They weren't "Populists necessarily and certainly not members of the Industrial Workers of the World."[18] Progressives were not liberals as is defined today, nor like the liberals of the New Deal that came in the thirties.

The progressive did not easily become a New Dealer. He or she saw too much use of federal power to solve problems and sympathized more with business leaders than young professors. Nor did the old progressive reformer find it as easy politically to penetrate the stock swindles and political mysteries as he had during earlier times. The movement consisted primarily of Progressives who criticized the White House after 1933.[19] Many of the surviving Progressives confronted industry head-on and believed that people could directly affect their government. Some pragmatic politicians were dragged kicking and screaming into the New Deal. As one member of Congress said, "...I have voted for this New deal..., but never with complete confidence. It does seem to me that there is a better way."[20]

The early progressive worked for a popular cause. K. Ross Toole, a Montana native and historian had it about right when he wrote, "...no thoughtful American at the turn of the century could look with either complacency or resignation at his economic, social, and political institutions.... The farmer was on the edge of peasantry; industrial development had been inspiring...but the process had depressed large segments of society...So there arose a new consciousness of man's inhumanity to man...A reform movement swept America."[21]

And what a reform it was. The progressive movement by the end of the first World War had secured a federal income tax, and a national banking system, and regulatory commissions to control transportation and manufacturing. United States senators were now elected directly by the people, and women had the vote–finally.[22]

On a national scale Progressivism produced two presidents, Republican Theodore Roosevelt and Democrat Woodrow Wilson. This suggests that the mantle of the reform movement was elastic enough to cover many differing ideals. Some of the many who called themselves

The Young Attorney

Progressive were isolationists. This was especially true in the West. Others were not. Some were anti-war. Others were not. Women's suffrage and prohibition occupied the energy of most of the early progressives. Montana leaders who fit the loose progressive mold, included Joseph Dixon, Thomas J. Walsh, Burton K. Wheeler–and Jeannette and Wellington Rankin.

Progressives flourished in Montana, partly because of the state's homestead heritage and partly due to disillusioned Republicans. The Progressives, along with the state's organized radical groups–the Populists and the Industrial Workers of the World (IWW)–clashed with established conservative powers such as the Anaconda Company, railroads, and livestock owners. The political result was often difficult to predict.

In 1910, Wellington Rankin found himself representing the liberal end of Montana's political rainbow. One of his first law clients, the Non-Partisan League (NPL), was not as radical as the IWW, which advocated Communism and "one big industrial union." It nevertheless confronted the conservatives of both established parties.

The NPL moved into Montana from North Dakota in 1916 but was present in the state before that time. For a short period, Rankin served as the NPL's legal advisor. He had sympathies for many of its causes. The NPL was anti-alcohol, and Rankin was a teetotaler. The organization supported women suffrage as Rankin and his sisters did. His representation of the League was audacious in the chaotic politics of the time, but it clearly established the direction the young attorney leaned. Although some described the League as a semi-socialist, anti-war, anti-draft group, most political candidates were glad to accept the votes that came with Non-Partisan League support.

If certain of his clients weren't enough to alienate the old guard of politicians and the legal profession, Rankin's personality was. By all accounts, the young attorney could be abrasive. This abrasiveness rubbed hardest on those who profited from the copper industry and established interests that went hand in hand. On one occasion he said, "I'm going to show those SOBs that I can be as big a SOB as they can."[25]

Charles Greenfield, a reporter for the *Helena Independent Record* and Rankin's close friend said, "He was a crusader out to reform the world politically as well as morally…"

A quick learner, Rankin understood the political machinations of his state and honed his political talents to a fine edge. Yet, from the start of his career, Wellington was unpredictable. In light of his times this doesn't seem unusual. Anathema to some, he was greatly admired by others.

Rankin was an indefatigable worker; he found time for a growing law practice and a total immersion into politics. In 1917, he suggested to other Butte Progressives that they start their own newspaper to combat Amalgamated's control.[24] This was the same year that he purchased his own paper, the *Havre Promoter.*

Early Life in the Queen City

"Well, she's like Elizabeth."

Rankin's personal life during this time was almost as chaotic as Montana's politics. Shortly after moving to Helena, in March of 1910, he met and married a local socialite, Elizabeth Wallace. She was a beautiful red-head, the daughter of a successful Helena lawyer. Rankin's courtship was not likely a social move or political union. However, it was rumored that Elizabeth, known as Bessie, married him over the protests of her father, William Wallace Jr.

Rankin never got along with Elizabeth's father. William Wallace, Jr., Elizabeth's father, was a corporate lawyer who became assistant U.S. Attorney General in 1914. Some have suggested that Wallace felt Rankin was after his money. According to legend, the father offered to buy the young man out of the union with his daughter. Rankin told a friend that Wallace asked him, "How much money do you want to give Bessie an uncontested divorce?"

Rankin responded, "If Bessie wants a divorce, she has no right to live with me, and by all means she can have it." Wallace, according to Rankin, broke down and cried, having misjudged his son in law. Wellington said that it was the first time the older attorney had shown any respect for him.[25]

With or without Wallace's influence, Rankin's marriage was soon on the rocks. One story that circulated around Helena pointed to a mismatch. Rankin was a total abstainer and disliked alcohol and those who drank it. When he came home to be present at a party Elizabeth had planned, he found her best china, silver, and accouterments for a lavish dinner on the table–including full wine decanters. Rankin allegedly lost his temper and in a fit of rage clutched the tablecloth, jerked, and pulled everything to the floor.[26] This possibly marked the beginning of the deterioration of the marriage.

Later in life, when Rankin would see what he considered a pampered, spoiled woman, he would remark, "Well, she's like Elizabeth."[27]

The dissolving union may have had something to do with the worldliness of a society girl and the rigidity of a Rankin. He was considered chivalrous to extreme degree. One account has it that while attending a play at Ming's Opera House, Rankin became incensed over a man flirting with someone else's wife. "I'd like to smash him," he told companions.

In a similar instance, on a train, Rankin did let his fists fly. He emerged in Missoula bruised and scratched after fighting with a porter who he considered overtly flirtatious with a female passenger.[28]

One source said that Bessie, as a society leader, spent a lot of money and that, shortly after the marriage, bills came that Rankin couldn't afford to pay. Deserved or not, his alleged reluctance to pay for services circulated later as one of many myths about his personality. This time however he may have been financially strapped. Occasionally his water and electric services were suspended, and according to his friends some merchants refused him credit. Stalwart conservative Republicans sensed this weakness in the young progressive, and told all kinds of yarns about him that added to his misery.[29]

Elizabeth undoubtedly had reasons for disliking her husband. Her changes in affection toward him obviously wounded Wellington, who kept a letter from her, written from Europe, asking him not to "hate" her his whole life.[30] Regardless of the root of its problems, the alliance was stormy, short-lived, and lasted less than a year. Rankin later mentioned meeting his first wife by chance, at which time she teased him about remarrying him.

Coping with divorce and the political climate did not hamper the young man's involvement in the exciting milieu of his time. Divorce was frowned upon, however. Divorce during this era was a very disturbing social issue. Some referred to it as "divorce crisis." Some even thought that it should be under federal control. Some states passed restrictive legislation. There were those who blamed women's liberation and immorality. It was a stigma and in some circles an unforgivable sin. It was viewed as asocial and even smacked of immorality. One can only surmise at the gossip that surrounded this young couple's troubles.[31]

The Progressive movement reached its peak in 1912 when the Republican candidate Theodore Roosevelt split the Republicans to form the Bull Moose Party and went down in defeat. So too did Wellington Rankin.

Only three years out of Harvard Law School, in 1912, Rankin presented himself as Montana's Bull Moose candidate for Congress. At the time he was head of the county Progressive committee and a Theodore Roosevelt devotee. He ran for the office of U.S. Representative in the first election held by popular vote in the State of Montana. He was defeated soundly. Of a possible 80,000 votes, Rankin received only 6,600.

His first defeat at national office was not a total failure. He gained the attention of local politicians and earned some degree of stature that went hand in hand with his membership in Helena's famed bastion, the Montana Club, where he kept Room 61. He gained mention in Helen Fitzgerald Sanders's *History of Montana*, published in 1913. Here on these pages he was described as "among the more successful of the younger members of the legal profession in Montana," and he was recognized as the owner of several mines, both coal- and gold-producing.[32]

As Rankin dealt with this early defeat, he sensed a wind of change coming to Montana politics. Already he was demonstrating his ability to fathom the complex affairs of the state. This particular wind, like a natural breeze, was due in part to geography. A man named Dan McKay traveled by horse from town to town and county to county selling the advantages of smaller counties to a ready audience. His pitch was this: smaller counties would increase the number of state senators and representatives. The action would also provide additional county court houses with a resultant increase in employment.

In 1915 the Montana state legislature played into the county-splitters hands and foolishly enacted the Leighton Act, which gave the counties a free hand to subdivide. By 1920 Montana doubled its number of counties to the fifty-six that exist today. The change was very expensive and cost the citizens a great deal, but with so many county seats, "government" was closer to isolated farm and ranch folk. This increased the agricultural representation in the Montana Legislature.

These changes influenced the state's radical-conservative debate, and gave the sparsely settled eastern prairies, with their Populists and other liberal-favoring people, more clout.[35] The political field was leveled.

4

JEANNETTE

A woman without sham and with tremendous courage.

Jeannette's biographer Kevin S. Giles writes of the relationship between Wellington and his sister Jeannette:

> Wellington was the Rankins' only son ...His mother's laconic expression "The Boy" conveyed blanket acceptance of Wellington's beliefs and activities, and Jeannette was annoyed often throughout her life that he would dare to rival her self-appointed leadership ...Jeannette privately criticized Wellington's consumptious lifestyle and poked fun at his devotion to Christian Science, while he accused his sister of being rash with her money and loose with her tongue.
>
> This epic rivalry persisted beneath an exterior of love and companionship.
>
> She was the philosopher; he the realist. He was a master in the strategy of law, real estate, and money; she was the master of ideas and people.
>
> This peculiar conflict between brother and sister had a profound influence on Jeannette's life.[1]

The influence was reciprocal and the two found much to agree with personally and politically. The cause of women's right to vote was the springboard that launched Jeannette into her political career. It was a cause that she and Wellington could agree on.

Jeannette had come home from Washington for Christmas vacation in 1910. While home, she learned that Dr. D. J. Donahue, then a member of the state legislature, had proposed to introduce a woman suffrage amendment. At the time, Jeannette was a member of the Political Equality

Club of Missoula. Her and her fellow club members were ecstatic at the news. The members chose Jeannette to travel to Helena and further pursue the matter.

When she arrived in Helena she was dismayed to find that Representative Donahue meant to introduce the measure only as a joke. In true Rankin style, she refused to let the issue die. She told the legislator face-to-face, "Well, now you've gotten the publicity, and you'll have to go through with it." Donahue acquiesced. The amendment was introduced into committee, which then sent it to the house. The members of the house then asked the young Jeannette Rankin to address them on this burning issue.

Wellington willingly coached his sister in the oratory skills he had learned at Harvard and helped her prepare for this momentous occasion. Jeannette recalled, "I worked on a speech and Wellington helped me and fixed it up, and I'd go on working on it and every time he'd leave me, he'd say, 'Now this is a very important occasion', and scare me to death"[2]

He coached her in politics and public speaking. She practiced among the shrubberies, trees, and lilacs of her mother's yard. She learned to "project her voice like Socrates."[3] With Wellington's help, and Jeannette's determination and previous speaking experience, she became a spellbinding orator. A skill she never lost.[4]

In the first decade of the nineteenth century Helena had become the capital of Montana. It was no longer the mining camp called Last Chance Gulch and its growing population sought sophistication and culture. There was money now and many fine homes and buildings. It was a busy, crowded town where Montana laws were made in a great concrete edifice crowned by a copper dome. It was a town where ambitions, both good and bad, reigned–a town where history was being made.

The Montana legislature met in Helena every two years, and during the sixty days it was in session there was almost continuous entertainment in hotel suites paid for by the Anaconda Copper Mining Company. The "entertainment" was reported to include gambling, prostitutes, and free liquor–free to all, that is, who voted for "King" copper.

Moral, intelligent, feminine, good-looking and forthright, Jeannette Rankin was not what Helena expected a suffragette to be. On the appointed day for her speech, February 1, 1911, the House was in a festive mood. The spittoons were removed and smoking was banned out of respect for the women guests. The members decorated the chamber with flowers paid for by an assessment of fifty cents from each member. The Representatives graciously invited the Senators to adjourn and join them. The Senate refused and remained in session. Many senators joined them which crowded the chamber.

Jeannette was given a bouquet of violets from California. A committee of other important Montana suffragettes escorted her. They included: Mrs. Mary Long Alderson, Dr. Maria Dean, Dr. Mary Moore Atwater, Mrs. James V. Sanders, and Mrs. May Murphy. All of them were prominent women who had worked on behalf of women in Montana. Most of the men in the audience were favorably impressed with Miss Rankin. They probably anticipated a more severe and less appealing woman. To the contrary, she was flawlessly attired, young, and attractive.

Intuitively, Jeannette began her speech, "I was born in Montana." Her statement was met with loud applause and cheers from the chamber. Some of those cheering were probably relieved to discover that this charismatic woman was not a "carpetbagger" from some eastern establishment, but was one of their own.

After the tumult subsided, she continued with all of the honesty, charm and skill she could muster, "We are not asking you gentlemen to decide this great question [of suffrage]. We are merely asking you to leave it to the intelligence and the sound judgment of the voters of Montana."

Unfortunately, when she concluded some members of the House poked fun in the speeches that followed. In Jeannette's own words, they gave "funny speeches about women suffrage, about all the things that would happen if the women got the vote–and they just had a field day and we were feeling worse and worse every moment."[5]

The ridicule stopped when House-member Judge Cornelius B. Nolan rose to speak. His spellbinding Irish brogue made his remarks all the more effective. He spoke of his mother and the hardships she faced both in Ireland and in Montana. When he had finished, fully a third of the men in the house had tears in their eyes.

Nolan was no stranger to the Rankins. Wellington had just left his law firm to open his own legal office. The two men were friends and it's not a stretch to suggest that her brother may have positively influenced Nolan's opinion on the matter of suffrage.

When the vote was held, a majority had voted in favor of suffrage. But it was not enough; two-thirds was required.[6]

Montana women were cheered by Jeannette's reception in the House and were now even more willing to renew their efforts in their campaign for voting rights Montana's struggle for suffrage, which started before the turn of the century, had gained little ground until Jeannette Rankin came on the scene.

They knew it was an achievable goal. Women in neighboring states had gained the vote already. Suffrage had been in place in Wyoming since 1869, Colorado since 1893, and Utah and Idaho since 1896. As state chairman of the suffrage committee, Jeannette spoke to any audience that would hear her. She traveled, campaigned, and worked with other women from every county in the state. She called on the organizational experience she had gained while working in Washington and New York.

She and her helpers pressured and bombarded men with every

means available. It was like a military operation. Wives, mothers, and daughters gave speeches, used cranky telephones, telegrams, ads, placards, and posters. Some quietly encouraged wives to use their feminine guile on their husbands. Burton K. Wheeler, a member of the House who voted to place the issue on the ballot, said later, "If I hadn't, I think my wife would have quit me."[7]

Montana women who lived in remote places in the state were deluged with information and propaganda. In time, the immense efforts paid off. In 1912, the major political parties agreed to place suffrage planks in their platforms. The suffragists had won some battles, but the war was not over.

Jeannette gained further national experience by acting as field secretary for the National American Women Suffrage Association in 1913-14, then returned to Montana to campaign even harder.

Wellington supported suffrage efforts from the beginning and guided his sister's political career as much as he tried to shape his own. During the campaign for woman suffrage in Montana, from 1911 to 1914, he headed the Montana Chapter of the Men's League for Woman's Suffrage. Other men who took a positive position on suffrage were subjected to ridicule but Wellington was dauntless and idealistic with a sense of fairness. It is unlikely that a rising attorney with such a strong physical presence as Wellington's was ever ridiculed to his face.

Wellington was undoubtedly influenced toward this cause, emulating his hero, Theodore Roosevelt. Roosevelt had spoken openly in support of woman suffrage while governor of New York. It was also encouraging to Wellington that his friend, Montana's Governor Samuel Stewart, supported women's rights.

In 1914 the issue of suffrage was finally placed on the Montana ballot. It passed. The vote was 41,302 to 37,588. It was no surprise that the majority of the votes against suffrage came from the older entrenched mining and agricultural areas where men had less respect for women.

Congresswoman Jeannette Rankin

Wellington Rankin to his sister, "Vote a man's vote."

It had been a long, hard struggle but Jeannette's political fight wasn't over. Suffrage had yet to be passed nationwide, and her love for social causes drove her to seek more influence. War raged in Europe and there were signs that Americans might soon be involved. She wanted to play a part in the future of her country, and the only way open to her was through political office.

In 1916, when Jeannette decided to seek a Congressional seat, she was discouraged by suffrage supporters who believed that it was too

Jeanette and Wellington Rankin in front of old Rankin home in Missoula about 1914. Photo: Montana Historical Society, Helena.

ambitious and too soon for a woman to run for national office. They told her the attempt would strike down their progress if she failed, and suggested she seek a state office such as the legislature instead. The suffrage movement had learned from years of political experience the importance of seeking one goal and one goal only–the vote for women. There was probably good reason for the leadership of the woman's movement to stress the importance of staying out of the limelight, avoiding any semblance of a threat to masculine domains. Even Montana's most prominent Progressive, ex-Senator Joseph M. Dixon, asked Wellington not to "let" his sister run.[8] Entrenched Republicans were not just a little embarrassed by her candidacy.

Jeannette wanted the national seat, and went to Wellington for advice. He disagreed with the feminists and others who had discouraged her, and urged his sister to run for Congress. He said emphatically, "Now you're going to run for Congress and I'm not much interested in whether these women go along with you or not. I'll manage your campaign and you'll be elected. I'll pay for the campaign and I'll elect you."[9]

Her platform was clearly progressive. She called for an eight-hour workday, prohibition, revision of the tariff, children's welfare, increased public knowledge about the business affiliations of political candidates, and suffrage as a federal law. She said about suffrage that her hope, "is to further the suffrage work and to aid in every possible way the movement for nationwide suffrage which will not cease until it is won."[10]

Although at the time the issue of war was not at the forefront, Jeannette's supporters knew that she was an adamant peace lover. She never missed an opportunity to stress this. Once on the campaign trail she said, "If they are going to have war, they ought to take the old men and leave the young to propagate the race."[11]

Wellington's Helena law office became Jeannette's election headquarters and from there he directed her strategy. Based on his burgeoning knowledge of the state, he instructed Jeannette to lean on her success in the campaign for suffrage, emphasize her support of prohibition, and give her blessing to the wool tariff. Many voters in the eastern part of the state raised sheep. The cattle industry no longer dominated the livestock business. These positions, he knew, would appeal to the voters of eastern Montana.

He suggested formation of a club of supporters to make campaign contributions easier, and sought endorsements of other politicians. At that time the population of Montana had increased to the level that called for two seats in the House, and they were both "at large."

With the experience gained during the campaign for suffrage, Wellington and Jeannette organized support. Women and their disciples mailed penny postcards on her behalf and her mother and sisters contributed their time and energy to the enterprise.

Jeannette traveled statewide, spoke at any type of assembly, and always made an impression on her audience—sometime positive, sometimes negative. She was always interesting. She was truly a face-to-face campaigner.

Often heckled, she stood up to rough talk and attempts to startle or shock her. Many years later in an interview Wellington said, "She was one of the best single-handed campaigners I ever saw."[12] Her opponents may have underestimated Jeannette's ability to take it to the "stump." As

Jeannette Rankin. Photo: Montana Historical Society, Helena.

a parting shot at their reluctance, the *Helena Independent*, no friend of hers, said that male candidates were too "dignified" for soapboxes.

Her campaign for Congress was not easy. Although their efforts proved successful, Wellington wrote, "I am shocked at the prejudice that exists against a woman going to Congress."[15] She and the other successful Republican candidate, George W. Farr of Miles City, won the primary. The two were now pitted against incumbent John M. Evans of Missoula, and Harry B. Mitchell, editor of the *Great Falls Tribune*.[14] Both of these Democrats were worthy opponents.

Fortunately for Jeannette, the one force that might have defeated her–the Anaconda Copper Mining Company, ignored her almost entirely. The state's largest newspapers, ACMC-controlled, gave her little publicity. They also did her little harm. Most likely the leadership of the copper industry was totally surprised at the outcome of the election. Most state newspapers took it for granted that she would lose the election.

When the polls closed, the vote tabulation was slow and early results were discouraging. Jeannette was ready to concede defeat. Wellington, on the other hand, was not as easily dismayed. Sitting in Helena on this cold November day, he studied the pattern of the voting returns already counted and predicted victory well before the final results were in.

Wellington had spent the previous five months studying Montana voting patterns. As he viewed the partial returns, he saw that much of the Farr plurality was reported in the more urbanized western half of the state. The tabulation of votes in the far-flung prairies of eastern Montana had been slower to come in, and Wellington predicted they would be the votes that would elect his sister to Congress.

He was right.[15]

Evans, the Democratic incumbent was returned to Washington D.C. with 84,000 votes. Jeannette was second with 77,000, seven thousand more than the other Democrat, Harry Mitchell. Mitchell was not vindictive. He refused pressure from some of his supporters disgruntled at his loss to a woman. They wanted a recount; Mitchell declined. He graciously stated that Miss Rankin had won fairly. He congratulated Jeannette and wished her well.

Jeannette Rankin's election had an immense effect on the country. The eyes of the entire nation were focused on her. Could a woman handle the responsibility of national office? Many were sure she could not. Other's had more confidence she would succeed. She was under extreme pressure. At 36 years of age, the first woman ever elected to Congress, she was literally scrutinized like a laboratory specimen.

History remembers Jeannette Rankin as a peacemaker and woman ahead of her time. Jeanette's life was dedicated to peace. Sometimes her methods were misunderstood and to many she was a pariah. However, time would throw a different light on her accomplishments.

On November 7, 1976, the Rankin Ranch at the mouth of Avalanche Gulch in Broadwater County was designated a National Historic Landmark and memorial to Jeannette. Merrill G. Burlingame, professor emeritus of history at Montana State University summarized at the dedication:

> It is particularly appropriate that we meet here today on the anniversary of one of Montana's most notable accomplishments—the election of the first woman to a major parliamentary body in the world to honor the memory of that first woman …She virtually originated the modern

movement of opposition to war …without a doubt had an influence in the formation of the League of Nations and the United Nations …"[16]

Whenever the opportunity presented itself, Wellington looked after his sister, and especially now. Wellington never missed an opportunity to stand behind her. As an astute moneyman, he arranged for Jeannette to earn some income while she traveled toward Washington. He contracted with the Lee Keedrick Speaking Bureau of New York City to pay the congresswoman $500 for each of a series of speeches. He also traded his legal services to a New York designer for the dress she wore on her first day in office.[17]

Interestingly there was a clause in the contract provided by the agency nullifying the contract if Jeannette voted against world war. This suggests that her reputation as a pacifist was already nationally known. Wellington conveniently ignored this provision, and signed her on.[18]

Young men in Europe were laying down their lives by the thousands, and Jeannette and others in Congress knew they would soon have to face the war issue here at home. The confrontation was unavoidable.

On the way to Washington, she and Wellington stopped to visit friends in New York City. While there, former President Theodore Roosevelt invited them to his Oyster Bay home. Wellington, nervous at meeting the man he had long admired, hoped that the former President would influence Jeannette to vote yes, or at least abstain, on the war question.

The trip to Oyster Bay was nerve-wracking for the politically attuned and hot-tempered Wellington. He recalled this experience many years later in an interview that is quoted here for its historical significance, and to shine a light on the personality of both Wellington and Jeannette:

> The night we went to see Roosevelt …Their chauffeur was supposed to know the way to Oyster Bay. So we started out about three o'clock. After we had gone for an hour or an hour and a half, that son of a bitch was further away from Oyster Bay than when we had started. Well, it was the most important engagement I had ever had in my life. I loved Theodore Roosevelt and admired him. I was so beside myself that I debated seriously just beating the hell out of this fellow. I just had the most terrible time controlling myself. I was just crazed.

> We couldn't phone Roosevelt and tell him that we were late because he had a private phone. All we could do was

keep going. It seemed like we were getting further away all of the time. We got there about eight o'clock. But when we got to the door, we couldn't find the bell—we couldn't find anything! ...Jeannette just broke down and she just laughed, and laughed, and laughed. I never suffered so much as I did then. But with it all, I don't think she suffered very much."[19]

The evening with Teddy went well. Wellington and Roosevelt discussed Abraham Lincoln. The shared admiration of Lincoln bonded the two men. Roosevelt admitted to reading something from Lincoln's writings everyday. To young Wellington this alone indicated that Roosevelt was "a pretty big man to recognize so clearly and firmly" the stature of the Civil War president.

Roosevelt did not live up to Wellington's hopes in one regard, however. He spoke little about the impending war and even less about what Jeannette should do with her vote. In fact, as Wellington later remembered, Teddy Roosevelt said that President Woodrow Wilson, whom he called, "that fellow in the White House," should see that there was no need for war at all "if he had a lick of sense."[20]

According to Rankin, Roosevelt then said that if he had been elected president he would have had some personal influence with the Kaiser. He showed Jeannette and Wellington pictures of himself taken with the German leader and implied that his past association might have been helpful in preventing war.

To put this visit in perspective it is important to remember that Theodore Roosevelt was the leader of the Progressive party. While Wellington and his sister were privileged to have this person-to-person contact with a man they had admired so much, it must have seemed a little like Dorothy and the Wizard of Oz. Vice President Roosevelt was thrust into the presidency in 1901 by the assassination of President William McKinley and kept the leadership of his country until 1909. During his time in the White House he made great progress in the eyes of those who felt a need for change.

He was a "trust buster." He arbitrated the 1902 anthracite coal strike, saw to it that the Northern Securities Railroad Combine was prosecuted for antitrust violations, and pushed the Pure Food and Drugs Act through Congress. One of his major successes was getting the Hepburn Act passed. This law authorized the Interstate Commerce Commission to regulate railroad rates.[21]

Roosevelt attracted young Progressive Montana Republicans like Wellington and Jeannette with more than just his achievements. He had strong Montana connections. In 1912, Missoulian Joseph M. Dixon had directed Roosevelt's bid for reelection when he split away from the mainstream and formed the Bull Moose Party. Although defeated, he won many followers like Wellington Rankin.

Thus, Wellington's disappointment when the old Bull Moose leader did not tell Jeannette how to vote on the issue that everyone knew would present itself—whether or not America should declare war on Germany.

Although Wellington believed his sister should vote yes on the issue of war, he nevertheless supported her. He advised her to "Vote a man's vote." This may not have been the best choice of words to give to a young flourishing feminist.[22] He knew that Jeannette was compelled to stand by her own convictions and that she had campaigned for election with the slogan, "Prepare to the limit for defense; keep our men out of Europe."[23] Wellington later recalled, "She would consider it more dishonest not to vote your conviction than to rob a bank or steal something."[24]

Wellington and his mother, Olive, stood proudly in the audience the day Jeannette was seated in the House of Representatives. He was less proud as he stood again by her side when the issue of World War I came at last to a vote. Jeannette's views were strong but Wellington did his best to change her position. "I tried to get her to vote for war," he said, "I didn't want to see her destroy herself."[25]

On Good Friday, at three o'clock in the morning on April 6, 1917, Jeannette Rankin cast her first vote as a member of the U.S. House of Representatives. All eyes were on Jeannette, the first woman ever to serve in Congress. After answering "present" on the first roll call, she answered "no" on the issue at hand: whether the United States should enter World War I. Her now famous reply was, "I want to stand by my country, but I cannot vote for war. I vote no."

President Woodrow Wilson had submitted the resolution. Jeannette voted her conscience. Her name thereafter would be linked with the cause of pacifism. Hers was only one of fifty "no" votes in the House. It was the one the country would remember.

Another prominent congressman who split with his president on the issue of war was Democratic majority leader Claude Kitchin of North Carolina. Among other things, he said, "...let me at once remind the House that it takes neither moral nor physical courage to declare a war for others to fight."[26]

After Jeannette's "no" vote, she met her brother. They walked together through the dark corridors of the capitol and onto the dimly lit streets of Washington, D.C. The support Wellington gave by his presence was shaken by his words. His was a tough love. He was overheard telling his sister that she had destroyed her political career and had made many enemies.

Belle Fligelman, Jeannette's secretary, remembered Wellington saying over and over to his sister, "Think of what you've done. Think of what you've done."

She replied, "I'm not interested in that. All I'm interested in is what they will say fifty years from now."[27]

The young congresswoman was subsequently attacked by some of her fellow congressmen, other politicians, the media, some suffragettes, and many men and women on the street for what they believed to be her nonpatriotic position. There were rumors that she had shown weakness and had broken down with tears and visible emotion at the time of the vote. These were false rumors meant to degrade her. Frontier women from Montana were expected to maintain their composure in public, and she did.

Others in congress did weep. Fiorello La Guardia of New York said he didn't know if the Congresswoman wept or not, stating, "...I could not see because of the tears in my own eyes." He voted for the resolution.[28] Jeannette and La Guardia remained friends throughout their careers.

Congresswoman Rankin was extremely stressed, depressed, and under great pressure as the whole country watched and speculated. She wrote to Wellington a week after the vote and said, "I'm sorry I had to disappoint you. I still feel this was the only way I could go."[29]

Wellington, always her closest friend and advisor, said a long time later, "I knew that she couldn't be elected again if she did vote against war [and] I didn't want to see her destroy herself [and] all of the things for which she had worked."[30] Later he expressed regret at the pressure he had brought on his sister at such a stressful time in her career.

As things turned out, many people in Montana never forgave Wellington Rankin for being Jeannette Rankin's brother. The label of pacifism attached to the Rankin family name did little to help Wellington in his future political aspirations. It was used against him frequently during his own political career and attempts to gain national office. The stigma of his sister's vote was tempered a little when Wellington served in the Tank Corps during World War I. He was in Officer's Training when the Armistice was signed. He never saw combat. Wellington and his sister were as patriotic as anyone. Nonetheless she was vilified, called a traitor and worse in much of the press, especially at home.

In 1917, patriotism throughout the nation flared to hysteria. Jeannette, who had campaigned as a pacifist and had received much support in her election by people who thought they did not want war, grossly misinterpreted the response her vote received. Especially in rural states like Montana the few people who raised even tremulous and tentative voices against war, were labeled communist or fascist.

Jeannette was right about one thing–many mothers lost their children to the war. There were 1,500 young Montana men killed in World War I. Because of a draft based on erroneous figures, a greater percentage of Montanans were conscripted than from any other state in the union. Almost 40,000 men either volunteered or were drafted–10 percent of the state's population.[31]

Jeannette fulfilled her term in spite of cries for her resignation or impeachment. After the furor over the controversial vote cooled, she served out her term trying to get some of the issues she supported passed into law.

She scrutinized each issue that came before the House to ensure that women and children were protected. She introduced a bill requiring the same wages for men and women in government work, and a bill for pensioning families of soldiers. She asked the House to give women a citizenship independent of their husbands.

Most of the issues she championed eventually became law during her lifetime, but failed during her term. She served in a Congress that was preoccupied with a war, and her issues were ahead of the times.

Her modest accomplishments during this period have been overshadowed by her first vote. On January 10, 1918, Jeannette addressed the House of Representatives on a joint resolution proposing an amendment to the Constitution, which would extend the rights of suffrage to women. A large proportion of American women still did not have this basic franchise. Hers was an impassioned plea, but the nineteenth amendment (suffrage for women) would not see the light of day until 1920.

She regained some popularity as she stood up for improved working conditions for Butte miners, argued for loans for farmers, and even advocated American recognition of the independence of Ireland. This last bold move earned her favor from a big segment of the Butte community. However, none of this helped her with the conservatives back home in Montana.

Her greatest legislative effort was exerted in an attempt to get the Rankin-Robertson bill passed. This bill was intended to promote women's health, and proposed instruction on venereal disease and birth control. It had strong support among the public, but it was defeated.[32]

When her term expired, she refused to leave the public scene. She entered the race for Montana's United States Senator. Surprisingly, much of the emotions against Jeannette had faded when she entered the primary Republican race for the U.S. Senate in 1918. In spite of the pacifist label, Jeannette was only narrowly defeated in the primary election by Oscar M. Lanstrum. Dr. Lanstrum was a respected Helena physician, newspaper publisher and leader of the Republican "old guard." He was the opposite of progressive, a Company man, and no friend of Wellington's or Jeannette's. Years later, the two adversaries, Rankin and Lanstrum, competed for control of the Montana Republican party.[33]

Jeannette was disappointed, but probably not surprised, at her loss in the primary to "the Company" favorite, Lanstrum. Wellington, who managed her campaign, re-entered her in the Senate race as an independent, a third party candidate. Now she was pitted against Democrat Thomas Walsh–Wellington's former employer–and Republican

Lanstrum. The fact that she had been defeated by less than five percent of the Republican vote gave them some hope of success.

She was supported primarily by a loose coalition of strange bedfellows–Non-Partisan League farmers, pro-war Socialists, anti-war Progressives, prohibitionists, and others dissatisfied with the two party system of politics.[34]

Their friend Cornelius Nolan, Walsh's partner and Wellington's former associate, who had supported Jeannette and woman suffrage with the utmost chivalry, discouraged them from continuing. He was concerned that Jeannette would split the liberal vote to the detriment of Walsh.

As the incumbent, Senator Walsh was leaving nothing to chance. Walsh was a formidable, charismatic, dominating leader who held the respect of a majority of the Montana population. Some say, as added insurance in this election, that he mobilized invaluable aid from his former enemy, "the Company," and wooed it away from Lanstrum.

It was too late for Jeannette to withdraw from the race. She might have abandoned the field before the election except for the spreading rumor that Jeannette had taken a Company bribe to quit. In the face of this, it seemed prudent to stay in.

Montana's senior Senator Walsh, as it turned out, had little to worry about. He carried the field. Jeannette was far behind both of the other candidates.[35] Although Walsh was a Democrat, he had much in common with Republican Jeannette. They were both Progressive in their thinking. The Rankins probably took some comfort in this loss since Walsh also defeated Lanstrum.

Before his terms in office ended in death in 1933, Thomas Walsh gained considerable praise as an "advanced progressive." He led the fight in 1916 to confirm the nomination of Louis D. Brandeis to the Supreme Court. He became a staunch advocate of enlarged federal programs including the retention of public lands. He favored the United States' involvement in world affairs. His most well-known triumph was the uncovering and prosecution of the so-called Teapot-Dome scandal.[36]

Jeannette, whom Wellington called, "a woman without sham and [with] tremendous courage" left the political arena–for the time being.[37]

5
THE YOUNG LAWYER

"...an experienced criminal lawyer, who added laurels to his specialty crown by winning a rather difficult victory."

By 1918, Wellington Rankin had gained a reputation as a promising lawyer who could hold a spell over a jury. He lived law every day of his life. He was the kind of man Montanans liked. A crusader, he was flamboyant and up front with his ideas and ideals. His reputation spread. At such a tender age he was already lauded as a trial lawyer and his cases were the stuff of conversation for many people.

Rankin's success as a lawyer was predictable from the beginning. His Harvard degree and his early start with the outstanding Helena firm of Nolan & Walsh were auspicious. His oratory skills, put to use in favor of Jeannette's causes, also served him well in the courtroom.

But his fame came from more than these alone. He also gained a popular reputation as a man who defended the underdog. The well-known Helena newspaperman and Rankin friend, Charles Greenfield, had this to say about Rankin's early years in law practice, "He let it be known that he would be glad to be appointed to defend persons facing criminal charges in the federal court who were without funds to hire counsel."

These were often tough cases and he had few successes, but Rankin sincerely believed in the innocence of his nonpaying clients.[1] He was known to pay court costs out of his own pocket when required. At one time he had about $14,000 invested in appeals for these hapless individuals and lost practically all of their cases. We are left to assume that he lost his money as well. At that time of the twentieth century, a dollar was a significant amount of money.[2]

Rankin's philanthropy gained him a great deal, especially in terms of reputation. He was well-known by ordinary citizens who looked for a legal hero. His political aspirations weren't hurt, either. While he traveled the state to try cases, he became acquainted with many different kinds of Montana citizens, in and out of court.

The young attorney also gained more than he lost financially. His prominence soon attracted clients who could pay for his legal skills. At this time in history, courtroom fame was the only way lawyers could advertise. Rankin, either consciously or unconsciously, took full advantage of this. His reputation expanded until he was known in even the more remote corners of the state.

If his reputation as a courtroom lawyer is as witnesses remember, he put on quite a show. Had television and radio and their modern preoccupation with the courtroom been available then, Wellington's reputation might have rivaled many of today's flamboyant attorneys. He would have been at par with men like Jerry Spence, F. Lee Bailey, Johnny Cochran, and others who play to a broad audience. More than likely he would have been invited to CNN's Court channel.

The Rodoman case, tried in Townsend, Montana in 1911, was one of the first to bring fame to Wellington Rankin. Mike Rodoman had been charged with the killing of Frank Jakleh, an Austrian immigrant on the Fourth of July. Rodoman was a Montenegran by birth, and some local people believed the killing was due to ethnic tensions between the two men. Defending Rodoman successfully, Rankin defeated the Broadwater County Attorney C. P. Cotter.

The local newspaper described Cotter as "being young in criminal prosecutions" but conceded that he presented his case in a "spirit of fairness." Whatever the newsman meant by this statement, the fact is that Rankin won. According to the newspaper article, the jury concluded that the tragic murder was related to racial prejudice, or as the writer termed it, the "equivalent to American Feudism." In addition, the article suggested, racism that leads to mayhem is to be expected among "foreigners."

There was a good deal of humor described among the jury and spectators in the courtroom over the "partial mastery of the English tongue by a majority of witnesses."[3] In flowery and dumbfounding words, the editor of the *Townsend Star* suggested:

> "The jury was made up of men of mature age, possessing analytical minds and that degree of discretion which counts for the conservation of justice and that permissibly protects the public treasury of the commonwealth without inviting tragedies or other wanton conduct by carelessly disposed citizens of whatever nationality that may constitute our mixed population now or in future."[4]

Whatever the writer meant to say, we are given a glimpse of frontier justice as it existed in Montana at that time. The headline in the November 4, 1911 issue of the same newspaper read, "RODOMAN ACQUITTED, Slayer of Frank Jakleh Pleads Self-Defense and Wins." This was 1911, the same year Rankin hung his own shingle and left Nolan &

Wellington Rankin. Photo: Montana Historical Society, Helena.

Walsh. *The Townsend Star* called him "an experienced criminal lawyer, who added laurels to his specialty crown by winning a rather difficult victory." This young attorney must have made a considerable impression.

Numerous tales about Rankin's prowess as a courtroom lawyer circulated around the state. Some were true, or at least based on truth; others were not. Rankin's name spoken in conversation from bar-stools, or in front rooms, or by cowboys hunkering around campfires, usually provoked a knee-jerk reaction causing someone to repeat a yarn about the man.

Many of the tales were similar to this undocumented anecdote: The young Rankin in 1912 purchased an automobile from a local dealer. Since he was a careful businessman and attorney he checked the contract of the purchase very carefully and discovered a major flaw in the way the document was written. According to the story, when he pointed out this error to "the Company," the owners were so grateful that they marked the contract "paid in full," and gave the car to him.

But there were differing versions of the story. Some not so complementary. Another version of the same story claims that when Rankin discovered the error in the contract he refused to pay for the automobile on the grounds that the contract was invalid.

Told repeatedly in Montana folklore, this and other myths create starkly different images of the same man. The tales were often colored based on the storyteller's personal opinion of Rankin. One version might paint him as an astute but honest businessman, another as a crafty, conniving character.[5]

Here's another legend that circulated at the time. Rankin had represented a client against the Northern Pacific Railroad. He won a $300 dollar judgment. "The Company" refused to pay. Rankin waited patiently until a train loaded with passengers from the west pulled into Helena. While the train was taking on coal and water, Rankin quickly placed a legal attachment on the locomotive. The train and its unhappy travelers were stalled until the money was paid.

"Insulting and Impudent"

There is ample evidence of Rankin's occasional abrasive behavior in the courtroom. In 1917, he became pugnacious while trying a case against the Helena Light and Railway Company. While riding one of "the Company's streetcars, Mr. John P. McDonnell had leaned on a door that unexpectedly opened. Mr. McDonnell fell out, was apparently run over, and literally cut in half by the large steel wheels. Rankin represented the widow at the coroner's inquest.

Rankin was winning the case until he questioned the coroner, Dr. Ben C. Brooke, a well-known Helena physician. Rankin and Brooke disliked one another, probably for political as well as personal reasons. Rankin was a progressive and Brooke was extremely conservative and a partner in medical practice with Rankin's political enemy, Dr. O. M. Lanstrum. According to Judge Henry Loble, Rankin committed a significant error that Loble suggests no attorney should make. He tried to put words in the witness's mouth.

"Doctor," Rankin said, "we assume that you are going to testify that the deceased died as a result of being cut in half by the wheels of the streetcar, isn't that true?"

To the surprise of everyone—especially Rankin—the doctor said emphatically, "No. That is not correct. The man died of a heart attack,

Wellington served in the Tank Corps during World War I. He was in Officer's Training when the Armistice was signed and never saw combat. Photo: Montana Historical Society, Helena.

then fell out of the car and was mutilated by the wheels."[6]

A shocked Rankin reminded the doctor that he had previously testified that the deceased man had died because of a fall. The doctor denied ever making such a statement. Brooke lost his temper and called Rankin a "prevaricator." He allegedly said the "P" word three times. According to the gleeful reports of Helena's *Independent Record* Rankin "swelled up," walked over to where Brooke was seated, clutched him by the coat, pulled him from his seat, and "struck him full in the face with his fist." Pandemonium followed.[7]

It was not surprising that he lost control. Tempers flared in Helena that autumn. It had been a scorcher of a summer, the driest July in ten years, and war in Europe raged on. The *Helena Independent* and its mouthy editor had fueled paranoia in a populace just eighteen months away from Prohibition, mourning the "cruel death for Barleycorn."[8] Rankin didn't drink, but he was anticipating entry on the side of those opposing prohibition. Being called a liar didn't calm him, nor did the prospect of losing the case.[9]

Rankin spent only a few minutes in jail and was released. The young district attorney in Helena at the time was Rankin's friend, Lester Loble. He had the unenviable responsibility of prosecuting Rankin who was not only a friend but also sometimes an associate. He dreaded the task.

With diplomacy, Loble urged Rankin to admit guilt and pay a nominal fine of $250. Rankin reluctantly agreed, probably more pained by the admission of wrongdoing than by the loss of cash. The court was relieved as well, apparently glad to settle the matter.

Brooke dropped the charges but exclaimed publicly, "I don't believe anyone that crazy knows right from wrong."[10] In the end, the coroner's jury ruled that McDonnell had died as the result of a fall from a streetcar. Rankin had won again and his antagonistic reputation as an attorney spread even wider. As president of the Helena Bar Association during this same period, Rankin was not likely censored by the group for his conduct in the courtroom.

His pushy courtroom behavior did not end with this event. On one occasion, he allegedly chased another attorney around the courtroom brandishing a pointer because the attorney had interrupted Rankin while he was demonstrating a chart.

In 1920, Judge R. Lee Ward of Lewis and Clark County had all he could take of Rankin's "insulting and impudent" remarks to the court during a case. He ruled Rankin in contempt and fined him $250 and sentenced him to forty-eight hours in jail. In a dramatic scene, the court delivered Rankin into the custody of the sheriff.[11] Rankin produced a $500 bond and was released from jail after a short time. He also paid the fine.[12]

It is interesting that although Rankin was seemingly not welcome in Ward's court, he was allowed to return and cross-examine some witnesses in the case. His associate, Mr. A. H. McConnell was not familiar enough with the medical aspects of the litigation and made a special request to the judge to allow Rankin back.[13]

If some judges were not happy with the young attorney's behavior, many lay people were. Without television or other entertainment, the courtroom became a showplace where people with time on their hands could enjoy a good debate, a fight, and a good show. Antics that would not be allowed today by officers of the court were tolerated at that time. Nothing short of a traveling circus or medicine show compared. Judges were not nearly so strict and attorneys played to the audience with little danger of censure.

Rankin's fame as a lawyer spread. In reference to Rankin, William Kitto, a longtime Broadwater County resident speaking about the "early days" said,

> How hard it is to separate the good defense lawyer that he is from the slogan that attaches to his name everywhere, that "you cannot beat Rankin." I need not tell you …to what lengths he will go to win his case. You, like me, have traveled miles to hear him present his final arguments before a jury.[14]

Rankin's deftness as an attorney began early in his career. Contrary to myth, he was not able to win all the time. Local Helena newspapers reported on one trial that he lost and wrote that it "read like a movie scenario."

Forty thousand dollars was stolen from the Union Bank & Trust Company in Helena. Charles Stevens, a young bank clerk was the suspected thief and was defended by Rankin. Stevens' behavior implicated him as the thief and led to his conviction. The paper reported with lavish detail and a great deal of poetic license a story that truly was worthy of film documentation. It could have played as a comedy starring the celebrated Charlie Chaplin.

The somewhat less than practiced thief, Stevens, managed to get custody of a large sum of currency that was in transit from the First National Bank at Butte to the Helena bank where he was employed. As testimony later revealed, the young man left a trail through the city of Helena making an effort to be seen and remembered by many people. While doing so, he made no effort to hide a package he carried in his hand. His actions were so obvious that someone even recalled that Stevens entered a building carrying the package. It was later established that this parcel contained the missing money. Witnesses testified that he had the package when he entered the empty building but came out without it.

A short time later Stevens was discovered in another building bound and gagged with superficial scratches and a slight abrasion on his forehead. He feigned unconsciousness, but on occasion asked for water and recognized acquaintances. His explanation for his predicament was that three men had subdued, bound, and gagged him. The press referred to one as "Scarface" (a well-known character in the contemporary "Dick Tracy" cartoon series). Stevens claimed he had a scar on his face, hence the label.

After the unsuccessful swindler had changed his story several times, he took the police to the abandoned building where he had hidden the money. It was gone. The corpus delecti had disappeared. Nonetheless, County Attorney Lester Loble satisfied the jury that fourteen years in prison for young Stevens was in the best interests of society.

In Steven's defense, Rankin could not convince the jury that his client could not have tied and gagged himself. Rankin appealed but the high court refused him. Stevens was sentenced to prison on March 10, 1920, one day after some of the missing money was discovered in the little town of Toston, Montana, a short drive from Helena.

Tracing the money discovered in Toston led police to Mrs. Oswald Watkins of Helena. Mrs. Watkins was a well-known alcoholic. On the day of the theft she saw Stevens with the package in his hand enter a vacant building and leave empty handed. She rightly assumed he had hidden it. Prohibition was in effect and hidden packages of this size and shape usually meant a stash of whiskey.[15] Thirsty people were always on the lookout for "booze" (the word used by the newspaper was "neckoil.")

Mrs. Watkins' husband and a man named Frank Smith were employed nearby as painters. She reported to them what she had witnessed. The "thirsty" three hurriedly searched the building. Instead of moonshine they found cash. By the time Stevens was on his way to prison part of the money had been spent and the rest buried behind an outhouse in Toston.

Oswald's brother became involved and now there were four people to share in the loot. They had difficulty calculating the shares. On several occasions, the four tried to count the money. Each time the result was different. They never did get an accurate tally. Their division of the plunder was inexact at best. Apparently, Smith was the better at math. The *Independent Record* said that he "departed to unknown places with the 'long end'" of the treasure."

To many who knew him well, Rankin was considered a philanthropist. His dealings were fair and honest. As an attorney, he represented people from all walks of life–the poor and the powerful. Untold numbers of clients were helped by Rankin: widows who needed help in the management of their affairs; divorced women abandoned and abused by the system; ranchers and farmers fighting government and bureaucrats.

He was an avowed enemy of corporations and oftentimes represented groups of laborers against big businesses like the Anaconda Copper Mining Company, the Montana Power Company, and the Northern Pacific Railroad.

A versatile criminal lawyer, he could defend murderers and get them acquitted–or as a prosecutor he could hang them.

Rankin was careful with money, but he supported social and political causes. As a young woman, Bozeman realtor Helen Johnson knew him well. She recalls many things that Rankin did for people she knew. She admired his selflessness and his efforts to support the Republican party. She said, "He used a lot of his own money." Ms. Johnson sent many troubled people to him for legal advice and recalled, "he was always able to help them, whatever the problem."[16]

The Young Rankin and Politics

*"...sometimes what appears to be the State
is 'the Company' and sometimes
"the Company" seems to be the State."[17]*

As a young lawyer, Rankin had political aspirations. Throughout his adult life he was a leader in Montana's Republican Party. Nonetheless, every attempt he made to achieve national public office had failed. Now his popularity, name recognition, and his well-deserved reputation as a lawyer, gave him access to the political stage once again, this time with more success.[18] In 1920, he ran for the position of Montana's attorney general and won. The same year Joseph M. Dixon was elected governor. To understand Rankin's political career, it is important to know his relationship with his contemporaries in the political arena.

Joseph M. Dixon

Wellington Rankin helped to spearhead the local Bull Moose Party in 1911-1912. This was a group that was decidedly "anti-copper." Their weekly news circular was headlined, "Put the Amalgamated out of Montana politics."[19] Both men, Dixon and Rankin, were allied politically, at least on the surface. Their ambitious paths had crossed on many occasions and their progressive beliefs were similar. In the beginning, there was also mutual respect. Underneath, the relationship between Rankin and Governor Dixon was less certain.

Dixon, a Southern Quaker, had moved to Missoula in 1891. A lawyer, businessman, and sometime newspaper publisher, he rose rapidly in local and state politics. He was elected as representative to Montana's Seventh Legislature in 1900 after serving for a short time as county attorney in Bitterroot County.

He then turned to the national forum. He was elected to Congress and was Montana's only voice in the House of Representatives for two terms, from 1903 to 1907. The folks at home appreciated his work. When he returned home for a visit five thousand people met his train.

During his congressional years, Dixon's Progressive colors showed. Acclaimed by many contemporaries as a fine speaker, he was also a natural and courageous leader. Joseph Dixon left his mark, a proud and progressive one, on the nation and his home state.

He always opposed the way "the Company" and its supporters controlled the State's government. He was disgusted with the "git and git-out"[20] attitude of most of the lumber, mining, and even some ranching interests that came uninvited, extracted wealth, and left without paying their share of taxes.

Even with the opposition of the industrial complex, Montana's legislature elected him U.S. Senator in 1907. In this office it was soon clear that Senator Dixon was not "a middle of the road" Republican. He became a devout "Rooseveltian" and bolted the main stream with the incumbent president to create the Bull Moose Party.

Teddy Roosevelt trusted the young senator to manage his campaigns. A full time job, it kept Senator Dixon away from Montana. While away, he could not debate his opponent and confront his enemies when his office was up for re-election. This and a Republican split gave his challenger, Thomas J. Walsh, an easy win. The Democrats swept the 1912 election.

Dixon lost, but so did Roosevelt. Dixon always felt that his sacrifice was worth it. Years later he wrote, "…I would not have taken a different course, even though I had known in advance that my action meant inevitable defeat."[21]

The 1912 election in Montana was not a total loss to the Bull Moose Party. Twenty Progressives were elected to the state legislature. The new Party carried the state except for "the Company" strongholds such as Butte and Anaconda; places that had a natural aversion to anything that smacked of progressivism.

One extremely important, almost sacred, progressive cause prevailed after the dust of the election settled. This was the issue of the direct election of U. S. Senators. Since the turn of the century twenty-nine western states had accepted this change in their constitution. The list now included Montana. No longer could the legislature, often controlled by major corporations and other special interest groups, nominate and elect who they wanted to represent the people's interests in the Senate.[22]

There was another breakthrough for the Progressives. Thomas A. Walsh, who defeated the incumbent reformer, was a strong Progressive himself. Now that Teddy Roosevelt had lost and the Bull Moose movement had faded, Dixon came home.

With the Bull Moose Party dead, Rankin and Dixon found themselves out in the cold without affiliation. Both Rankin and Dixon squirmed back into the Republican Party. Their relationship had changed however. Eight years later, working in nearby offices in the Capitol, the former colleagues now mixed like oil and water.

Burton K. Wheeler

On a cold, October day in 1905, Wheeler, a tall, thin, twenty-three-year-old Massachusetts Quaker, with only a diploma from the University of Michigan Law School in his pocket, disembarked from the Northern Pacific train at Butte. Only five years later, in 1910, he was elected to the Montana Legislature. From this time on, his life was devoted to public service.

In the campaign for governor in 1920, Dixon overwhelmed Burton K. Wheeler, the Democrat.[23] He received significant help from "the Company." They had good reason to fear Wheeler. Early in the contest Wheeler was quoted by the *Butte Daily Bulletin*, "If elected governor of Montana, I will not put the A.C.M. out of business, but I will put it out of politics."[24] This was a challenge that could not be ignored. Political control was the life blood of Montana's industries—especially the copper dynasty.

Wheeler was a man who would survive more than thirty-five years of political tumult. He would later say during his retirement, "Controversy has sparked my public life…I've been called …Communist to Fascist…almost everything but timidity."[25]

Always a controversial figure, Wheeler's involvement in the 1920 campaign for governor of the state was no exception. Newly fired by Senator Thomas Walsh from his appointment as United States Attorney, where he had inflamed the hatred of many Montanans, Wheeler challenged Dixon.

The memory of World War I was still fresh on the minds of Montana voters. Many irate citizens would never forgive Attorney General Wheeler for his defense of, and refusal to prosecute, many people who were accused of "unpatriotic behavior" during the war with Germany. This background and his open support by the radical Nonpartisan League, seen as socialists or "Bolshevics," made him vulnerable to verbal as well as physical violence.[26]

There was a frenzy of paranoia in America during 1917-1918 that spilled over into the remote and sparsely populated West. "Spy fever" prevailed.

In Montana, yellow journalists fueled that fever. Will Campbell of the *Helena Independent* warned Montanans in headlines that spies might masquerade as ordinary people: "Your Neighbor, Your Maid, Your Lawyer, Your Waiter May Be A German Spy."[27]

According to the news media, people were frightened by reports that enemy "airships were seen crossing the country…"[28] Unfortunately many people believed these bizarre rumors and neighbor turned against neighbor. This was especially true in those communities where there was ethnic diversity like Butte. Agricultural areas that had attracted Germans speakers from Europe to farm in the area provided plenty of suspects.

The Montana Council of Defense was created to foster economic and moral support of the War. It was not meant to limit civil liberty or to promote mob violence. However, the local group fell under the control of zealots, such as journalist Will Campbell, who spread propaganda and misinformation. Consequently, some Montanans were jailed illegally. Citizens under suspect had their rights trounced upon in the name of patriotism. There was at least one lynching. German books were burned.[29]

United States Attorney Wheeler tried to keep a lid on the frenzy that gripped much of the state. He refused to charge many of those accused of sedition. As an officer of the court, he saw it as his duty to uphold the rights of all citizens.

When Wheeler didn't conform, he was called before the Council himself. For many days the group subjected Wheeler to a biased inquisition. He did not relent or bend under pressure. He was combative and stood firm. Piles of worthless, irrelevant, and prejudiced testimony accumulated.[30] In the end, all of the participants went home exhausted.

Judge George M. Bourquin

"This court may be wrong, but not in doubt."

Another Montanan that was stained as unpatriotic in the minds of the so-called "patriots" was Federal Judge George M. Bourquin of Butte. Fortunately for Wheeler, Judge Bourquin agreed with him and said that the Espionage Act was not intended "to suppress criticism or denunciation, truth or slander, oratory or gossip, argument or loose talk."[31] These were not federal crimes, Bourquin said.

As United States district judge, his rulings in the so-called "slacker" cases during this period of turmoil hurt his reputation just as bad as it did Wheeler's. He was called arrogant and irascible. He probably was, but he was fair and just and humane. He was the kind of judge who said to one defendant that was charged with a minor liquor violation, "The court finds you not guilty, but don't do it again."[32]

In the highly visible cases prosecuted under the National Espionage Act of June 15, 1917, in America, many militants wanted the courts to make federal cases of sedition based on minimal and often hearsay evidence. A few of the Montana cases were not entirely without some merit.

In one case, for instance, Judge Bourquin found the accusations about his country "unspeakable." However, there was not any evidence presented, in the Judge's opinion, to justify a guilty verdict.

Other cases were simply ridiculous. Take for instance the case where one man was fined and sentenced to hard labor in prison for refusing to kiss the flag, even while ruffians and thugs were trying to force him to comply. Bourquin reversed another court's decision in this case and reinstated the victim's freedom.

In Montana, especially in these early years, judges had to be strong. As the noted law professor Roscoe Pound said in his book, *The Formative Era of American Law*: the West depended on a strong judge. One who knew "how to use the precepts of the law to advance justice…"[33] There simply were not many judicial decisions recorded. A good judge had to use common sense and common law and adapt to changes with little reference to precedent.

In the frontier days of the West, courts achieved social justice by natural law and reason instead of authority. It was more important to be tenacious than erudite. One legal historian commenting on the contribution of the West's first judges said that they "did not know enough to do the wrong thing, so they did the right thing."[34] Judge George M. Bourquin was probably right when he said, "This court may be wrong, but not in doubt."[35]

"Boxcar Burt"

Many groups of people in the state would never forgive Wheeler. During his campaign for the Democratic nomination for governor, he was prohibited by the Dillon City Council from speaking at a rally at the courthouse. His supporters gathered in the countryside where he spoke from the bed of a truck. A group of men crying, "Get a rope," drove him into a boxcar where armed friends guarded him through the night.

After this episode, many of his enemies called him, "Boxcar Burt." Others preferred, "Bolshevik Burt!" These outrageous names stayed with him for the rest of his life, but he wore them like badges.

The *Billings Gazette* attempted to cast a shadow on Wheeler's reputation by accusing him of advocating "free love." The Nonpartisan League, an organization that supported Wheeler, apparently had published some books discussing the subject of "free love." Wheeler told a crowd in reference to the publisher of the *Gazette*, Charlie Bair, "Now let me ask you…If there was free love in North Dakota, do you think Charlie Bair would still be in Montana?"

Stories were circulated among Lutherans that he was a Catholic and Catholics were told that he was anti-Catholic. Wheeler's reply: "My mother was a Methodist, my father was a Quaker, I attended the Baptist Sunday school as a child, I am married to a Methodist, and like most of you men, most of my religion is in my wife's name."[36]

After he was defeated by Dixon and went home to Butte, he was attacked and beaten severely on the street by toughs. When the stooges who beat him were brought to trial, the Butte judge dismissed the case and said, "Any man with red blood in his veins would have done the same thing…"[37]

This was the lowest point of B. K. Wheeler's career. To the surprise of many, he recovered and was elected to the United States Senate in the next election. Here in this lofty position of authority he remained from 1922 until 1947.

Dixon the Reformer

"there is [no] lesser evil offered in this case."

Dixon won the governorship in spite of his open opposition to the Amalgamated Copper Mining Company and its ruthless twin, the Montana Power Company. Both organizations opposed anyone with a progressive past or present. Neither candidate was acceptable to the "Montana Twins," but Wheeler was even less so. The Anaconda Copper Company's paper, *Butte Miner* said, "there is [no] lesser evil offered in this case."

Wellington Rankin summed up this characteristic of the industry many years later when he said, "Those outfits [the Company] never wanted an independent person...[they prefer] a person who will never rock the boat."[38]

Dixon campaigned primarily for Governor on one issue: to increase the tax upon mining interests in order to shore up Montana's sagging post-war economy. Although he won the governorship, he was defeated during his tenure in every way by "the Company," by drought, and by the depression. His attorney general was no help either.[39]

Whether or not Rankin preferred Wheeler as governor we will never know, but he did not like Dixon in the office. This became clear after several months of combat between the governor and the state's new young prosecutor.

From its start, Dixon's administration faced challenges. It was a bad time to be in charge. When Dixon assumed office, the state had a $2 million deficit brought on by a severe drought and depression. In the agricultural areas of Montana there were over 20,000 foreclosures between 1920 to 1925. Two million acres of agricultural land had passed out of production and twenty percent of the state's farms were vacated.

There was a great deal of public support for increased taxation to correct the deficit. Governor Dixon offered an inheritance tax, income tax, a tax on oil and coal, a higher license fee for automobiles and taxation of mining production.

In 1923 Dixon reported that $20 million worth of metal had been extracted that year from Montana mines with a total tax on the mining industry of less than $14,000. Furthermore Governor Dixon reminded the people that Montana's "stricken farm" industry paid in thirty-two per cent, livestock more than ten per cent, and railroads seventeen per cent of the State's revenue. The mines, on the other hand, contributed less than nine per cent.

Nevertheless, the State House of Representatives, influenced by the mining industry's lobbyists, ignored his figures and refused his administration any more revenue. Although he confronted the industrial powers in a way that few other Montana politicians had, Dixon was hamstrung in all his efforts to increase taxes on mining interests. His administration was crippled by its inability to solve the financial difficulties of the state, and to a lesser degree by the burgeoning animosity of his state's attorney general.[40]

Attorney General Rankin

Rankin did a good job as an elected official, but he was not a team player. As attorney general he prosecuted a wide range of cases–from bootleggers to murderers. He didn't always win his cases but he represented the people to the best of his ability.

Rankin waged some of his battles from his seat on the Montana State Board of Equalization. In August 1921, as attorney general and as a Board of Equalization member, he questioned the right of the Northern Pacific Railway to hold and sell mineral rights on land–grant parcels. Rankin ordered "the Company" to show cause why it should not be assessed $5,000 or more per acre for mineral rights, saying, "I don't believe it was ever intended that the Northern Pacific Railway company should keep this right. There is a surface right, a district right and they contain valuable oil, gas and coal…."[41]

Rankin's challenge came to nothing. It did help to establish him as a voice against corporations taking resources without paying. Like many politicians of the era, he waffled this position throughout his tenure for political expediency.

Attorney Frank T. Hooks, who practiced in Broadwater County for forty years, opposed Rankin in court ten times, and he said, "they split fifty-fifty."[42] One notable case of Hooks versus the young Attorney General was *State v. Doughty*.

An influential stockman, contractor, and railroad builder A. B. Cook, who ranched in Broadwater County, had accused a man named Doughty of stealing sheep. Rankin, as newly elected attorney general, decided to prosecute the case himself. Twice the case went to court, both times it resulted in hung juries. Rankin was anxious to impress Cook, his good friend, an influential Republican, and a contributor to Rankin's campaign.

The young attorney general returned to Townsend a third time, but the case was dismissed. The Broadwater County sheriff's office had allowed the skins of the sheep, the evidence, to disintegrate. The *corpus delicti* upon which his case depended was gone. Rankin was furious and threatened to prosecute the sheriff himself, but he didn't.[45]

Rankin's most famous and controversial case as attorney general was a politically motivated parody. The case involved Frank Conley, the well-known and politically savvy warden at the Montana State Prison. Conley had thirty-five years' association with Montana law enforcement and the prison at the time of the trial.

An ambitious lawman and entrepreneur, Conley came to Deer Lodge in 1886 to work as a guard in the prison. It was a federal institution at that time. Conley had come to Montana in 1880 and served as deputy sheriff of Custer County for four years. That alone suggested that he was tough and able to take care of himself. Miles City, the county seat of Custer County, was notorious for law-breakers of all kinds.

In 1889, the State inherited the prison from the federal government. Conley and a partner made a contract with the state to manage it and act as wardens. During this period, the prison was essentially a private enterprise. The system continued until 1908 when the State assumed control. Conley continued as warden after the transition.[44]

A photograph of the warden taken circa 1920 depicts a large, balding man with heavy, dark eyebrows, a thick mustache, blunt features, and cold, penetrating eyes. He was reported to have a congenial personality. He was well connected socially and politically with formidable and influential friends. Among his most powerful supporters was "the Company."

Dixon's administration detested Conley. Governor Dixon suspected, for good reason, that the warden was cheating the state. He hired a New York accountant and attorney, T. H. MacDonald, to investigate the prison finances. After five months, the investigation was completed. MacDonald discovered that Conley, on a salary of $4,000 a year, had amassed a fortune of $200,000. As one accountant said, "if the eggs could be unscrambled" the total Conley fortune would be closer to a half million dollars.[45]

MacDonald concluded his analysis of Conley's record with this comment, "Every avenue of curtailment of expenses has been diverted into the private treasury of the former warden and every industry at the prison has been prostituted to his enrichment."[46] Dixon accused Conley of mismanaging state funds and fired him. This started a controversy that would plague him the rest of his term.

Newspapers controlled by the copper mining interests and anti-Dixon forces kept the Conley case in the limelight. Will Campbell, the editor of the *Helena Independent*, and a well-known Dixon-hater, accused the governor of "coddling slackers, seditionists, highwaymen, rapists, porch climbers, and jail breakers" while prosecuting "good men." The newsman had a way with words, but his phrases often made little sense.

Cornelius B. Nolan, Rankin's former associate and good friend, represented Conley. It was Rankin's responsibility to prosecute the warden. Rankin and Governor Dixon were openly antagonistic over this issue.

The feud might have been anticipated since the two had argued on most matters brought before the Board of Prisons and the Board of Equalization, on which they both served.

Rankin lacked the desire to prosecute Conley because the young attorney general had higher political goals, and did not want to be tarred by the same brush that was smearing Dixon. The garish Conley, a fellow Republican, had friends in high places. He was well-known for his lavish parties and other entertainment that included hunting and fishing trips on his ranch holdings.

Always the strategist, Rankin had his eyes on the upcoming congressional election and hoped to unseat Senator Henry L. Meyer in 1923. He knew he needed all the support he could get, at whatever the cost. Dixon's biographer, Jules Karlin, summarized Rankin's dilemma as follows:

> Rankin, who held the balance of power...was unsympathetic from the outset to an investigation (of Conley). He even refused to assign an assistant to participate in MacDonald's probe. After all, the attorney general was indebted politically to Conley...[47]

Rankin may have feared that prosecuting Conley would place him on the wrong side of the Republican leadership as well as conservative Democrats. Politically, by opposing Dixon, who was the "whipping boy" of his own administration, he felt somewhat protected. The economy was bad and Dixon took the blame for everything from the drought to the depression.

By stalling the prosecution of the Conley case, Rankin curried favor with the Northern Pacific Railroad and the Anaconda Copper Mining Company. Apparently, the industrial leaders felt, and they were probably right, that if they kept the heat on, Dixon and the Board of Equalization might be prevented from increasing state taxes on their mineral wealth. Attorney Rankin's behavior must have pleased them.

Karlin writes:

> Dixon and his associates all bore the Republican label; their relations were consistently unharmonious. Attorney General Wellington Rankin was an enigma.... handsome, brilliant, and dynamic, Rankin could also be magnetic and pleasant when he desired, but he was a victim of his own qualities. He was overweeningly ambitious, intensely selfish, erratic, mercurial, vituperative and temperamentally undisciplined. ...During this era, Dixon had hailed Rankin as "my friend and a thorn in the side to 'the Company' and the old guard." Rankin's senatorial ambitions virtually

compelled him to…. oppose Dixon at every turn. Thus, although Rankin could hardly be classified as a "Company Man," his performance could not have been displeasing to it.[48]

Rankin's anti-Dixon positions gained him temporary approval of that powerful political force, the Anaconda Copper and Mining Company sometimes known as the "Kerosene Crowd" or the "Standard Oil Gang." At the same time, Rankin lost credibility with pro-Dixon forces that were not insignificant.

Rankin stalled and postured and in the end asked only for an "accounting" from Conley. He did not charge him with any criminal acts. This was far less than Governor Dixon had hoped for. He saw it as a "friendly suit with no teeth."[49]

Rankin escaped his quandary, but with consequences. Governor Dixon was enraged. Conley and "the Company" were pleased. Judge A. J. Horsky presided over the trial without a jury. After three thousand pages of transcript and untold amounts of press from Company controlled newspapers in his favor, Conley was acquitted.

The judge did not exonerate Conley of bilking the State of Montana. He ruled that none of Conley's activities in running the prison had violated any statute.[50]

Judge Horsky's verdict aggravated the antagonism between Dixon and Rankin. The vocal battles between the two made news, and the media played up every skirmish between the former allies.

Rankin accused the governor of making political capital out of the Conley affair. Dixon responded, "If there is any man who has subordinated every official action to politics, it is yourself." Rankin denied it but later admitted that he himself had been on trial.[51]

One interpretation of the Conley miscarriage might be that once Rankin became state attorney general, he realized that, nationally and locally, the Progressive movement had withered. His struggle for prominence and increasing conservatism led him to butt heads with Governor Dixon. As a leader of the decaying Progressives he wittingly or unwittingly became a friend to king copper, which he had previously fought at every turn.

As Rankin obstructed Dixon's efforts to bring about tax reforms and dragged his feet on the Conley prosecution, he inspired even more public rancor toward Dixon's administration. Such publicity benefited none except those already in power. Rankin essentially did their bidding as he strove for attention. What we cannot say is whether he knew he was currying favor at the detriment of his former colleagues. And if he knew, was his conscience bothered? Whatever his thoughts, it is obvious that he worked toward his ambition–to be the Senator from Montana.

Rankin the Reformer

*"Some of the worst bootleggers in the state are holding
public office and I intend to smoke them out."*

Meanwhile Rankin had a job to do. His office had more than the
Conley matter to contend with. He was "the Law" for the state and just
over the mountain from Helena was Butte, a community teeming with
people. It was the largest city between Spokane and Minneapolis and
north of Salt Lake City until 1930.

In Butte, fourteen thousand five hundred of the approximately
eighty-five thousand inhabitants worked underground, and many of
these were foreign born. A place that Joseph Kinsey Howard called, "a
very bully of a city, stridently male, blusteringly profane, boisterous and
boastful." An "island surrounded by land," it was labeled, entirely
dependent on copper. A smoky overcast place where the *Butte Miner*, the
Company's voice declared, "The thicker the fumes the greater our financial vitality."[52]

It was also a place that enjoyed the smell of whiskey fumes. In 1910,
when Carry Nation brought her hatchet to Butte in her battle against the
evils of drink, she was physically beaten and tossed out of one drinking
and whoring establishment by none other than May Maloy, Butte's legendary madame. Carry's saloon smashing crusade that worked in
Kansas did not work in Butte. This was eight years before the Volstead
Act was passed.[53]

Drinking was a big part of Butte culture. Prohibition was a dirty
word on the streets of Butte. It altered, but didn't cure, the problems
related to alcohol. A miner, off duty after hours in the bowels of the
earth digging ore, needed a "Sean O'Farrell," (a drink of whiskey with a
beer chaser). After prohibition, moonshine and a glass of home-brew
worked just as well. A miner explained the value of this mixture as follows, "...whiskey to cut the copper dust from their lungs, and the cool-
ing beer to slack the thirst accumulated during eight hours in the
'hole'..."[54]

Mary Murphy in *Mining Cultures, Men, Women and Leisure in Butte, 1914-
1941*, wrote, "Until the advent of Prohibition, drinking in Butte was gov-
erned by clearly defined and understood social rules. Saloons were male
preserves...Any woman who drank in a saloon was assumed to be a
prostitute at worst, 'loose' at best. Prohibition changed all this."

An industry of underground moonshining was born. Women
cooked liquor on the kitchen stove and husbands and wives ran blind
pigs, moonshine joints, and "home speaks" competing with saloons that
had been hastily veneered to appear as soft drink parlors to the unsus-
pecting. Women began to drink in public and participated in the fun. It

was no longer a man's world. Now women were involved in a business that men had previously dominated.

Regardless of the law, Butte remained "wide-open where a man could buy a drink, place a bet, or visit a prostitute at any hour…without worrying about being arrested."[55] Drinking was a way of life in most mining towns, and especially Butte. Police, juries, and judges were inclined to look the other way.

The enforcement of prohibition backfired in Butte. It was hard to catch and prosecute those who were breaking the law. The county attorney in Silver Bow County prosecuted only about a hundred cases for bootlegging. during a two year period, and in Cascade county, a much smaller community, the prosecutor took two hundred and seventy-one to court. In Lewis and Clark County, one hundred and sixty-eight were brought to justice.[56]

Law enforcement was confronted by an almost impossible task in attempting to do its duty. Many citizens didn't like the restrictions placed on them, and there were those paid to uphold the law that were easily corrupted. Although it was hard to prove, many believed that Prohibition contributed greatly to graft and payoffs."[57]

Unfounded rumors had circulated about Attorney General Rankin for some time. It was said that he closed his eyes to the alcohol trade in Butte. His friends knew it was not true. Mary O'Neill, a Butte political activist, suffragist, and one of Jeannette Rankin's best campaigner allies wrote to warn Rankin of this "word on the street" in 1921. She said:

> While I (O'Neill) was in the office of Sheriff Larry Duggan this afternoon arranging a little business matter he told me of a piece of news which had been told to him earlier in the day… 'A traveling man came to me (Sheriff Duggan) today and told me 'This order of Wellington Rankin to close up gambling rooms, suppress bootleggers, etc., etc. is just the same old game of his predecessors.' I was told by several men in Helena that Rankin had given out information where it will scatter best that he had been forced to issue this order to enforce the laws, but that he would let them alone in a few weeks."

> I believe I convinced him that you, too, are in earnest and will back him up in his determination to clean out the deplorable conditions here.

> When you come over to Butte please make it one of the most important matters that you see him and talk over the conditions here, and assure him that there is no four-flushing coming out of the office of the Attorney General while you control it….[58]

The accusation was ironic, since Rankin was a teetotaler himself, a supporter of temperance societies, and long known as a "dry." This spurred him to action. A short time after receiving this letter he addressed the state's county attorneys: "Some of the worst bootleggers in the state are holding public office and I intend to smoke them out...., I do not propose to spend my time prosecuting whisky runners but I do intend to weed out those officers who, under the cloak of official authority are committing crimes, and also those officers who through spineless timidity, follow the line of least resistance and deliberately and willfully neglect their duty." These were strong words. This was Wellington Rankin at his best.[59]

He honored his word. On October 16, 1921, the Missoula county sheriff, W. H. Houston resigned. He had been caught selling and delivering whiskey. He had also notified and warned bootleggers when raids were contemplated.

In another case, John Morgan the sheriff of Liberty County resigned after he confiscated liquor and then allowed several cases of that booze to be taken from his automobile while his back was turned.

In 1922, the *Missoula Sentinel* singled Rankin out as an opponent of those who ignored prohibition. He was active in prosecuting as many as were arrested for bootlegging or operating clandestine bars and speakeasies. The *Sentinel* article noted that Rankin's liquor-busting activities in Billings had led to the corralling and conviction of a large number of lawbreakers.[60]

Rankin's efforts in Butte could barely have stemmed the flow of liquor to the parched mouths of thirsty miners. And the problem was not confined to Butte. Hunting down bootleggers in the thousands of square miles of Montana with its remote and sparsely populated areas proved to be not only difficult, but impractical. Bootlegging was a statewide industry.

The Federal Writers Project Almanac declared, "Baffled federal blotters ranged this huge state in a vain effort to dry up millions of gallons of 'mountain dew' made for 537,606 prospective drinkers who had 94,078,080 acres to hide in."[61]

Even the most ardent prohibitionists, the Anti-Saloon League, eventually lost heart. The young attorney general had about all he could handle and more in dealing with the overwhelming problems of alcohol in this huge area. He was only able to scratch the surface, but scratch it he did. At least he did enough to keep the newspapers following his progress.

While the Conley case and bootlegging problems received the most publicity, Rankin had many other matters that occupied his time. He received high marks for his aggressive stand against the livestock rustling, especially in Eastern Montana. Cattle rustlers along the Powder

River, headed by a notorious character named "Poker Jim," were getting the best of the authorities. Rankin ordered enforcement of the law and required inspections of all animals moved from county to county. For this popular move the *Independent Record* editor was unusually kind to him.[62]

Rankin's forward thinking administration prevented at least one injustice. He secured the adoption of a resolution providing that when a prisoner at the state penitentiary applied for parole, pardon, or reduction of sentence, the county attorney in the county where the convict was tried was to be consulted before action of the board of pardons was taken.

This action prevented at least one murderer from being paroled from Deer Lodge Penitentiary. J. C. Miller had been incarcerated for several years for murdering a young man named Green. The board of pardons was being petitioned by well-meaning citizens to release Miller. Allegedly, the victim's father, who lived in Spokane, had made a deathbed confession to the murder himself. The county attorney at Spokane, Washington, when consulted, exposed the confession as total fiction. He said that the death and confession of the murdered man's father was, "slightly exaggerated", and Mr. J. W. Green was "alive and well and in my office, this morning..."[63]

One of the most important cases Rankin prosecuted as attorney general was the "Smoke Case." It received little press from Company owned newspapers because it cast a shadow on Montana's mining industry. Oscar B. Goon had asked for $27,000.00 because the ACMC smelter at Great Falls released arsenic and zinc fumes that killed his cattle. Twenty-five other livestock owners filed similar cases against "the Company." Wellington Rankin represented the plaintiff but returned to Helena in defeat. The trial ended in a dismissal because the jury in Fort Benton where it was tried failed to reach a verdict.[64]

During the same month in Eastern Montana, Rankin took only three days to convince a Hysham jury to convict Joe B. Reagan for murder. Reagan had killed an undersheriff when he attempted to steal from a bed-ridden woman.[65]

Rankin's fame in the media made him a frequent target for criticism. In February and March of 1924, his attorney general's office was the focus of a federal grand jury investigation. Once again, Rankin was accused of failing to enforce the Volstead Act in Butte.[66] There is some evidence that the case was part of an orchestrated smear campaign against him. When the dust of Rankin's indictment settled, facts involving corruption of Butte officials became known.

U.S. Attorney Joseph Slattery, who triggered the investigation, was accused of refusing to present certain evidence to the grand jury. The dry Anti-Saloon League of Montana and the Butte Citizens Law Enforcement Committee supported Rankin and joined him in denying any wrong doing.

Both organizations made it clear that they always had the full cooperation of Rankin and his office in combating whiskey related crime. The League and the Enforcement Committee had enlisted the help of the President Coolidge White House, the U.S. Attorney General of the U.S., and the Burns Detective Agency to bring charges against Butte officialsnot against Rankin.

These groups claimed that "for a year the United States Attorney's office (Slattery) has not supported efforts to secure a cleanup in Butte and Silver Bow County."[67] There were assertions that sinister influences and mysterious interplays defeated justice in Butte in all cases involving liquor, gambling, or vice. Rankin's office, privy to the illegal activities in Butte, had waited for the federal agencies to act. Rankin said pragmatically, "The likelihood of securing a conviction was greater in the federal court than in the state court."[68]

Once exonerated, Attorney General Rankin marched triumphantly into the turmoil of Butte. According to the *Anaconda Standard*, Rankin said, "We have just begun.... We are in Butte to stay until law is respected."[69] This was a courageous, if not, calculated move. The mining town of Butte was a dangerous place and drinking liquor was not just a pastimeit was a way of life. Any one threatening this liberty could be in harm's way. In spite of the danger, Rankin immediately filed thirty-six abatements against places where liquor was being sold. Rankin and George W. Bourquin, Butte's courageous county attorney, tried all the prohibition and bootlegging cases like a police court without a jury, processing dozens of cases each day.[70]

Rankin emerged from both the Conley matter and the grand jury proceedings with a mixture of friends and supporters from both parties. One of the most prominent was the Democrat, U. S. Senator Burton K. Wheeler, who continued throughout his long career as Wellington Rankin's friend.

Both Wheeler and Rankin considered themselves enemies of big business and stayed at odds with "the Company" throughout their political lives—except when it was expedient to be otherwise. As Rankin campaigned at home in Montana, Wheeler was in the U.S. Senate battling with the egregiously corrupt Harding Administration.

Shortly after Harding's death in 1923, Wheeler introduced a resolution to investigate corrupt U.S. Attorney General Harry M. Daugherty. According to Wheeler, some of Daugherty's outrageous illegal transgressions were "prison sentences shortened, pardons sold, paroles granted, and cases not prosecuted—all for money. Daugherty participated in stock market pools and owned shares of stock in companies he should have prosecuted."[71]

As a result of Wheeler's inquiry, President Calvin Coolidge discharged Daugherty from office. Before Daugherty left office in disgrace in April of 1924 he arranged for the FBI to secure an indictment against

Wheeler for allegedly accepting a retainer to influence the issuance of oil and gas property permits in Montana.

John L. Slattery, the U.S. Attorney for Montana who had also attacked Rankin from time to time, prosecuted the claim. The respected Senator Thomas J. Walsh was the principal defense counsel for Wheeler. Rankin sat with Wheeler in a show of support throughout the long and painful ordeal. This period of comradeship between the three men sealed the Walsh-Wheeler-Rankin friendship. Wheeler was exonerated when the principal witness for the prosecution admitted to perjury.[72]

One of Rankin's last official acts as state attorney general was his attempt to cancel the now infamous championship boxing match held in the little town of Shelby in Toole County. Basking in the afterglow of the discovery of oil in nearby Shelby people had visions of grandeur. A few entrepreneurs in the town conceived the idea of holding the Jack Dempsey-Tommy Gibson heavyweight title bout in this obscure location. The fight was scheduled for July 4, 1923. It was expected to draw thousands of people to Montana.

Rankin, a boxer himself, initially approved of the event. In the weeks that led up to the planned exhibition of fisticuffs, newspapers reported rampant vice in the little High-Line hamlet. Publicity attracted quite a few shady characters. The papers reported there were "side-shows, girly shows, and even rodeos."[73]

Attorney General Rankin was forced to respond to the rumors of such corruption. From Helena, he made his intentions known, saying "Shelby shall not be the rendezvous of thugs, yeggs, plug-uglies, pickpockets, gamblers, rum-runners, or any other class of anarchists who make a living by defying the law and the Constitution." After this pronouncement he visited the town and concluded that the reports had been exaggerated.[74]

The fight was held with a smaller and tamer crowd than expected. Overall, it was not a very exciting event. Gibbons, a relatively unknown but likable contender, lasted fifteen rounds in the summer heat. Dempsey won by a decision. The contract stated Dempsey was to get most of the money, regardless of the outcome. Gibbons capitalized on the publicity and was indirectly rewarded. The town of Shelby was the big loser. Four banks closed after the event, and several financiers lost their fortunes because the fight did not attract a large enough audience.[75]

In 1924, as political opportunities presented themselves, Rankin pulled himself up to higher places. He had lofty ambitions. He advanced methodically from attorney general to the Supreme Court of Montana, and finally to the towering position of United States Attorney for Montana.

Like some before him and others to follow, he hoped to use the position of attorney general as a stepping stone to higher political office.

6

HIGHER AMBITIONS

The Mavericks[1]

Rankin's next attempt to reach the illustrious destination of national office, the U.S. Senate, came in 1922 while he was serving as Montana's attorney general. He lost a close primary race for the U.S. Senate Congressman Carl W. Riddick, of Lewistown. In an example of Republican solidarity, Rankin crusaded vigorously against Democrat Burton K. Wheeler on behalf of Riddick.

Every community has its power elite. They are usually a fraternity of men. Sensing power in the brotherhood, they borrow status from one another. It is a reciprocal attraction. The class distinction crosses boundaries of age, background, and political affiliations.

In older establishments education, community standing, and (especially) ancestral connections form pools from which leaders evolve.[2] Not so in young, developing states like Montana from which Rankin sprouted. The Treasure State was unique and isolated, and it developed its own power elite. Those who rose to the top of the political pyramid did so by sheer force of will, personality, and shrewdness. At this time in history, it was popular to be progressive and to battle corporations. Some Montanans who aspired to power gained voter approval by confronting the state's Goliath industrial complex. This was a dangerous endeavor. In most instances, it was preferable to have "the Company" as a friend rather than an enemy.

Burton K. Wheeler was a furious anti-corporation candidate. He overcame almost impossible barricades created by propaganda and character assassination to finally win a seat in the U. S. Senate. He was hardheaded, practical, and a quick learner. Certainly, he did not conform to any established set of rules or party.

Thomas J. Walsh, a quieter opponent of "the Company, always seemed to do the right thing at the right time in the eyes of Montana voters. He was liberal and proud of it.

Wellington Rankin

Then there was Wellington Rankin, who was born on the frontier and well-educated. He was a man of strong character, impeccable morals, and masculine looks. Nonetheless, he was never able to grab the "gold-ring" of high political office. He was his own man and stayed his course regardless of the consequences.

Politics, and the behavior of those caught-up in the discipline, are confusing to sideline observers. In many ways, the behavior resembles that of a sporting event. Opponents do battle. Sometimes the loser is angry and considers his successful adversary an enemy. This may last for a long time. Sometimes the wounds of that conflict never heal. Very often the combatants find that they have more in common than they thought. They become friends and support one another. If one fellow runs for office, the friend, who was previously an adversary, may give him all the help he can.

There, of course, is no guarantee that they will not oppose one another again if different circumstances present worthwhile advantages. If this happens, whatever the result, they return to their friendship and life goes on as usual.

Although they were never opponents for office, Rankin, Wheeler, and Walsh were of different camps and often supported different candidates. Walsh, Wellington's former associate in law practice, had to fend off the Rankins politically in his bid for re-election to the Senate. On occasion, it was necessary for him to distance himself from Wheeler to garner conservative support. Nevertheless, during their long careers, all three remained friends and supported one another in many ways.

Burton Wheeler

In the 1922 election, Wheeler defeated Riddick who had defeated Rankin. This time Wheeler, the young campaigner, was more careful, wiser, and far less combative. His defeat by Dixon in the race for governor just two years earlier had taught him some valuable lessons.

Wheeler was careful to suppress his support from the agricultural Nonpartisan League because of their "liberal" ideas and the stigma that had developed against them during the recent war–particularly in conservative minds. He made it clear to them that he saw their point of view and wanted their support, but he did not want their open promotion.

His campaign was helped immeasurably by Montana's depression, and Governor Dixon's inability to prevent the economic decline. This disastrous period vindicated Wheeler in the minds of many Montana citizens. To support this exoneration he told a playful story from platforms all over the state during his canvass: "A man applying for citizenship was asked by a judge to name the governor of Montana. To this question he replied, 'Wheeler'. After he was corrected by his interrogator, the man said, 'All I know is that all the papers, the bankers and the politicians said that if Wheeler was elected all the mines would close, the banks would foreclose the mortgages on the farms, and everybody and everything would go broke. Now the mines have closed, the farmers are losing their farms and it looks as if everybody's going broke–so I think Wheeler must be governor.'"

Wheeler also benefited by "the Company" closures forced by the economic slump. This unpopular action on the part of the mines lost the industry much of its support, and voters who usually followed its lead began to think for themselves.

Many of Wheeler's detractors felt confident that he could not succeed anyway since he had been so badly beaten by Joseph Dixon in the governor's race. But, win he did, with fifty-six percent of the vote. The man known as "Boxcar Burt" or "Bolshevik Burt," described by some as "an accident in politics;" a man who was nearly lynched by a Montana mob just two years earlier; had won a resounding victory.

His long and illustrious career in the Senate had just begun. Only two years later Wheeler was chosen as the Progressive Party's vice-presidential running mate of Robert La Follette of Wisconsin. This effort at a third party fizzled, and Wheeler wisely realigned himself with the Democratic Party as soon as he could. [5]

The 1922 Senate Primary: Rankin vs. Linderman

That same year, Wellington lost yet another bid for the Republican Senate nomination. As president of the Helena Bar Association, he was becoming a greater political force in the state. His competitor, Frank Bird Linderman, was just as well-known. In the June primary election, the majority voted for Linderman.

It was a close contest. Linderman was Montana's premier man of letters in the early twentieth century. He wrote with great skill and perceptiveness about Montana. In particular, he was a voice for the state's Native Americans. His books did not make him rich, but they sold well and some are still in print. During his long Montana career, he was a trapper, assayer, insurance salesman, businessman, newspaperman, state legislator and innkeeper. Always actively engaged in the support of his Native American friends, he was instrumental in getting Rocky Boy's Reservation established in 1916. Some of Montanan's most respected pioneers such as Charlie Russell and Paris Gibson called him friend.

He was not as successful as a politician. Linderman ran for national office three times, but was defeated each time. He was a proud man of the old school. Throughout his political career the loss that hurt him the most was his defeat by Jeannette Rankin in 1916 for the House of Representatives. In the primary contest he was only one of eight candidates.[4] In his private letters and other writings, he said that "immigrants" and "feminists" defeated him. This revealed a side of his personality that was not readily apparent. Losing to a woman was extremely painful and discouraging to him. He later said, "The Warbonnet has passed from Buck to Squaw. Soon the peace pipe will too!"[5] This statement may have been partially right. Jeannette Rankin spent most of her life organizing peace efforts.

Both of the primary Republican candidates, Linderman and Rankin were progressive within their party, but Linderman held more support from the "Republican center" than did Wellington. Linderman was a close ally of Dr. O. M. Lanstrum, the powerful Republican leader. Lanstrum was a man that did not hold Wellington Rankin in very high regard.

Linderman and Lanstrum had served in the legislative assembly together. According to one story, they had agreed between themselves to vote against Thomas H. Carter, "the Company's choice, for the U. S. Senate. Linderman kept his agreement and voted against "the Company" man, Carter, but Lanstrum succumbed to pressure and voted "the Company" line. Nevertheless, Linderman and Lanstrum, remained the warmest of friends[6]

Several of the smaller newspapers across the state supported Rankin's candidacy against Linderman. In the Miles City Star, Rankin was perceived as "… a man of considerable force, with a strong personality and the ability to make friends. He is an eloquent speaker and presents a good appearance on the platform…. Mr. Rankin has been on the side of the people."

Others agreed. The *Boulder Monitor* added, "It is generally conceded that Wellington D. Rankin will be the Republican nominee for United States Senate to oppose Walsh … the Republicans are fortunate in having a man such as Attorney General Rankin to vote for."

Although he had some support and fought hard for a chance to challenge his friend and former attorney associate, Senator Thomas Walsh, his attempt was unsuccessful. Sometime during Rankin's early law practice and entry into politics, Walsh and Rankin had developed a mutual respect. Such was the political aura of the time. Unfortunately, their burgeoning friendship gained Rankin the reputation as an even stronger progressive than he really was.

Thomas J. Walsh

Walsh had become a powerful, national figure during his short tenure in the Senate. He was a fearless muckraker. His success in rooting out "evil" in government in the case of the Teapot Dome Reserve scandal was lauded throughout the nation. He was praised by numerous periodicals as an honest and forthright man who was "tireless," "unchanging," "dogged," as well as "respected."

At the 1924 Democratic National Convention Walsh was made the permanent chairman. He turned down the vice-presidential nomination.[7] He was re-elected in Montana defeating Frank Bird Linderman in the process.

Walsh garnered powerful support from many corners, and he needed it. Corporations, in this case the oil groups, who saw themselves tainted by the Teapot Dome scandal opposed him.

Burton Wheeler announced his support of Walsh because Walsh's defeat would be regarded, in his words, "as a repudiation of his magnificent fight against corruption. He has aligned himself with the progressives on almost every issue during the last term of Congress…" As usual, the voters listened to Wheeler, who had such a forceful way with words and a powerful way of saying them.[8]

A Man of the People

Never pick a fight with anyone who buys ink by the barrel.

The "gods" that ruled national political office in Montana seemed to never smile on Wellington D. Rankin. One biographer described the young politician as a powerful presence who might have been equally strong politically:

> …a 190-pound dude with a hard fist, ready at any time to accept a physical challenge as he was to accept a court test of legal ability. He was a handsome man, and had been urged in his college years to become a dramatic actor, and his speaking voice compared with any this writer has heard. He did not utilize his great talents to the limit, as he did in the practice of law, when he ran for political office.[9]

Winfield Page, an occasional political opponent of the Rankins, believed that Wellington's biggest handicap to political success was "his arrogance and the everyday friction he had with people." Those who were close to Rankin were discouraged by his refusal to mingle and meet with potential voters. He would not "glad-hand" or kiss babies. His sister, Jeannette, criticized him for his aloofness. She thought that he simply did not like so much closeness with people or perhaps he saw it as a loss of dignity.

Another factor that contributed to Rankin's defeats was Jeannette's image as a liberal woman and pacifist. He stood too close to her to not get splattered by the conservative vitriol aimed at her. This "guilt by association" effect cannot be overestimated.

For example, the *Washington Post* interviewed Jeannette in 1917. The interview undoubtedly made an indelible impression on the Anaconda Company and its supporters. She made statements that they could not forgive or forget. Blunt statements such as, "They'll [the Company] try to do to me just what they have done to everyone who ever tried to oppose them... They own the state. They own the government. They own the press... All the mud and all the bricks in the state will come hurtling in my direction," infuriated them. She ended her censure of "the Company" viciously, and said, "they probably won't assassinate me because they use more subtle methods now."[10] And to add salt to Wellington's political wounds, Wellington's political enemies never, ever, let him forget that his sister had voted against War.

When Rankin first entered the political scene, he used his educational background to impress the voters. Later he discovered that an education at Oxford University lost him votes, especially those from the blue-collar Irish miners in Butte. In his speeches, he reminded potential supporters that his namesake, General Wellington, was an Irishman.[11]

The same constituency viewed him as anti-labor. This, of course, was not the case. Rankin had stood up for and sometimes represented unions in court. But in politics, labor groups seldom trust Republicans.

He did his best to project his image as a man of the people. He was proud of his Montana family and heritage. In his campaigns, he reminded audiences that he had driven four-and-six-horse teams as a boy on the family's ranch near Missoula, and that he knew what it was to work hard. However, nothing he said gave him that final boost to national office.

To his friends, Rankin claimed he was shy and professed a dislike of public fame. In view of his accomplishments, in the court, as a public speaker, as a land baron and as a politician, this is surprising–and probably a subterfuge.

Rankin's ambitions outweighed any social unease he felt. His goals stretched beyond material things. He drove a black Ford with little chrome. His choice of office space in his Pittsburgh building in downtown Helena was certainly not ostentatious.

In August 1924, Rankin resigned his position as Montana's attorney general. One can only imagine the relief afforded Governor Joseph Dixon when he found a way to get the "incorrigible" and usually hostile Rankin out of his hair. Dixon appointed him associate justice to replace Judge Charles H. Cooper (father of Gary Cooper, the actor) who had resigned from the Montana Supreme Court. It is also likely that Rankin wanted to escape the Dixon administration's sinking ship.

U.S. Attorney General Rankin

The Montana Republican party was splintered. Dixon and Rankin factions had taken sides. Linderman had just defeated Rankin in the primary for United States Senator. Cooper had resigned as associate justice. He and Rankin claimed that the governor had "failed to keep faith with them during the campaign." Whatever this may mean, the feelings were so strained between Governor Dixon and Rankin and Cooper that Cooper refused to hand the governor his resignation until Rankin had the Governor's appointment in his hand. The Governor simultaneously accepted Rankin's abdication as attorney general. The whole process took only a few minutes.[12]

Rankin sat on the Montana Supreme Court for only one year. In December 1925, he was appointed by President Calvin Coolidge to replace John Slattery as U.S. Attorney for the State of Montana. Rankin was relieved to get away from the state Supreme Court. It bored him. Now he was ready for action in a much more important position.[13]

"Silent Cal" Coolidge probably cared little who was appointed to the U.S. Attorney position in scarcely populated Montana. Montana political leaders such as Senators Thomas Walsh and Burton K. Wheeler, and Representative Scott Leavitt did care. Wheeler had a good memory and an axe to grind. U.S. Attorney Slattery had prosecuted him.[14] Now was the time for debts to be paid.

Senators Walsh and Wheeler and Republican Congressman Leavitt sponsored Rankin for Slattery's position. In an unorthodox move, Wheeler and Walsh brought Rankin's nomination for U.S. Attorney to the Senate out of the usual order. They had it unanimously confirmed without reference to a committee.[15]

Leavitt's reason for supporting Rankin is of interest. He and Rankin were of the "New Guard" of the Republican party and this unconventional appointment was a slap in the face to the "Old Guard"–Republican party leaders who probably would have selected someone less progressive for the job, someone other than Rankin.[16]

The 1928 Governor's Race: Rankin vs. Erickson

In 1928, Rankin was soundly defeated in yet another political bid. He entered the race for governor but lost to the incumbent, John E. "Honest John" Erickson. Erickson, a Kalispell attorney, had defeated the incumbent, Dixon, for the job in 1924. He not only had the support of "the Company" but also of Walsh and Wheeler and their liberal supporters–another example of the confusing and enigmatic boundaries of Montana politics.

During this period it is unlikely that Rankin had anything positive to say about his archenemy Dixon. He very well may have supported Erickson against Dixon in the 1924 election.

Things were different in the years that followed, and Rankin wanted Erickson's position. The Anaconda Copper Mining Company

(ACMC) always sought to control the State through the executive office. Rankin certainly was not their kind of candidate. Erickson didn't choose to make an enemy of "the Company, but he wasn't in their pocket either. Although the nation voted Republican and elected Herbert Hoover and many Republican candidates were ushered into office, Rankin was left behind. He put up a good fight but lost.

Just as Rankin had used the ill-defined "whipping boy," the Board of Equalization, to further his goals in the Dixon administration,[17] he was not against using the same agency in an effort to dislodge Governor Erickson, even though it meant a 180-degree turnabout. Rankin assault-ed the Anaconda Copper Mining Company. He condemned the Highway Board (the chairman of which was O. S. Warden, the general manager of the *Great Falls Tribune*) and the Board of Equalization under Governor Erickson, because they had reduced the assessments of Montana's railroads. According to candidate Rankin, this would hurt ordinary taxpayers. A few short years before, Attorney General Rankin had stood on the other side of the fence and prevented Governor Dixon and the Board from increasing the railroad's taxes.

This chameleon-like behavior did not go unnoticed by the media. Tom Stout of the *Lewistown Democrat-News* in an editorial published in the *Great Falls Tribune* summed-up Erickson's administration as follows: "There has been… a spirit of mutual co-operation and friendliness among those vested with the duty of conducting the state's affairs. The governor has gotten along with republican state officials without bicker-ing or discord. This contrasts favorably with the situation which obtained during the previous administration when the relations between Governor Dixon and his attorney general [Rankin]… were those of extreme personal hostility and constant discord." Further, the editor wrote, "This newspaper has only the kindliest feeling towards Wellington Rankin… He is well educated, comes of a fine family, and is possessed of a most attractive personality. But even the best friends of Mr. Rankin admit that he has a decidedly erratic temperament…"[18] Attorney General Rankin's antagonism to then Governor Joseph M. Dixon had not been forgotten.

Rankin in his bid for governor contended that the ACMC controlled state government and suggested that they did it by telephone. He said that to save money for the state he would have the private telephone line between the Butte office of the Anaconda Company and the capitol removed. This allegation of a "private line" from the ACMC to the Capitol building was often made by candidates but never proven. Rankin, grasp-ing at straws to link his opponent with "the Company," claimed in September that Governor Erickson's office had placed two calls to Swan Lake, summer home of some of the officials of "the Company. One call cost as much as $1.30. That was a grand sum in those times.[19]

The ACMC-controlled newspaper, *Anaconda Standard*, blasted him with an editorial entitled, "RANKIN AT HIS RANKEST." He was further criticized for running for state office while still U. S. Attorney.[20]

With big business as the enemy, Rankin said to the voters that the real question was "whether you are going to have a government owned body and soul by the Anaconda Copper Mining Company."[21] During his gubernatorial run Rankin depicted himself as the common man–a good tactic, but one that gave him little chance of being heard.

Like Joseph Dixon, who had purchased a Missoula area newspaper, Rankin himself was a publisher. Since 1917 he had owned the *Havre Promoter* and could at least depend on its good press. But one rural paper was not enough to defend against the yellow journalism of "the Company-owned papers.

One incident vividly illustrates what Rankin faced. Toward the end of Dixon's administration in 1924, the *Helena Independent* published a preposterous, unfounded tale. In conspicuous headlines, Will Campbell's fanatical pen accused Governor Dixon and Attorney General Rankin of having sympathy with the Ku Klux Klan and for financially supporting a Klan newspaper in Helena. The article elaborated on the fictitious paper's staff and finances, and even alleged that the governor was soliciting further Klan support.

The entire story was a hoax. Twenty-four hours later, a small retraction was printed in an obscure corner of a back page.[22] This shoddy journalistic behavior was nothing short of outright lying and was similar to the kind of news coverage found in today's supermarket tabloids.

To Rankin, "the Company-dominated newspapers described him in ways that were anything but supportive. During his campaign against Erickson, the *Anaconda Standard*, a Company-dominated paper, described him as having "...all of the dignity of a baboon, all the self-restraint and poise of a tomcat, all the calm deliberation and judicial decision of a jackass, all the finer emotions and sentiments of a yellow dog, all the nobility and character of a snake."[23]

Rankin told his campaign-trail audiences that the ACMC owned eleven newspapers and that they all campaigned against him. There was evidence to support his contention. However, O. S. Warden's *Great Falls Tribune* denied that there was any press "bombardment" of Rankin. In October 1928, before the election, the editors of the *Tribune* had claimed that their review of the *Missoulian*, the *Montana Standard*, the *Livingston Enterprise*, and the *Billings Gazette* had "not a word" against Rankin.[24]

In fact, the editorial columns of the *Tribune* had taken him to task. One editorial even reproached him for his brief time spent at Oxford, saying, "his sheepskin from that old British institution serves him poorly when it comes to discussing Montana affairs."[25]

It was not unusual to slander an opponent not favored by "the Company" in those fiery and uninhibited times. Any candidate that did not support the Anaconda Company was treated the same. A politician who was sympathetic to industry was okay. In later years, the policy changed. Instead of attacking foes, "the Company" press simply ignored them and blacked out controversial candidates and issues. The editorials focused on irrelevant and locally unimportant matters, hence the term "Afghanistanize."[26]

"The Company-controlled press–fifty-five to sixty percent of the daily newspaper circulation in Montana–was especially malicious in dealing with gubernatorial candidates they didn't favor. They campaigned heavily in turn against Burton K. Wheeler, Joseph M. Dixon, and finally Wellington D. Rankin. Through its many connections and ties, including Adam's-rib type companies such as the Montana Power Company, smaller independent weeklies were influenced and even dailies like the *Great Falls Tribune* felt the pressure.[27]

Rankin might have done better to follow the old advice, "Never pick a fight with anyone who buys ink by the barrel." Nonetheless, his tactic of punching back at what some called the "Great Gray Blanket" of the press at last paid off. Shortly before the election in November 1928, he was rewarded for his pugnacity. He accused the *Great Falls Tribune* for refusing to print speeches that he made and he publicly challenged the newspaper to publish his views presented in a speech in Great Falls.

Consequently the paper printed Rankin's views with headlines and extensive quotations.[28] In his speech, Rankin charged that the incumbent governor Erickson was "robbing the sheep and cattle men by charging them too large rentals on lands leased from the state." He also said, "Rentals on agricultural and grazing lands owned by the state of Montana should be reduced. The present rentals are more than the farmer and stockman can afford to pay."[29] Here he was treading on thin ice. As a rancher himself he stood to benefit personally. This did not withstand the scrutiny of some voters.

The rental at that time was twelve cents an acre for grazing, and less than seventy-two cents an acre for agricultural lands–about one-third what it cost the average owner to use his own land. The money from the rentals went toward education, and Rankin was accused of "appealing to selfish interests" at the "expense of school children."[30]

Rankin had acquired the support of some prominent Montanans. Among them, his friend A. B. Cook of Townsend, was a well-known and respected cattleman and engineer. In a letter sent to his friends just before the election, Cook stressed Rankin's fidelity and character:

> During the many months of battling in the courts to prevent the sale of this wonderful herd he stood by me, even during the Primary when they were calling on him...staying in Helena and fighting for me every day and night and jeopardizing his own nomination, thus showing real friendship.

> I appeal to you to vote for your own townsman regardless of political affiliation because a vote for Rankin means individual state government, better roads, greater recognition of agriculture, labor and individual enterprise, and because he is fearless, has ability, character, and independence.
>
> If you will do this, you are doing me a personal favor and you are electing your OWN Governor—NOT the Anaconda Copper Company's Governor.[31]

Cook's words failed to breath life into Rankin's campaign. Rankin was not only defeated, he was beaten badly. The nation voted Republican and elected Herbert Hoover. Although many Republican candidates won office on Hoover's coattails, Rankin lost the race for governor.

Rankin probably took some consolation in the current election. His political enemy, Joe Dixon, was sacked soundly during this same election by Burton Wheeler who was reelected to the United States Senate in 1928. It is doubtful that either of the two defeated men saw much humor in the Will Rogers Column in the same Great Falls paper that announced their defeat. The country's foremost humorist and political critic said that he was elected as a candidate of the "Anti-Bunk" party by the silent vote. He claimed at the start of the election that he would resign if elected and "...that is the only campaign promise I am going to stick to." Will claimed further that he was, "The only cheerful loser in the race."[32]

Back to Law

Two years later, in February of 1930, with the influential support of Montana's Republican and Democrat political leaders in Washington, Rankin was reappointed to the position of U.S. Attorney by President Herbert Hoover.

Rankin's opponents for national office were especially stalwart, but like the boxer he had been in his youth, Rankin returned to the ring round after round to be pounded. His next political defeat occurred in 1934 when Scott Leavitt, the former congressman (1923-1933) and Rankin's ally, defeated him in the Republican primary for the U.S. Senate. Rankin had not given up his senatorial dreams, but fortune avoided him. Leavitt was a Spanish-American War veteran, a nationally recognized Rotarian, and Forest Service employee.

Luck also eluded Leavitt. In spite of winning the primary, Leavitt lost in November to James E. Murray, a wealthy, liberal New Dealer. Murray remained in the Senate until 1961, longer than any other Montanan to this date.

Although the disappointment of so many defeats must have been painful, Wellington seldom demonstrated emotion externally. Deep down he must have felt something. Years later when he was unseated as head of Montana's Republican Party one of his friends commented to him that, "…well it isn't any big deal, what the hell…," Rankin fired back, "Save your philosophy for somebody that needs it."[55]

Rankin continued to be one of the state's most prominent lawyers and expanded his respect in the Montana courts.

7
MONTANA TRIAL LAWYER

The key to winning a case was to get the jury to like you.

The phenomenal growth and the booming agricultural economy in the West waned by the end of the second decade of the 1900s. The great land rush to the Rocky Mountain region was essentially over. Falling prices, a lack of moisture, periods of depression thinned the ranks of ranchers and farmers. The few that held on would be saved by the New Deal that was about ten years away. The same period saw the beginning of the Great Depression.

In Montana, things were just beginning to look better. The drought of the 1917-1918 era was easing. The "War to End All Wars" (World War I) had ended and most Montana "boys" had come home. The terrible worldwide Spanish flu epidemic that killed 5,000 young Montanans was a fading nightmare.

On October 24, 1929, the stock market failed. At first few people in the west had much concern. Depression was not a new experience to most people in the state. Montana had been in a slump since the end of World War I. People out west, for good reason, had never trusted Wall Street anyway, and most people thought that the eastern speculators deserved what they got. Reality set in, however, when Westerners recognized that there was no longer market for the commodities they produced. When cattle prices fell sixty-six percent and wheat went from $1.87 to $0.38 per bushel and copper dropped to $0.05 per pound, the effect on the people of Montana was devastating.[1]

The distribution of financial failure was not uniform. Some places were less affected. Mr. Dewey Street, president of the Security Bank and Trust Company of Bozeman during the 1960s and 1970s, remembered the depression well. Raised on a farm in the Spring Hill community of the Gallatin Valley, Dewey graduated from Montana State College at Bozeman in 1929. After graduation, he went to work for the Security Bank. He said that none of the Gallatin Valley banks failed, and that somehow they carried the ranchers, farmers and business people who were indebted to them through the thirties. A few businesses failed, he said, but no more than in good times.[2]

Many bank failures were attributed to over-zealous speculation by entrepreneurs. Practically anyone who wanted a bank could have one. By the late 1920s, banks could be found in places that didn't even have a post office. This came to a head in October of 1920 when the money-changers that served as banks began to fail. In 1924, one hundred and ninety-one Montana banks failed and depositors lost about $30,000,000.00 over a four-year period.

By 1929, most institutions that were sick had already died.[3] This created a scarcity of money. Some of the big cattlemen, sheepmen, and farmers were so much in debt that there was little to do except abandon their ranches and farms.

Politically the Democrats swept the country and brought in the New Deal. Many reluctant Montanans were saved. A large number of the hardened, independent men of the soil tried to make it on their own, but eventually they were forced to accept help. President Franklin Delano Roosevelt made the federal government a dispenser of relief, a creator of jobs, and a source of capital. From 1933-1939, through federal programs, the West received a disproportionate amount of per capita payments. The people of the Rocky Mountains were given $716.00 per head in contrast to $380.00 per head received by citizens in the Great Plains region.[4]

The mining city of Butte in 1929 had never seen a better economy. Miners there were paid the best salary ever–six dollars per day. When copper prices dropped, so did the jobs and the salaries that went with them. Families survived on less than ten dollars per week. People who had known poverty before were faced once again with the prospect of hunger. Some miners took to the hills to prospect hoping to glean out enough gold dust to keep their bellies full. Others took up "bootlegging," and found profit as long as they could stay out of reach of the law. For a period of time the only relief available to those who could not provide for themselves came from private charities. Those funds were soon exhausted.[5]

The great drought and dust bowl that devastated much of Colorado, Oklahoma, Kansas, and New Mexico from 1935-1940 avoided Montana. But many conservative Montanans would have preferred the "dust bowl" to the liberalism that did invade their state. A strong Democratic majority dragged conservative Westerners kicking and scratching into the New Deal era.

The Pittsburgh Building

*"My office is humble because many of my legal clients are
humble. As headquarters of a ranching operation,
I don't want a brand new office."*

During the depression, everyone worked long, hard hours to make
a living. In the 1930s, Wellington Rankin was Montana's top trial lawyer.
He was well-known in the state's capital, but was equally recognized in
rural areas. His astonishing career was the product of hard work.

A dedicated professional, he practically lived in his law office. It was
a place where he was always available. It was said that one of his outstanding characteristics was his willingness to take the time to visit with
people. He welcomed not just people that were considered important,
but anyone who needed to talk about his or her problems.

A diligent worker himself, he expected the same work ethic from
others. The following anecdote illustrates his demanding nature. When
another attorney asked how a young clerk in his office was doing,
Rankin answered that the man's work was satisfactory but questioned
his dedication. Apparently the young assistant had asked for the Fourth
of July off.[6]

According to some observers, the business atmosphere of the office
relaxed slightly during baseball's World Series, but for little else. There
were lighter moments, however.

During Jeannette's first campaign, Rankin's office was in the Gold
Block of downtown Helena. In a nearby office, another lawyer persisted
in poking fun at Jeannette. Jokingly, he made remarks about women in
politics and how "the weaker sex" shouldn't abandon their traditional
roles. The banter was tolerated mostly with good humor but Wellington
decided to teach the man a lesson.

In an interview, Bella Winestine (Fligelman), a close family friend,
recalls, "I remember one noon, he (Rankin) had two assistants in his
office that had just graduated from the law school in Missoula. And he
and these two boys–young men–went into this lawyer's office and took
out, while the lawyer was gone to lunch, took out every stick of furni-
ture…and hid it …the man came back from lunch, opened his door and
the room was empty."

When the young lawyer came to Rankin upset by his loss, Rankin
advised him to go immediately to the police station and report the theft.
While he was gone, Wellington and his helpers moved everything back
into the office so that it appeared exactly as it had before. Winestine
(Fligelman) said that, "When that man came back with two policemen,
the office was in a normal state and they thought the man was crazy."

The depression taught everyone to be frugal. Later Rankin and his associates practiced law on the fourth floor of the Pittsburgh Building in downtown Helena, an ancient building that he owned. It was ever on the verge of decay. Friends sent him Charles Addams cartoons of a run-down mansion and suggested they looked like the Pittsburgh block.[7] Some of the electric lights in the building were switched on by turning a key that hung conveniently by a string from the ceiling near the bulb. *Great Falls Tribune* writer C. T. Sullivan later described Rankin's office as:

> …an ancient building on Last Chance Gulch … that has survived earthquakes and fires in the Capitol City. His offices utilized an entire four-story building in the down-town business center. Walls of office after office are lined with law books. Obviously not much has been spent on upkeep. The elevator in the building ran between open latticework of ornamental iron so its passengers could look out and down into the well of the aged building.[8]

One couple who visited Rankin's offices in the early 1960s described the elevator as one of the first that Otis ever built. Another visitor to the building remembers a whistle hung on a string by the elevator. "You'd blow the whistle and this old attendant, a little foreign-looking fellow, would show up. We said, 'Good morning,' and he said, 'I ain't no god-damned Arab.'"[9] Its operator, Abdo, was often described as a Turk or a Greek. His foreign appearance added to the aura of Rankin's office build-ing. However, his religious biases showed. In later years, during some of the troubles between Israel and the Arab states, Abdo allegedly refused to give Helena attorney Lester Loble a lift, saying "Jew, you walk."[10]

After riders were on the elevator, Abdo pulled a lever and engaged a noisy pulley. This produced a high-pitched, disturbing squeal as the elevator cage lifted slowly. Leaving the elevator, a passenger entered a dark hallway and passed stores of ranch supplies–tools, sacks of feed, saddles and other items–illuminated by rays of sunlight streaming through a dusty skylight above.[11] When the elevator was not in working order, Rankin's clients passed through tunnel-like halls and climbed an ancient, creaking staircase.[12]

Gallatin Valley rancher Harry Brainard said, "I was in his [Rankin's] office a lot of times. Once when I was there a mouse run across the floor and Rankin reached in there and got a little piece of cheese and throwed it to him and fed it."[13]

In response to questions about this distinctive choice of office space, Rankin said, "My office is humble because many of my legal clients are humble. As headquarters of a ranching operation, I don't want a brand new office."[14]

Rankin was attracted to big disputes, those with news appeal, like a bug is lured to light. No litigation was too trifling, however. In the mid

1930s, he sued the City of Helena and the Helena City Health Department on behalf of several victims of an outbreak of typhoid fever. All parties agreed that it was unwieldy to try so many cases separately. One case was selected for trial and the rest were to be settled based on its outcome. Rankin represented Ralph E. Safransky in the test case, and had fifty-four other victims of the illness waiting in the wings. His side won, and all the people he represented got a settlement. A total of $473,537.00 in reputed damages were filed against the Queen City. The decision can be counted among the first so-called "class action" suits and was upheld by Montana's Supreme Court.[15]

His cases were not all as lucrative. In 1941 he represented "Doctor" Wong Sun, a venerable Chinese herbalist who sold his cures and practiced his art in Great Falls, Helena, and some other places. Wong Sun was charged with practicing medicine without a license and was convicted. The court did not see any value in his ancient Chinese remedies of ground dragon teeth that purportedly made his clients "fit as a fiddle." There was also the fact that he hadn't paid for a license to practice. This was just the kind of case that Wellington Rankin liked—defending the little guy against the establishment. His Christian Science beliefs may have encouraged him in opposing the rules of organized medicine. Since the court had not given Wong Sun a bill of particulars upon whom and where and when he had practiced medicine without a license, Rankin took his case to the Supreme Court and won.[16]

As a winning attorney, Rankin worked late into the night and required little sleep. Sometimes he transacted business, arranged meetings, or called clients extremely early in the morning. While representing a group of ranchers in a land purchase and conducting lengthy discussions with them late at night, Rankin called the owner of the land, an elderly lady, who lived in Florida. One of the clients said, "It must be early in the morning there. Won't she be asleep?"

"At least we know she'll be home," Rankin answered.[17]

Just as undocumented stories circulated about Rankin's law practice, myths concerning his dealings with creditors made the circuit. According to some of these legends, Rankin did not like to pay bills. Allegedly, he sometimes ignored statements from the Mountain Bell Telephone Company and Montana Power until those companies were forced to send collectors to his office. He kept the emissary waiting in his outer office, or used up time instructing the innocent employee about the shortcomings of his employer, the telephone or power company. It was said that he relished the inconvenience this caused his creditors.[18]

Another yarn about Rankin's alleged tardiness in paying his bills was that the telephone company once discontinued Rankin's service due to a late payment. Furious about this, Rankin allegedly threw the "dead" phone out the window to the street below.

Another mythological tale recounts how Rankin bought a deep-freeze appliance from a local business. After it was installed in his basement, he renovated the floor of his house, which made it impossible to remove the appliance without tearing out a door and part of the foundation. He then refused to pay the company and told them to come and get it. When the owners of the business sized up the situation, they dismantled the freezer by removing the motor and other vital functional parts. Rankin was left with a mere shell of the appliance taking up space in his basement.[19]

The force of Rankin's personality helped to catapult him to legal success. His knack for surrounding himself with talented people also contributed to his ongoing advancement. Many clerks and invaluable assistants worked for him over the years. Of these, partner Arthur P. Acher was perhaps the most important to Rankin's legal career.

Acher became Rankin's associate in 1927. A shy man, Acher preferred the background to the limelight. Other lawyers knew him as one of the finest minds in the legal business. In Judge John Harrison's opinion, Acher's personality had been absorbed totally by Rankin. He said, "If Rankin said, 'Jump out the window,' he (Acher) would have looked for which window." The judge did admit that Acher had a fine legal mind, but seldom tried cases himself.[20]

Other attorneys agree that Acher was seldom in the forefront. Nonetheless, he was essential to Rankin's research and understanding of the law. He also held down the Helena office as if it were his own fort and managed much of Rankin's real estate and ranch empire.

Bozeman attorney Ben Berg described Acher as a plodder, a worker who probably knew more about the law in Montana than any other individual and who demonstrated this skill behind the scenes. Acher closely followed the progress of each case and advised Rankin, slipping forward into the fringe of light with written notes and reminders. As Rankin aged and was too vain to wear glasses, Acher's notes had to be bolder and in larger print. Eventually the scribbled messages were so large that everyone in the "pit" at the front of the courtroom could see them plainly.[21]

It was rare to see a team like Acher and Rankin. Complete opposites in demeanor, each supplied something missing in the other-some absent fabric of character. Their collected power was greater than the mathematical sum of the parts.[22]

Rankin's brilliance was as a trial lawyer, and he took most of his firm's cases to court himself. He won cases because he knew people and understood them. He used common sense, logic, and everyday language in the courtroom. He pointed to the facts rather than the twists and turns of the law. Theirs was an age of realism and the judicial system and "law" was tested on the frontier. It could be bent and molded but it was pragmatic. Good attorneys looked, saw, described, and spoke clearly.

Rankin spoke to real people on the juries he played to-farmers, ranchers, and average folk–and gained their support for his clients. Like other lawyers early in the twentieth century, he was granted freedoms in court that today are usually frowned upon, belittled, or no longer tolerated. He was riveting in front of a jury.

A risk taker, he tried the patience of judges–but packed courtrooms with people who came just to watch him. Observing the justice system was an inexpensive form of entertainment available to most citizens. According to the style of the time, Rankin made long speeches and summations. He was an actor and he played his part well. Furthermore, he handpicked his most important audience–the jury.

Rankin often said that given enough time he could disqualify any prospective juror if he wanted to. He researched the jurors and surprised them with his questions. He studied their families, their habits, and their acquaintances. When he was interrogating them he would be as friendly as if he had known them all his life. He went on the assumption that the key to winning a case was to get the jury to like you.[23]

To accomplish the same end, other attorneys used different tactics. For example, one Great Falls attorney sent flowers to the families of everyone listed in the obituaries of the local newspaper on the basis that a prospective juror might remember the flowers and who sent them.[24]

Like the famous attorney Clarence Darrow, Rankin used devices to gain and keep the attention of juries. Most lawyers who practiced at the same time as Rankin were in awe of his mastery. Bozeman attorney Ben Berg, with a successful record himself, remembered Rankin as one of the best attorneys he ever knew, and noted, "He was a showman, brilliant and psychologically astute, and quick witted." According to Berg, Rankin worked long hours planning his courtroom strategy.

Rankin was described as a "big man, always in a dark blue suit and usually a tie of a similar color, a reddish-ruddy complexion and a broad face, and he seemed to dominate the courtroom. He would try all sorts of things to intimidate the judge... but wasn't very often successful."[25]

Rankin had better luck with juries than judges. Berg recounts how Rankin distracted the jury by tossing coins or pacing back and forth while his opponent was examining a witness, presenting his case, interrogating, or summarizing. (Yet, when a lawyer by the name of Billy Meyer used the same tactic on Rankin–walking to and fro and juggling coins–it made Rankin livid.)[26] Rankin's style was showy and commanding.

Attorney Louise Rankin Galt saw her husband from a somewhat different perspective.

> He took center stage on anything he was in. He had a good sense of humor, which did him well in the courtroom, but his greatest strength, I think, was understanding human nature and what arguments would appeal to people. He reasoned things out, and he picked things out

before he went to court. He wasn't near as spontaneous as people would think. When he was thinking, he always had silver dollars in his hand, whether it was the court-room, in the office, at home; he'd pace up and down and shake these silver dollars, and you knew something was on his mind; in court it was unconscious. He wore out more pockets with silver dollars. A lot of younger lawyers thought he did it to distract the jury, but he didn't. It was just a habit he had; take these dollars and you could just see the mental processes working as he worked the dollars in his hand. He didn't have any tricks; he didn't need them. He was always so prepared—that was his strength. Not only in the law, the briefs, but on the facts—the reasoning of it; he'd have those worked out pretty well ahead of time.[27]

In his later years, Rankin's false teeth clattered when he talked, and some suspected he used this slight imperfection to encourage jurors to pay better attention to him, in the same way that a speech impediment can make people listen more carefully. Judge Robert J. Nelson who practiced on Rankin's side in some cases and opposed him in others said, "Either way, it was a war of nerves."[28]

Rankin could browbeat less-experienced attorneys and dominate entire courtrooms. One spectator who had witnessed Rankin in action referred to him as a "bull of a man," and physically intimidating. He told about a time when Rankin was called as a witness in a cattle-rustling case in northern Montana. A man was accused of stealing cows from Rankin. By the time Rankin finished his testimony from the witness stand, he had practically taken over the judge's mien and had even lectured the accused man about his deportment. The defendant was convicted.[29]

"He was outstanding and cut from a different mold—not likely to be duplicated," said retired Circuit Judge Henry Loble of Helena.[30] Loble knew Rankin well. His father, District Judge Lester Loble, and Rankin were contemporaries. Both Lobles sometimes opposed Rankin in court. The younger Loble described him as an intense, tough opponent who fought every case as hard as he could. He was always prepared, cold, and calculating. "He had many enemies," Loble added. In reference to this he said, "Any lawyer who fights hard for his clients makes enemies. This can happen, win or lose."[31] Wellington Rankin certainly had his share of detractors.

Regardless of the outcome, Rankin's cases were good drama and often in support of the underdog. The following case illustrates this. In 1936, an elderly Irish lady came to see Rankin hoping to retrieve a $1,000 investment. The woman, a cook who supported a crippled husband and several children, had been told to trade her sound Great Northern Bond in to buy an Insull Bond. She was assured that the bond was secured. "As good as a thousand dollar bill," she was told and backed by ownership of all the utilities and power companies of Chicago. By the time the case reached court, the Insull Bond was worth $1.75.

Rankin took the case to court, and the bank that sold her the bond admitted misrepresentation. The district court granted her a judgment for $910. The Montana Supreme Court reversed the decision, on the basis that the exact value of the bond at time of purchase had not been established, and denied a rehearing.

Associate Justice Walter B. Sands dissented. Such cases, he said, "make laymen lose confidence in courts." In his minority opinion, as the sole dissident, Judge Sands said:

> I liken the case to a banker's organization to fleece purchasers into buying glass diamonds by taking advantage of the confidence imposed in them....The plaintiff here is denied redress because it is claimed she has not proved the value of the fake diamond at the exact time she purchased.[32]

Rankin and Acher were more successful when they were involved in a dispute known as the "one-eye case." A client had lost an eye in an accident, and his attorneys had obtained compensation for him. Ten years later, he lost the other eye in a similar accident. The compensation offered this time was for the loss of but one eye. Rankin and Acher won him restitution for total blindness.[33]

Rankin was not one to overlook any weakness of his opponents. When he represented a client he paid attention to detail. A rancher in Park County who was accused of stealing sheep had a large, unsightly, scaly wart on his nose. Rankin agreed to represent him, but before the trial, at his own expense, he sent the accused to a doctor and had the wart removed. When asked why he did this, he answered, "You can't believe a man with a wart on his nose."[34]

Rankin was the favored attorney of ranchers and cowboys when they got into trouble. He often received pleas from men in jail asking that he review their circumstances and defend them. Mary Leffingwell, who has ranched all her life near Clyde Park, Montana, north of Livingston relates the following story in her book, *Diamonds in the Snow*. It is a tale that is nearly biblical–brother against brother.[35] The story tells of two brothers who worked on Mary's family ranch and tended sheep in the mountains. After a bout of drunkenness, the more dominant of the two beat the other one severely. The injured brother, whom Leffingwell calls "Fred," walked bleeding and bruised to the nearest neighbor's house. In addition to superficial injuries, he had multiple shallow stab wounds in his back. The Leffingwells reported the incident to the Park County sheriff, but were told there was nothing he could do unless charges were filed. Fred refused to do this.[36] Two years later, during another fight, Fred used a .22-caliber rifle to threaten retaliation. According to the story, the aggressive brother grabbed the gun by the barrel and it discharged accidentally into his chest. Fred's brother died. Rankin was asked by Fred's friends to defend him against the murder charges.[37]

Mary Leffingwell was a young woman at the time. She and her sightless mother were character witnesses for the accused at the trial. Between court sessions the Leffingwells became well-acquainted with the famous defense attorney. She described Rankin as a short, heavy, powerful man who resembled the Italian dictator Benito Mussolini. When Rankin discovered that Leffingwell's mother was blind, he used Christian Science to try to help her. Mary says he would come to their room in the Park Hotel every evening and deliver orations about Christian Science healing in the hope that her mother's vision could be restored. Leffingwell says, "He was very convincing, but her eyesight didn't improve."[38]

During their short acquaintance, Mary, who knew that Rankin was a big landowner, asked him jokingly what he was going to do with his property when he died. Rankin responded by whispering in her ear, "I'll tell you a secret. I'm not going to die."[39] She says she wasn't persuaded about this, but Rankin did satisfy the jury of Fred's innocence and he was acquitted. Fred was not a young man and he died a few years later while working on one of Rankin's ranches to pay off his legal expenses.[40]

On the high-altitude Montana prairies, water is a valuable commodity. An attorney practicing in Montana must be competent in the law of "water rights." Rankin was an expert on the subject. He was selected in 1937 to represent a group of ranchers and farmers against the Montana Power Company—an Anaconda Copper Mining Company subsidiary—in the famed "Broadwater-Missouri" case. Rankin once again stood for the common folk against "the Company."

The outcome of this case would be crucial to future water laws in Montana. The state's system of water usage allotted water rights to whoever was "first in time" on the land. This rule evolved during the placer mining period and was inherited by agricultural, power, and domestic users. In time, unreasonable over-conscription of this perishable commodity resulted. Historical use of the water might be claimed by more than one of the users. This arbitrary and historic method of dividing water has caused many disputes in dry years when the demand is greater than the supply. For example, a rancher or farmer might admit to have historically used more water than a little creek contained even at spring runoff. This often led to conflict.

As long as there was plenty of unused water, there was no problem. However, drought parched the state in 1937, and the mighty Missouri

River at Great Falls dropped to a level so low that the Montana Power Company's generators couldn't run. A drastic power reduction followed and factories were forced to close and lay off workers. All parties, previously indifferent, were forced to recognize that water was precious. It was an unpredictable asset that was affected by silt, weather, changing channels, and numerous other factors. Fearing a similar catastrophe farther up the Missouri River, Montana Power sued the agricultural users above a crossing spot called Canyon Ferry and contended that the utility had prior rights on the whole river.

The Broadwater-Missouri lawsuit opened Pandora's box. As it turned out, Montana Power wished later that it had not raised the issue in the first place. Wellington Rankin brought his renowned, intimidating courtroom style with him on the side of the ranchers. There were many attorneys in this important case representing different factions. The U.S. Department of Justice assigned experts to assist in the ranchers' defense against Montana Power, and what began as a simple adjudication over water rights became a showdown in the spirit of the Old West. To quote Mark Twain, "In the West, whiskey is for drinkin'—water is for fightin'."

In court, Rankin and his associates claimed "the use of water for raising food is superior in right and equity to the use of such water for power purposes when power can be developed by other means."[41] This argument was prophetic. Today a similar philosophy is used in the continuing struggle over the west's diminishing flows.

Rankin represented a group called the Broadwater-Missouri Water User's Association which had been spawned by the state legislature. The group managed water that supplied irrigation to 21,000 acres near Townsend, Montana. After years of litigation, Rankin and the water users prevailed on January 4, 1944.

The controversy attracted the attention of the U.S. Army Corps of Engineers who were working on behalf of Bonneville Power in Washington State. The Corps, always looking for something to dam coveted the Missouri's potential as one of Montana's great water resources—and began another battle. The agricultural water users and Montana Power now had a common enemy: the federal government in the guise of the Corps of Engineers. The whole affair was similar to two dogs fighting over a bone just to have another dog sneak in and steal the prize.

The Corps of Engineers won in the end—ten years later it raised an impressive concrete dam at Canyon Ferry. However, ranchers, farmers, and Montana Power gained from the outcome. Once the lake was filled, everyone had enough water. In fact some had too much. The small town of Canton, for instance, and thousands of acres of low-lying ranch and farmland are now lying at the bottom of Canyon Ferry Reservoir.[42]

In the resulting lawsuits, Rankin was involved in all aspects of this fight, including a successful attempt to get the government to pay more for the condemned and flooded ranchland. One of the ranchers whose land was inundated by water was Harry Brainard. He says:

> He [Rankin] represented me in court. I had some land
> over north of Townsend. I wouldn't take what the Bureau
> of Reclamation offered me, and they condemned it, and
> they didn't give me time to get all my buildings off when
> the Canyon Ferry dam backed the water over my proper-
> ty. It was a good place, so Rankin took them to court. The
> other attorney was all dressed up and had a bow tie—
> cocky little bastard. Rankin says, "I'll take the air out of
> him, don't worry." So when he [Rankin] gets up he starts
> calling him [the other attorney] "snotnose," and the judge
> says, "You can't call him that," and fines Rankin twenty
> dollars. Rankin pulls a twenty dollar bill out of his pocket
> and gives it to the judge and says, "I don't care what his
> name is; he's still a snotnose." He won for me, and we got
> $88,000; they'd offered $28,000. Rankin took $23,000.[43]

The Broadwater–Missouri case and all its aftereffects piqued the
interest of the state government, including Governor Sam Ford, the state
water conservation board, and thousands of citizens who had prevented the Kerr Dam on the Flathead River from being raised seventeen feet.
These few feet of dam would have flooded communities, fertile land,
cherry orchards and even part of the city of Kalispell. Rankin had stood
on the side of agriculture which only amplified his political power in the
mostly rural state.

Switching from defender to prosecutor Rankin aided the state attorney general's office in State v. Simpson, a murder case that was tried in
1938. He was invited to participate by Golden Valley County Attorney
Nat Allen to help keep a lower court's conviction intact before the
Montana Supreme Court.

In April of that year, W. L. "Lee" Simpson, a resident of Golden Valley
County, had abducted livestock on his land. A mare and colt that
belonged to someone else was in his possession. Simpson knew that the
county sheriff was coming to take possession of the horses and had
directed his employees, Robert and Gerald McDonald, to take the colt,
hide it in the timber, and cover up their tracks in the snow.

When Sheriff E. J. Dolve arrived, Simpson tried to give him another
colt instead. Recognizing that it wasn't the foal in question, the law
enforcement officer refused to take it, and went away.

Simpson had threatened others who visited the ranch later when he
had armed himself with a rifle and was reportedly acting strange. When
the sheriff and his deputy, Arthur Burford, went back to Simpson's ranch
to check on Simpson's peculiar behavior, the two lawmen were unaware
that Simpson had murdered the McDonald boys earlier. The officers

pulled up at Simpson's place. Deputy Burford waited in the car as Sheriff Dolve walked toward the house. Simpson shot at the sheriff three times but missed; the lawman escaped around the corner of the house. The sheriff and deputy returned fire; the gun battle lasted several hours before Burford was hit and fell near the police car. Out of ammunition and thinking that his partner was dead, Dolve walked to Ryegate to get a posse. But Burford wasn't dead–yet. As soon as Dolve left, Simpson walked to where the deputy lay and shot him in the head with a pistol.

When the posse arrived, Simpson was gone. He turned himself in that night to the sheriff in Lewistown and made a full confession, which included the killing of the McDonald boys and the location of their bodies. He had shot Robert McDonald first, then later in the afternoon of the same day had killed Gerald McDonald with an axe.

Simpson later confessed that he wrongly thought the officers knew about both the stolen horse and murdered boys. In a summary of the case the Supreme Court said, "His [Simpson's] attitude was akin to that described in the old proverb, 'The guilty flee when no man pursueth.'"[44]

Ryegate, a small town on the Milwaukee railroad, was not accustomed to such excitement. One Montana doctor, a schoolboy at the time of the trial, remembers how he and his brothers would see the light burning in the jail cell at night and say to one another, "Well, Simpson ain't gone to bed yet."[45]

Rankin managed yet again to insert himself into a spectacular case. The defense team tried to show Simpson was insane, but prosecutors disagreed. In his verbal argument for the prosecution, Wellington Rankin announced to the jury:

> Every bit of this evidence of insanity is sham. They have proved nothing. Nothing. That burden is upon them. They have told you, "Return a verdict of not guilty by reason of insanity." Do you know what that means? Do you know when you walk into this jury room and come out and that door there of the jury room and you walk up here with a verdict that reads "Not guilty by reason of insanity" that this defendant walks out of this courtroom and there is no power under the law to stop him until some new order is issued?[46]

If Rankin shifted the usual burden of proof to the defense, the court did not mind. Its members found the defendant guilty as charged. Simpson was sentenced to death. In a most direct means of restitution, Sheriff Dolve himself hung Simpson in Ryegate, the Golden Valley County seat. Simpson was one of the last men hanged in Montana. County Attorney Nat Allen later said:

> I had gone in to say good-bye to Simpson and he said probably the sanest thing he ever said, "I don't hold it against you." It is a strange thing when a man is hanged, everybody connected with it believes he did it. The prosecutor, of course, thinks he did it because he presented the case. The defense attorneys think they may have done it, because they poorly defended the case. Each juryman thinks he is responsible because, after all, without his individual vote, the man could not be hung. The judge, of course, thinks he did it because, after all, who pronounced the sentence. As a matter of fact, nobody hung Simpson except Lee Simpson himself.[47]

Later in the 1930s, Rankin was asked to defend, in separate incidents, two ranchers for killing elk. The cases were similar but unrelated. Each rancher had complained many times to the Game and Fish Commission of Montana that wild elk were destroying their crops. Each said his pleas were ignored. Consulted by phone in both cases, Rankin advised his clients to each kill one bull elk and then carefully prepare the carcass, but not use nor waste any of the meat. They were to notify the authorities immediately after this was done.

From Augusta, Montana, on March 3, 1939, the Montana Fish and Game Commission received a telegram from C. R. Rathbone of the Circle H Ranch. It read, "We are killing elk on our ranch. Advise quickly disposition of carcasses."[48] The Montana Department of Fish and Game responded immediately.

Rathbone was charged with violation of wildlife statutes, and in the subsequent trial the lower court in Augusta ruled against him. In a show of support for a fellow rancher, the Montana Stockgrowers Association and the Montana Woolgrowers Association pooled their money to have Rankin appeal Rathbone's case to the Supreme Court. Here Rankin prevailed and the verdict was reversed. His not-guilty plea had been based on the right of "any person to keep or bear arms in defense of his home, person, and property."[49]

The other elk-killer's trial, a similar case, was held in Townsend. The Broadwater County Courthouse was filled with people throughout the proceeding, and most armchair lawyers were sure the Montana Fish and Game Commission would win. But a not-guilty verdict was declared. Rankin had won. And according to the defendant Joe Greaves, a successful Broadwater County rancher, he "wasn't charged a cent."[50] There is no record of who paid Rankin for his defense but more than likely, it was the Montana Stockgrower's Association.

Rankin made Townsend news again that same year. On October 5, 1939, a front-page report in the *Townsend Star* would lead him to a case: "Toston Man Shot Early Sunday Morning Following a Minor Quarrel."

and "Duck Season Opened Earlier Than Planned." The duck hunters were happy, but James T. Olary wasn't. Jim Bembrick, was a miner, sometime butcher, and city marshal. He should have gone duck hunting, but instead had shot and killed Olary after a confused and drunken Saturday night. The tragedy occurred on the banks of the Missouri River in and around the small town of Toston. Events moved between the Paskavan Saloon and the Tostonian Bar, which Jim Bembrick owned.

Rankin was called to Bembrick's defense. Jury selection for the case was slow, and tedious, and required three days. For the first time since suffrage, Montana women were called for jury duty in a criminal case, but none of the nine women who responded were accepted as jurors. The jury chosen was completely male.

The courtroom drama was worthy of Rankin. During the proceedings, and from the stand, the fourteenth witness for the defense, Douglas Pease, smashed prosecuting attorney Frank T. Hooks twice in the face. Hooks was trying to find out how the deceased, Olary, had come through the back door of the saloon. On the surface it was an innocuous question, but it seemed to have been resented greatly by Pease. District Judge George W. Padbury, Jr. fined him ten dollars. After the "smashing" of Attorney Hooks face, court was adjourned for the day.[51]

Rankin's power before a jury once more played well. According to the local newspaper, "His [Rankin's] psychology and knowledge of law, and especially the law of self defense, was noticeably exercised during his appearance.... He took three and a half hours to make his plea."[52] Bembrick, a longtime resident of Broadwater County, had many relatives in the crowded courtroom to support him. The jury found him innocent of murder.

Another slant to this incident comes from ninety-year-old rancher Dan Sullivan of Townsend, who knew Rankin casually, and had watched him in court:

> He [Rankin] was a helluva lawyer ... great criminal lawyer. And I was drawed for jury but I didn't want to sit on the goddam jury because the guy [Bembrick] was as guilty as could be, you know, and when the judge said "You're excused" that's just what I wanted.... The guy was so goddam cold-blooded ... murderer, you know. I had my mind already made up. If I was in a tight place ... everybody [who] was in a tight place got Rankin. He could sure influence a jury... One fellow working on Rankin's ranch got caught trappin' beaver—it's against the law, you know—and Rankin got him off.[53]

Rankin's record of representing ranchers was nearly unblemished. He also drew attention by representing labor. In 1938, he stood for the

Montana State Federation of Labor against a chain store. In what would turn out to be a test case, the issue at hand was the store's contention that the employer had the right to determine whether an employee would work a straight shift or split shift-even if the status changed daily. The Montana Supreme Court agreed with Rankin that this kind of dictatorial whim was illegal.[54]

Rankin's success and reputation as a defender of the little people also included a personal side. Some remembered him fondly for his eccentricities and humanity. Successful Seattle businessman Bob Davis says that Rankin befriended him in the mid-1940s, when he was a street kid in Helena nicknamed "Stinky." Stinky sold papers and had Rankin as a customer. He recalls:

> I always thought he was bigger than life. The kind of man everyone called 'Mister,' a controlling type. I remember he had a beautiful gold chain and a watch and he had lace up shoes, and he always had them shined to a real high gloss. I made a deal with him. He wanted his paper first and he gave me strict orders that he would take a paper from me five days a week; the Independent Record Herald. It was downtown in those days. In fact it was right across from Ida's Rooms at 19½ South Main. What I had to do was get the paper and run down to his office. The building was actually a warehouse, he kept barbed wire in there, cases of food, sacks of grain, everything you could imagine.... on Friday he wanted me in his office soon as I could get down there from school. I always picked up a big, brown envelope to deliver to Eddie Barnhart at the Stockman's Bar. Later I found out I was delivering payroll for the workers [Rankin's ranch hands] that came in on Fridays and were paid out of the Stockman's Bar because they hung out there.[55]

Davis said that the friendship with Rankin gave him a certain amount of status on the Helena streets. People knew him as a Rankin protégé and gave him respect he wouldn't otherwise have received.

Rankin also kept track of Davis and knew when he was in trouble. "Stinky" was a fighter. His mother told him once, "You've had a black eye for ten years." Davis and a friend named Tom, who lived in nearby Marysville, decided that they would break into the ghost town's old assay office, then owned by Judge George Padbury, and dig in the foundation for gold dust that may have been dropped there when the mines were open. After gaining entrance into the building, the two boys found and took several slot machines, illegal in Montana, but nevertheless valuable.

Davis, a high school student, received an anonymous note a few days later: "Davis, bring those machines back." He did, and he thinks that Rankin interceded for him.

"Lester Loble took us in his chambers there and reading the riot act to us and I smart talked him," he said. "I'm sure that Wellington had his hand on my shoulder."

I always thought that he [Rankin] had kind of a twinkle in his eye, kind of a sense of humor. When I was about ten, maybe a little older, I got bit by a dog. It got infected and I was limping a little bit. So he said, "What's wrong?" When I told him, he said "I want you to go see Dr. Cline or Dr. Cashmore right now." I said, "I have no money to pay for that," and he said, "You get over there." And so I went and they dressed it and cleaned it up. I got a shot and I never heard anymore about it.

He always knew when my birthday was, he never asked me, and he'd always give me a dollar for my birthday, a silver dollar—I'll never forget that—and three dollars at Christmas. And those days, that was real money. He'd say, "Now, get out of here, Happy Birthday."[56]

8

AGAINST WAR, AGAINST WASHINGTON

"Jeannette would go to the stake for a cause."

Wellington Rankin may not have known how to win his own campaigns, but he had the know-how when it came to those of others. In 1940, Jeannette, with Wellington's help, ran for a second term in Congress–and won.

At sixty years of age, Jeannette sensed that the time was right to make a political comeback. Many Montanans felt threatened by FDR's war machinations and she thought she could run for Congress and take advantage of those fears. Returning to Montana from Georgia, where she had been living on a small farm, she entered the campaign with the leverage of her brother's political connections.

In the June Republican primary she beat Jacob Thorkelson (the incumbent), W. R. Allen, and Winfield E. Page. Her opponent in the general election was Jerry O'Connell, an FDR Democrat and former Congressman who spoke out in opposition to Senator Burton K. Wheeler, campaigning now as a conservative in spite of his more liberal Democratic Party affiliation.

To combat O'Connell, Wellington and Jeannette were able to win bipartisan pro-Wheeler forces–including Wheeler himself–to their side. Wellington and Wheeler were old friends. In 1940, together with gubernatorial candidate attorney Sam "Model T" Ford, they were the state's most influential politicians. They were three "tired Radicals" who ruled the state of Montana as a "triumvirate"–an obviously bipartisan "axis." Holding to the middle of the line they were assailed by the extreme factions of both parties who wanted fewer moderates and more Party line votes.[1]

Rankin supported Ford as the Republican candidate for governor in 1940. Some of Ford's supporters saw Rankin as a liability. This editorial and an accompanying cartoon in the *Missoula County Times* speaks volumes:

In the current campaign, Montana Republicans again find the name of Rankin emblazoned across their banners.

> Wellington D. Rankin, prominent in Republican campaigns since 1912… is busy this year with a double-barreled blitzkrieg.

> Rankin, brother of Jeannette Rankin… again is assisting his sister in her effort to return to that [congressional] post. In addition to assisting his sister, Rankin has been given the ear of Sam Ford in the gubernatorial campaign…. With [Rankin's] record of defeats, political observers are speculating whether Rankin's approval for a candidate may not mean—The Kiss of Death.[2]

Rankin had the last word, since both Ford and Jeannette won. His political savvy did not go unnoticed. Another source noted:

> It is noteworthy that signs point to the achievement by Mr. Wellington Rankin of his long-cherished ambition to supplant the old leaders who have so often defeated him…. With his sister nominated for congress, and his loyal friend [Sam Ford] named for governor, Mr. Rankin has now pushed the old timers out of the Republican picture.[3]

Jeannette's campaign for office was based on peace. War was raging in the world and the United States, although neutral, was taking sides. Jeannette advocated staying out of the war in Europe, and she campaigned on her anti-war record. For the previous ten years, she had worked as a lobbyist for the National Council for the Prevention of War (NCPW). She advocated the use of American military force only in defense of the continental United States. Her campaign slogan was, "Prepare to the limit for defense; keep our men out of Europe."

The former congresswoman took her message directly to the people as she had always done. At Broadwater County High School in Townsend she delivered a speech to students entitled, "How To Keep Us Out Of War." In it she said:

> Public opinion can prevent war… has stopped war between the states, between the United States and Canada, also South America… why not stop all war? War is a habit in Europe; let's not make it a habit in the United States.[4]

Surprisingly even the *Butte Daily Post*, an Anaconda Copper Mining Company newspaper, printed a similar speech. "the Company" was neutral in this campaign where it liked neither candidate. Jeannette had taken labor's side against "the Company" in the Butte Mine strike of 1917, but that was forgotten. Since that time she had been away from the state and was not a threat. Fortunately O'Connell, Jeannette's opponent, had committed a more recent error in the eye of "the Company." In 1938, he had pointed out that Anaconda had evaded an excise tax on imported copper and initiated legislation to stop its importation.[5] "The Company" probably considered Jeannette the lesser of two evils.

Regardless of who else was on her side, Jeannette had the peace vote. She campaigned as a peacenik, and won.

Once again in Washington, Jeannette was able to strengthen her bond with Senator Wheeler by arguing against Lend-Lease legislation, which when passed gave the Roosevelt administration power to wage war without declaring it. Both Wheeler and the nation were leaning right, and a sudden change in circumstances set Jeannette against most Americans, most Montanans, and even, once again, against her brother and advisor.

On December 7, 1941, Japanese aircraft bombed the U.S. military base at Pearl Harbor, Hawaii. In the uproar following the attack, Congress convened to vote on the issue of whether or not to join a second world war. Most Americans believed in the right to defend their territory but Jeannette did not want to put more lives at risk, and according to one historian, was "seemingly oblivious to the dramatic reversal in public opinion."[6]

She could have avoided the vote because of speaking engagements, but she chose to return to Washington to exercise her responsibility. She took a roundabout train route and avoided calls from Wellington, who once again advised strongly against casting a "no" vote. When he finally got through to her apartment, he spoke in terms of political strategy, pleading with her to vote "yes" for war in order to protect herself and her career.[7]

In the House chamber, Jeannette was unable to attract the Speaker's attention and join in the pre-vote debate. When it came time to answer the roll call, she responded, "As a woman I can't go to war and I refuse to send anyone else." The final tally that introduced the United States into World War II in the House of Representatives was 388 to 1–the lone "no" coming from Representative Jeannette Rankin. After voting, Jeannette was mobbed in the chambers by angry congressmen, news reporters, and others. Stationing herself behind the protective glass doors of a telephone booth, she had to be escorted to her office by police.

If Jeannette had grossly miscalculated the sentiment of the nation, Wellington had not. After she escaped the mob Jeannette made a single call to her brother in Helena; he told her unsympathetically, "Montana is 110 percent against you."[8]

A few days later when pressed for a statement, Wellington's family loyalty prevailed. He referred to Jeannette's record and campaign promises, saying, "You can always depend on a Rankin to keep his word."[9]

Dan Whetstone, a powerful Republican and longtime editor of the *Pioneer Press* in Cut Bank, Montana, sent her a telegram just a few hours after her polemic Congressional vote. It said, "Messages from all parts of Montana indicate disappointment over your attitude in failing to support the war declaration. I urge and beseech you to redeem Montana's honor and loyalty by changing your vote as early as possible." Others sent messages such as, "Your vote a terrible disappointment..."[10]

Winfield Page, a former political rival of the Rankins who visited Jeannette in Washington before Pearl Harbor, claimed she didn't intend to run again for the office anyway. Page and his wife met with Jeannette to test the political waters. Page wanted to enter the race for Congress himself. According to the Pages, Jeannette told them she had promised "the Company" she wouldn't run against Mike Mansfield whom they favored.[11]

Former U.S. Senator Mike Mansfield, who succeeded Jeannette in office, rebuts this suggestion as follows:

> As far as Winfield Page's statement is concerned, Jeannette Rankin at no time agreed not to challenge me when I first ran for the House of Representatives. As a matter of fact, when I was defeated in my first race for the House, Jeannette came to see me at my office at the University, to request my support. I told her that I could not give it to her because I was indebted to the Democrats.
>
> Jeannette Rankin would not conform to any "request\insistence" of the Anaconda Company, or to anyone or anything else except her conscience. This she did throughout her life and in doing so set an example that few were able to follow...[12]

Regardless of her motives, the "Lady from Montana" found herself hated in her home state. Many Montanans were furious about the vote. Some demanded impeachment, calling her a traitor and worse. She held out, completed her term, and managed to pass some vital legislation. History has given her a better reputation than the war proponents could have imagined. Years later, in a homily in the Capitol rotunda during a dedication of a statue of Jeannette, her efforts were praised by her niece, Virginia Ronhovde, quoted here in part:

She was not the extreme pacifist some would picture, hating all the military. She said she admired President Eisenhower because he warned against the "military-industrial complex," and he spoke of war as a method to be "outlawed." She was a fighting humanitarian who detested and found despicable the profits made by the "munitions-makers" on both sides of the wars. She befriended the "used" soldiers, considering them the victims of the stupidity of war... She introduced the bill in 1919, which led to the enfranchisement of all U.S. women citizens, though it was passed when she was no longer in Congress. She secured the right of American women who had married foreigners to retain their American citizenship. She helped to reduce the staggering maternal and infancy death rate in Montana and nationally through securing the services of the Children's Bureau. She pushed for legislation banning the commercial use of child labor. She induced the U.S. Treasury Department to improve working conditions at the Bureau of Engraving and Printing. Told that the change would take months, she persevered and achieved it in a day. Capital newspapers called it "the swiftest change ever made in Washington...."

The *Washington Star* in a January 23, 1968, editorial, again praised her at the time of her march protesting the Vietnam war: "However one may disagree with her now...when all else fails, everyone must nevertheless respect her feminine consistency in her passion for an end of the killing... Her brigade set new records for peace demonstrations.... She was, first and last, a convinced and inspired humanitarian."[13]

Jeannette earned a place in history, but in doing so, she pushed her brother out of the limelight and under a spotlight he preferred to escape. Letters to Jeannette from Montanans slightly favored her debatable vote. Wellington struggled against his sister's pacifist reputation for the remainder of his political life. It was weight added to a record and personality that did not need the extra burden, and it may have made him too sensitive to criticism. Nevertheless, he supported Jeannette even though her unpopular postures worked against him, saying, "Jeannette would go to the stake for a cause."[14]

With the arrival of war, Montana became more conservative. During the trend Wellington Rankin decided to run again for office. He made a complete reversal from liberal to conservative.

At the start of the 1940s, the political party lines were still unclear. Voters often crossed over them. This was particularly true in the case of Senator Wheeler, who had been considered a possible candidate for the presidency, and was still smarting from his defeat at the Democratic National Convention. His treatment by the Convention was especially painful since he had received more votes in his home state than did FDR. He was strongly anti-war, and patronized Jeannette's anti-war campaign to the hilt.

Now Wheeler supported her brother Wellington as the 1942 Republican senatorial candidate opposing entrenched Democrat James Murray, a firm Roosevelt champion. Wheeler believed that if Murray was to be defeated, 1942 was the time. He was almost right. Wellington, with his political history and statewide influence, was presented as an attractive alternative for Montana neo-conservatives.[15]

The recognized leader of the state's Republican Party, Rankin began to campaign against Murray in September, 1941. He played on voters' wartime discontent and Murray's loss of favor with small business. He ran strongest in southeast Montana. He also gained the support of the Butte Irish who were not pleased with Murray's approval of the Lend-Lease agreement, which allowed munitions to be sent, at practically no cost, to Great Britain.

Throughout the campaign, Murray was on the defensive, but his son Charles Murray managed his campaign with skill. Murray went with the fervor of the times and asked his audiences to judge Rankin "by the Congressional record of his pacifist sister," whom Murray labeled "un-American." One of the more extreme things he said was, "Nazi newspapers in Berlin would hail his [Rankin's] victory. We can only judge him on his sister's record."[16] Not willing to settle for the damage caused by his statement in the newspapers, Murray made his scurrilous remarks on the radio (a new weapon in political campaigns).[17]

Rankin countered weakly that the draft was unfair to Montana men, and Murray was somehow responsible for this. Murray's tactics worked with the voters. Jeannette's vote in Congress against entry into World War II was still ringing in many Montanans' ears.

Wheeler and fellow Democrat Barclay Craighead, of the Unemployment Compensation Commission, did all they could for Rankin's campaign, but they could hardly do enough. The tenacious Wheeler, once called "Bolshevik Burt"[18] or sometimes "Boxcar Burt"[19] was in any corner that fought against his archenemy Franklin Delano Roosevelt. He expressed his concerns about Rankin's chances shortly before the election:

> With reference to Rankin's campaign, my own view is that it has been miserably handled but he may win yet. I am receiving a lot of letters from women in Montana protesting the taking of boys 18 and 19 and that is bound, in my judgment, to hurt Mr. Roosevelt and Murray.... All the letters I am getting from Montana from women and farmers

and people of that kind indicate there is a tremendous change in sentiment—a very definite undercurrent against the Administration (Roosevelt). I don't think that Rankin has shown as much courage and guts as he should have. He has been entirely too timid because of the severe criticism that Jeannette got.[20]

Instead of taking an active stand and proposing change that Montanans might welcome, Rankin adopted a defensive strategy. In November, it proved to be a poor method. He lost to Murray by a very narrow margin. Craighead wrote to Wheeler after Rankin lost, saying, "I agree with you that Rankin was a little bit timid in some of his campaign material. However, on the whole he did a very good job after he once got on the stump."[21]

As testimony to the fickleness of politics, some believe that Rankin would have won the Senate race in 1942 if he had destroyed a piece of real estate he owned. The Pittsburgh Building in downtown Helena had been condemned, and many voters considered it a blemish on the beauty of the city. Some alleged that Rankin might have lost as many as two thousand votes in his own district because of this.[22] Murray's victory was particularly sweet. He had defeated Rankin and he had proven his strength against Wheeler's bi-partisan patronage. The bitterness of the campaign did not ruin the Rankin-Murray friendship. They remained staunch personal friends. When Republican Wesley D'Ewart of Wilsall, Montana, later challenged Murray, there were significant rumors that Rankin crossed party lines again and used his influence to help Murray's campaign. Word was that he and D'Ewart, both strong personalities, differed over who would get the spoils of patronage if D'Ewart won. D'Ewart would not relinquish these plums, so Rankin refused to support him.

Montana Republicans had no federal patronage since the Hoover Administration until Eisenhower was elected. It was customary for the National Committeeman and Committeewoman to play a large part in recommending people for the jobs of U. S. Attorney, Federal Marshall, and some department heads. Rankin, Mrs. Gladys Knowles, the National Committeewoman, and D'Ewart discussed this at the National Committee meeting in Washington D.C. According to Rankin, D'Ewart was abrupt and discourteous to him and Knowles, and implied that if he was elected only he would decide on the appointees. This angered Rankin.[23]

Wellington had once more gone to the stake for his own cause-his own ambition—and lost. The 1942 race affected his pocketbook as much as his morale. Law partner Arthur Acher wrote letters such as this one asking for repayment of old debts:

Jeannette Rankin and Senator Mike Mansfield. Photo: Montana Historical Society, Helena.

The campaign is over and we lost out by less than 1,700 votes. That was very close indeed. It was very strenuous and we all were exhausted at its conclusion, but are now getting into the legal end of things, and funds are exceedingly low, due to campaign expenses.

Mr. Rankin suggested that I write you again…. Anything you can send at this time would be very much appreciated…[24]

Rankin returned full time to the world of law and land ownership setting aside politics–but not entirely.

9

LABOR AND POLITICS

His fee was probably punishment enough

Wellington Rankin hated anything corporate, and in the
early 1940s, much of his law practice involved cases against corporations–property damage against public utilities, or personal injury suits
against automobile insurance companies. Rankin was known primarily
as a friend of labor who could handle anything. His reputation as a
tough contender in court was well-known. Gretchen Billings, publisher
of the left-leaning newspaper *The People's Voice*, remembered Rankin as
steely, saying he was sometimes "so cold that he urinated ice water."[1]

In 1941, he represented miners in a conflict known as the "Collar to
Collar" case. His win strengthened mine workers' rights. The case hinged
upon mining practices. It was customary for miners to reach the face of
the drift where they worked, which might be deep in the mine, on their
own time. It sometimes took as long as an hour for them to struggle their
way through the long dim tunnels and shafts. The reverse was true, also.
A miner's wages ceased when he left the face, not when he left the mine.

Rankin convinced the court that this practice was unfair. He argued
that the miner's eight-hour day commenced when he reported for work
and ended when he left the mine. As expected, the suit was welcomed
by labor and opposed by the Anaconda Copper Mining Company. For
the working miner, Rankin's winning verdict meant that more hard
earned wages filled the ore-digger's pocket.[2]

In 1942, Rankin represented the Butte Miners Union No. 1 against
the Anaconda Copper Mining Company for an increase of compensation benefits. He won. Not surprisingly he alienated "the Company. He
paid a price for these victories as "the Company" and its influence always
helped defeat his political goals.

He was popular as a representative in court for many labor disputes.
He shielded unions against liable and local ordinances that attempted to
criminalize peaceful picketing. Unfortunately, even this record on the

side of labor failed to capture him their support during his political campaigns.

The decade of the Forties was not without personal events. In 1947, Wellington's mother died at 93. For several years Olive had lived with Jeannette. They spent the winters in Georgia's milder climate and the rest of the year at her son's Avalanche Ranch in Broadwater County.[3] If his mother's death affected him, Rankin tried to conceal it. The son held great respect for the mother. She lovingly referred to him as "The Boy" and after the death of his father, he managed affairs so well that she was financially secure throughout her long life.

Still powerful in Republican politics in 1948, at age 64, Rankin made another unsuccessful bid for the "golden ring"–the U.S. Senate. This time he was defeated in the primary by Tom J. Davis, a Butte lawyer, respected community leader, Rotarian, and former president of the Montana Bar Association. In the campaign, Rankin targeted the federal government for taxing Montana excessively and not returning enough for highways. Other states in the West such as Nevada, Utah, Wyoming, and Idaho were favored, according to him, by large amounts of money in highway subsidies.

Another giant that Rankin confronted in the race was Bonneville Power and its management. "We don't need the Bonneville dam management to tell us what to do with our rivers and land in Montana, and we don't intend to let them make western Montana a reservoir or dumping ground for waters they wish to use at their convenience for hydroelectric power," he announced.[4]

In this contest Rankin attempted to use his influence to gain allies from both parties. His political machinations did not go without notice. Emmet Glore, a Missoula lawyer, was asked to evaluate the state for the potential candidacy of Senator Robert Taft in 1948. In a letter, he succinctly and humorously analyzes Montana's political personality.

> Montana politics can be understood only by Montana politicians. This is a rugged state. So are its politics...only one [columnist] had even a passing conception of what was going on in the Wheeler-Erickson senatorial shuffle that ended, to the amazement of all hands, with the election of Zales Ecton.
>
> ... The Republican people's governor Ford, a potent Baptist every Sunday, is a company-bound disciple of the ex-democrat senator (Wheeler) ... who was originally elected as the people's advocate and promptly went over to "the Company. This ex-senator was defeated last fall in Montana, by one Leif Erickson because his opinions on Germany offended some of the wealthy Jews in New

York City. All the Butte chaws and cousin jacks voted for Erickson. Does this make sense? Absolutely in Montana. Wellington Rankin, a republican, now expects to defeat the incumbent democrat Murray with the assistance of Ford and this same ex-democrat senator's machine, which, incidentally, elected this republican people's governor…. It's all fascinating and on one's better days, hilarious. If he must have Montana, my advice to senator Taft is to buy it: from B. K. Wheeler, Sam Ford, Wellington D. Rankin and J. Burke Clements, and from the Monopoly. In Montana politics, that approach is most direct, least expensive, and best understood.[5]

Overall, in spite of his anti-corporate stance, Rankin's list of goodies for voters was a bland one. In spite of his promises for "lower taxes, lower living costs, governmental economy, encouragement of free enterprise, and more housing," he was not expected to reopen old sores or rock the Republican boat; nor would his campaign rankle the Anaconda Copper Mining Company.

What was the reason for Rankin's timidity? Memories. Rankin had entered the race still tormented by recollections of his extremely narrow defeat in 1942 by Senator James Murray. The incumbent Murray had asked his audiences across Montana to judge Rankin by the Congressional record of his pacifist "un-American" sister.[6] Rankin was a patriot and these kinds of unfair comments were undoubtedly painful and damaging. Also hurt in his previous campaign by Murray's use of the radio, he was stunned again by the same media.

A lawyer and former employee of Rankin's, who was wildly opposed to him, paid a Helena station for fifteen minutes of air time on the night before the primary election. The broadcast was treacherous, and a jolting blow. To the delight of Rankin's enemies, the broadcast "took Rankin apart."[7] During the tirade the assailant went on about Rankin's references to his service in the army during World War I, and said, "It's a great thing to be a veteran, particularly right after a war. And now, ladies and gentlemen, I want to tell you this. There were GIs in World War II under chloroform longer than Wellington D. Rankin was in uniform."[8]

This, of course was an unfair insinuation, since Rankin was in officers' training when the armistice was signed in 1918. He never pretended that he had served in any other capacity. But the attack and others that followed it regurgitated Jeannette Rankin's positions on U.S. involvement in war along with Wellington's own foibles, and rankled enough voters to have an effect. It was a well-planned strategy and Rankin had no time to challenge the insults.

Rankin may not have pressed enough hands to make a difference.

Labor and Politics

According to advice from attorney Howard C. Gee in Lewistown, who suggested good local venues for Rankin to visit, Rankin had, in his opinion, "missed the boat." He hadn't met enough people. It was Gee's idea that in primary campaigns the voter supports the candidate that makes the best impression.[9]

Gee thought that his letter should go to Wellington's sisters Jeannette and Edna, who were campaigning for their brother across the state and who, Gee felt, had "more than the ordinary political horse sense needed in this particular campaign."[10]

Between the lines, Gee intimated that the sisters might encourage their brother to adopt a more populist posture–less aloof, accessible and amiable.

Davis won the primary, but he had no chance against the entrenched Murray, partly because of his image as a "Company man." He lost the general election by a large majority in a virulent battle. Murray carried Montana's population centers and labor fortresses.

The candidates smeared one another incessantly. Davis was characterized as "an enemy of labor" and "tool of Anaconda Copper." Murray was the victim of anti-Catholic radicals and called a Communist.[11]

The liberal Murray kept his seat and stayed in the Senate from 1935-1961, longer than any other Montanan. From as early as 1913 Montana had a predilection for liberal Democratic Senators. Its voters apparently preferred fiscally conservative politicians at home and liberals in Washington. Murray's son Charles claimed that Rankin was one of his father's best supporters after he lost the primary to Davis. In an interview Charles Murray said:

> Wellington for some reason or other liked me. I think he thought I was a crooked politician just like he was. And, by God, I used to go to his office, I'd get on an extension of his phone and he'd call several people around the state…. I remember the Montana Power Company claimed that they were going to be neutral and I told Wellington that. He said, "Oh, don't let them take you in like that." He said, "Come on up to the office." He called Bob Corette, the general counsel for Montana Power at that time and I got on the extension and he said, "How's D'Ewart doing?" He [Corette] said, "Well, if you'll get out and do some work, Wellington, and put a little money in, we can beat Murray! We can get rid of the son-of-a-bitch!" So that proved to me where Montana Power stood.[12]

Defeat did not keep Rankin down. He proved to be a rallying force at the 1949 statewide Republican Party convention in Helena. Here he kept up his fight against an unfavorable press. Waving a copy of the

Lewistown newspaper in his hand, he condemned its publisher Ken Byerly as a "carpetbagger from Wyoming," who had falsely said the Republican Party was dead. Byerly printed what began as a news story favorable to Rankin in response, and printed again a picture of Rankin dating from the early 1930s:

> The old guard leadership of Montana's Republican Party is plenty OK! In brief, this is the opinion of Wellington D. Rankin, one of the greater orators in the history of Montana.... Rankin, who has established an awesome record as a brilliant, biting and almost unbeatable barrister, concluded that things were pretty close to OK among Montana GOP party leaders and policies.

Byerly then smashed the icon:

> The speech went over well with some of the old guard, but many other Republicans afterwards expressed considerable skepticism. "He's never been much of a party man before," one said of Rankin. "How come he's pouring oil on the troubled waters and trying to make out everything is wonderful, when we know it isn't."

> Many GOPsters feel that the Helena attorney has never been one of the real insiders in party circles, even during the years when Rankin was defeated in his race for the United States Senate, and for governor.

> They feel Rankin is trying to get in good with the present party leaders, and wonder why.[13]

Rankin also took issue with other news media. He fired off a rebuttal letter to the Associated Press office in Helena, refuting their charge that he said democratic power in Montana rested on wholesale bribery. Correcting them he stated, "I did say, speaking of the last presidential election, that the promises of the national administration and its tremendous expenditures and giveaway programs operated as a wholesale bribe to the voters."[14]

For Rankin the conference was not a total bust, if only for a personal reason. One of the attendees was Ms. Louise Replogle, Lewistown's county attorney and voice of the young Republicans, who, the newspaper noted, had caught Rankin's eye. The paper stated, "Rankin has shown interest in the young MSU graduate's legal career, and there is much talk that he may back her for congress in Montana's eastern district in 1952 when Wesley D'Ewart runs for governor."[15] It appears in retrospect that politics wasn't his only interest in the young lady.

Byerly did his best to cut down Rankin's protégé, too. He quoted young Republicans who said Replogle did not speak for them, that in fact, no one could, since they did not have a voice. Rankin would not have minded the political comments. His interest in Replogle would soon go beyond an interest in her legal mind.

Rankin's most recent election loss had not affected his legal practice. His clients were found across the state, and his methods of fighting for underdog defendants drew more and more of them. Joseph Gary, a retired circuit court judge in Bozeman, began law practice in Montana in 1949 and tried cases against Rankin. One stood out in his mind. Michael O'Connell, the Gallatin County attorney, with Gary as his assistant, prosecuted a high-school student for manslaughter. The high-school senior had taken a pistol with him to a "kegger" beer party, and after a few drinks had discharged his gun. The bullet had gone through the window of a nearby house and struck an elderly man in the stomach. The man was taken to the hospital where he died a few days later. The young man's parents hired the best–Wellington Rankin–to defend their son.

Gary and Mike O'Connell had never met Rankin, but they were awed by his reputation. The two young prosecutors were prepared to dislike Rankin because they had heard he was a rascal. Gary recalled:

> I'd never met him … here he was, a big, handsome guy, very straight and erect, very charming. God, he was charming as hell.… He was very formal: "Mr. Gary" or "Mr. O'Connell," and he just charmed the hell out of us. We were just young attorneys and we didn't know too much yet and he'd say things like, "Mr. O'Connell, you're doing the most remarkable job …" And I couldn't talk to Mike … his head was getting bigger and bigger all the time.[16]

Rankin called two witnesses during the trial. The first was Ed McGivern, a national champion pistol shot and gun expert from Great Falls, who testified that the bullet that struck the deceased had ricocheted, and that the death was therefore an accident. McGivern testified often for Rankin in cases involving guns and impressed courts all over the state. He was a short, jolly individual, and even though it was a murder trial McGivern soon had the jury and judge laughing. "They laughed us right out of court," Gary recalled.

The prosecution witness for O'Connell and Gary was a ballistics expert from the Federal Bureau of Investigation (FBI). In cross-examination, Rankin asked him, "Have you ever made a mistake?" The expert then made the mistake of answering no. Rankin prodded, "You mean you have never made a mistake in your whole life?" The FBI man said, "Never, not in my business." Rankin proceeded to work over the apparently superhuman witness until the poor man was excused. Gary said,

"He appeared relieved to leave the stand."

Rankin's next witness was a respected Bozeman physician. The doctor had great dignity and presence and testified that the injury from the bullet actually did the old man a favor since he was suffering from so many ailments: high blood pressure, diabetes, heart trouble, and cancer. Further, the doctor assured the jury, the wounded man's last few days were enhanced by his hospitalization and the nursing care he received.

"When we were trying to make our argument to the jury," Gary said, "he [Rankin] was flicking these silver dollars in his hand, and the jury was looking at those damn silver dollars instead of listening to our argument." Rankin won an acquittal, and Gary said, "His fee was probably punishment enough."

It wasn't the last time the two would meet in court. According to Gary:

> I had a couple more cases against him after that and I was getting a little more self-confident and so I said to the judge, "Would you please request that Mr. Rankin doesn't drum those dollars through his hands while I'm arguing to the jury because it's diverting their attention?" Well, Rankin was incensed about that.[17]

John Harrison, who also tried cases against Rankin, said he flipped pennies in his hands rather than silver dollars, hoping to show the jury he was poor and honest as opposed to the wealthy Rankin.[18]

Rankin and Joseph Gary clashed again in what was at first a simple divorce settlement. Gary represented the husband, and Rankin spoke for the wife. After the divorce, the ex-husband became ill and was admitted to the veteran's hospital in Helena. Property settlements were to be arranged later. On the appointed day in court, when the couple's assets were to be divided, Rankin accompanied by the wife said, "Your Honor, I move to dismiss this case." When Gary objected and asked why, Rankin said, "The parties were remarried yesterday."

An astonished Gary later discovered the details:

> Well, what he had done, he'd gotten an ambulance, went out to the Veteran's Administration Hospital, got our client, put him in the ambulance, took him out near Toston, brought a Unitarian reader from Bozeman who was capable of performing marriages, remarried the parties, signed the certificate, took him back to the hospital and dumped him off and that was it. That blew our case completely out of the water. We could have set it aside for fraud, but the daughter of our client said, "Let's forget it."[19]

• • •

Rankin's office was busy; busier than he and Acher could handle. They needed help. In 1951, he brought Louise Replogle into his firm after she beat him and Arthur Acher in court. The case was against a prominent citizen of Lewistown for sodomy, State v. Searle. Rankin and Acher were counsel for the defense, and tried to get a change of venue by producing affidavits from citizens suggesting that the accused wouldn't get a fair trial in his hometown. Louise Replogle had just as many affidavits from others giving the opposite viewpoint. The judge ruled in her favor. It was a difficult case, since children were required to testify, but the prosecution prevailed. It was appealed after Replogle left Fergus County and was reversed by the Montana Supreme Court on technicalities.[20]

Before joining Rankin's law office, Louise Replogle had gained considerable prominence in a test case against a nightclub. This was another that went to the state Supreme Court. In *State v. Joyland Club*, she pled the state's side successfully and is credited with preventing the use of slot machines in Montana. The defendants and their Helena lawyer had incorporated as a private club and brought in slot machines. They planned to organize many bars around Montana into their "club," thereby circumventing the law. As Fergus County Attorney, Replogle raided the Joyland premises and seized five slot machines. The club was then locked and sealed by her office.

During the course of the case, state and national newspapers had a field day with cartoons and pictures. One of these showed Louise as a young, slim, attractive woman with a sledge hammer in her hand destroying a slot machine. The images were reminiscent of pictures of Carry Nation, the militant temperance advocate who gained notoriety at the turn of the century by destroying saloons with a hatchet, and who had passed through Montana thirty years earlier.

A Minneapolis newspaper said, in an article entitled, "SLOT MACHINE FIGHT OPENS IN MONTANA," that "faces are long today in Montana, gloom stalks the streets, and sobriety hangs like a pall." The *Montana Kaiman*, the University of Montana student newspaper, entitled its article about alumna Louise Replogle, "HAVE AT 'EM." Other headlines were "DECISION MAY BAN DEVICES FROM MANY BARS IN MONTANA," "CHIEF JUSTICE ADAIR 'SEES NO LEGAL MACHINES'," and "SUPREME COURT RULING BANS SLOT MACHINES IN 'SOCIAL CLUB' CASE."[21]

At the time there were six thousand slot machines with federal licenses grinding away in private clubs in Montana. By 1950, when the state Supreme Court rendered its final decision in the matter, the contraptions were no longer legal anywhere, not even in private clubs. With state and national attention focused on the young county attorney,

The funeral of Thomas J. Walsh. Judge Lester Loble is at the front of the right hand line with Wellington Rankin immediately behind him. Intending humor, Loble said to Rankin, "Hang on tight, Wellington, this may be as close as you ever get to the U.S. Senate." As a politician whose greatest ambition was to be elected to this important national office, Rankin found little humor in the quip. Photo: Montana Historical Society, Helena.

Mademoiselle magazine selected her as one of its "Ten Outstanding Young Women of 1949."

Replogle came from strong Montana stock. Her father was an attorney and state legislator in Lewistown. He was a disabled hero of World War I, who had said in a colorful speech at a legislative banquet in his honor, "Down south when I was a boy we learned to fight by raising mules and the mules were just about as dangerous as the German Army, but not half as stupid." One citizen of Lewistown, pointing out that Louise's father wasn't perfect, said he had one bad habit: "He chaws tobaccy." Replogle had raised his daughter to fight and shoot a rifle, skills that could be helpful to a Montana lawyer in a rough and ready state.

To Rankin's firm, Replogle brought the experience she had gained as Fergus County attorney and in her Lewistown practice. She also brought a shared Republican viewpoint.

She graduated from the law school at the University of Montana in Missoula in 1946. While at the university she was president of the State Young Republicans, an accomplished musician, and a student office holder. Elected Fergus County Attorney in 1946, shortly after her graduation, Louise had been re-elected to a second term. She was also co-chairman of the Young Republican National Federation in 1948, and functioned as assistant secretary of the GOP national convention.

Once established in Rankin's firm in Helena, Louise conducted research and assisted the colorful senior partner who disliked reading law books. He would tell assistants Acher and Replogle, "Well, there should be a case on such and such a point" and wouldn't take no for an answer. "This is bound to be the law; now get to the library and find it." Generally, he was right.[22]

Wellington spent forty-five of his adult years as a single divorced man living alone. He was a strong masculine figure–athletic, muscular and handsome–and had an active social life in his interval as a bachelor, with many friends and perhaps just as many romantic connections. Helen Johnson, a regally attractive former legislator (1961) and an unusually successful real estate broker, knew Rankin socially in the 1930s. Johnson was active in Republican politics, and the two were good friends for the rest of his life.

> I just thought he was wonderful. He was magnetic and his conversations were always interesting. Because I felt he was so much smarter than most of the people I talked to, I maybe overrated him. A friend of mine who lived with me was engaged to him for a few years. He used to visit her every weekend. And I'll always remember him because he always brought her a huge box of candy from Gamer's, and I got all the bon-bons because she didn't like them. He was thirty years older than she was, and…she lived at my house for quite a while…one night she went out with a young, good-looking man that I thought she would really enjoy. When she came home, I said, "Did you have fun?"
>
> "It was boring, he was so boring after Wellington," she said.[23]

For several years Rankin was said to have dated a woman named Marjorie who had once been his secretary. A date to marry was set occasionally, but each time something…a case in court, a political meeting, a business trip…would interfere and the marriage was postponed. Finally, the lady married someone else.[24]

Judge Henry Loble considered the three partners a superb legal team. Rankin must have agreed. In 1955, three years after bringing her into the firm, he married Louise Replogle.

Wellington's young wife was welcomed into the Rankin clan by his sisters. In a letter to Louise dated December 3, 1957, Edna Rankin McKinnon says that the previous summer her visit to Montana was made especially pleasant because of Louise's presence. "...I am so pleased that you and Wellington are so happy together. You know you have done for him what none of the rest of us have been able to do and I am so grateful to you." Louise says her favorite sister was Mary who spent many vacations with her and Wellington. She saw Jeannette rarely, but they corresponded frequently, and Louise handled her tax returns and other business.[25]

Louise was much younger than Wellington, but seemed his equal partner in law and politics. Now she was his partner for life.

10

INVESTMENT RANCHER

"You can't go wrong on land"

Wellington Rankin loved to ride horses, and he rode them well. From his childhood days on Grant Creek to his adult life as one of Montana's–and the nation's–largest landholders, he cut a fine figure in the saddle. Like her husband, Louise Replogle Rankin was also an experienced rider. The Rankins had plenty of space in which to ride. In 1964, they possessed one million acres of land.

One participant of a roundup on the 71 Ranch near Martinsdale recalls a time that he and some other veteran cowboys were unable to find or catch a group of horses hidden in the foothills. After climbing to the top of a hill, the riders saw Louise in the distance. He recalls seeing "the biggest cloud of dust way down country from us…. There was Mrs. Rankin, Louise … she must have had a hundred to one hundred fifty head of horses down in that corner and was holding them by herself."[1]

The story of the building of Rankin's empire is closely tied to the history of the settlement of Montana. That story begins with Daniel A. G. Flowerree, one of the first livestock producers in Montana.

Floweree, a Montana pioneer, brought cattle up from Missouri in 1864, and his herds of cattle grazed freely on huge pastures in what is now Lewis and Clark, Teton, Cascade, and other counties. He was a respected steward of wealth, and was credited with saving a Helena bank from bankruptcy during the silver Panic of 1893 by borrowing $400,000 from a Chicago bank and depositing it locally. This single act bolstered the financial credit of the entire state.[2]

Rankin first took the role of landowner by acquiring a Flowerree family property shortly after World War I. He was connected to the Flowerrees through Elizabeth Wallace, his first wife, who was also D. A. G. Flowerree's granddaughter. When Elizabeth's uncle, Dan Flowerree, Jr., died during the first world war, his mother sold the Avalanche Ranch, which had supposedly been bought to keep the young Flowerree out of the draft.[3]

The ranch changed hands several times and Rankin bought it in 1927 from A. T. Hibbard.[4] This fine property rested on the western slope of the Big Belt Mountains southeast of Helena, at the foot of Avalanche Gulch. Established by pioneer J. V. Stafford, who had also run a ferry across the Missouri River nearby, the ranch was known chiefly for its orchard.[5]

The Avalanche was the only property in which Rankin ever took more than a commercial interest. He maintained a summer house there, and it served as home for visiting members of his family.[6] Olive, Jeannette, Hattie, and Hattie's daughter Virginia Ronhovde spent many vacations there, basking in the beauty of the rolling hills and valleys, roaming its handsome hillsides of wildflowers on foot or horseback.[7]

The Matter of the Cook Ranch

The next ranch property Rankin obtained, for strictly commercial reasons, was part of the A. B. Cook Ranch in Broadwater County. The purchase of this ranch ultimately became a complex and agonizing transaction.

A. B. Cook was a self-made man who had come to Montana in 1883 and found work on the 79 Ranch in the Big Coulee Valley south of Ryegate. He was a well-known and respected Montanan. He was an engineer and helped lay the bed for the Great Northern–Montana Central Railway from Great Falls to Butte. By the turn of the century, Cook held the position of state auditor. His land purchases included large holdings in Broadwater and Meagher Counties, where he developed a fine herd of Herefords.

Cook is described as a large, impressive man over six feet tall who could look others in the eye with clear "optimism." Montana had advantages for cattlemen, he said:

> Our bunch grass and blue joint pasture are highly nutritious. Blue joint hay will put fat on an animal just like timothy and clover with grain. The altitude increases lung power. The lime in the hills and water develop bone. The cold climate gives cattle plenty of hair, develops their power of resistance and makes them hardy and healthy.[8]

He had chosen a good spot to begin his own herd, a spring-fed ranch in Broadwater County called the Dunlavy place. Three shrewd Irish brothers, John, Anthony, and Pat Dunlavy originally developed this ranch. They bred an impressive herd of cattle and became wealthy in the process. Commenting on the size of the Dunlavy herd, a neighbor said, "Even the jackrabbits down that way were branded PD [the Dunlavy brand]."[9]

Investment Rancher

Cook's ranch was successful. The main reason was that he knew how to inspire people. Axel Holmstrom managed Cook's ranches from 1917 until 1929 as if they were his own. When hired, he was told, "Axel, I've got 30,000 acres of land here in Meagher County, see what you can do with it." A loyal friend and employee, Holmstrom played a major part in the development of a quality herd. Cook's cattle became famous nationally and topped many sales.[10]

The ranching business had its vagaries. By the late 1920s, Cook was indebted to First National Bank in Helena for a large sum, and bank official Thomas A. Marlow called the loan. Cook insisted to the money-lenders that he would regain solvency if given time, but the bank was adamant. Cook was forced to put his entire herd up for sale at auction.

He was heartbroken, and he was mad. Some postulated that this decimation of his pride led to an early death. Cattlemen, when they heard about the sale, came from all over the United States. The choice animals sold for a great deal more than Cook owed the bank.

Not long afterward, on November 24, 1928, Cook died. He died suddenly and unexpectedly, the result of an infection. His will bequeathed his property to his wife Mary Agnes Cook, and appointed her executrix.[11]

By a terrible coincidence, Cook's wife died two months later. Her will bequeathed one half of her entire estate to the Cook's only child, Gloria Braid Cook. The other half went to her son by a previous marriage, Frank H. (Hervey) Cook. To her daughter, Hervey Cook's full sister, Mary Agnes Patenaude, she left the sum of one dollar.[12] For three years after Mary Cook's death until he resigned, Rankin acted as Gloria Cook's legal guardian.[13] However, Gloria Cook Walker claims she removed him from that role of guardian when she was fifteen.[14]

The dissolution of A. B. Cook's property and Rankin's role in representing Gloria still inspires rancor in the Cook family. They suspect that "cattle baron" or "Rasputin" (their terms) Rankin may have somehow cheated them. The story is a complicated one. Judge W. H. Poorman presided over the hearings before the District Court of Montana's First Judicial District. The principals involved included Frank Hervey Cook, who was administrator of the estate; and his attorney Wellington D. Rankin; W. R. Church, as guardian of the Estate of Gloria Braid Cook (A. B. Cook's daughter), a minor; and her attorney M. S. Gunn.[15]

After Rankin resigned as Gloria's guardian, other guardians were appointed including her older half sister Mary Agnes Patenaude. This seems unusual since her mother had essentially disinherited her. Mary Agnes Patenaude threatened a lawsuit, but she eventually settled with the estate and accepted $22,500,[16] 25,000 shares in the New Gould Mining Company, and some silver as her portion.

Cook owned five ranches totaling approximately 40,000 acres at the time of his passing. But the property was not free and clear. He was in debt and owed $45,000 on the Havey Ranch in Meagher County alone.

That ranch was turned back to the creditors. The estate, also in Meagher County, paid another $38,000 owed on the Newlan Creek Ranch.

The transactions and legal ramifications became more complicated and cloudy after that point. Enter Lena Cook, Hervey's wife, who supplied the $42,500 to purchase Gloria's part of the estate. Sanctioned by the judge, Gloria's guardian, W. R. Church, and her lawyer, M. S. Gunn. This payment was not only for real property but also for 438,000 shares of New Gould Mining Company and the estate's livestock: 586 cattle, about half of which were purebred Herefords, and 141 horses. Farm implements and two cars are listed. There was also about $5,000 of outstanding debt to individuals incurred by Cook before he died.

Tragedy enters the picture once again. Lena Cook died in August of 1933. Her will left the balance of her estate to her husband Hervey.[17] In April of 1935, Rankin purchased part of the original ranch in Broadwater County from Hervey Cook.[18] This purchase became one of Wellington's earliest additions to his expanding empire.

These complicated transactions involving the Cook estate took place before, during, and after the worst depression the United States had experienced. Money was tight and many people were in debt. Land and commodity prices fell and people were unsure of the future. There were many failures and banks were no exception. The whole process of settling the estate was done as amicably as one could expect for such complicated legal wranglings.

Rankin's role always remained within the bounds of the law. The family's lingering bad feeling is not based on any documented facts. There is no proof that Rankin acted beyond the limits of law or ethics. However, in all fairness, both viewpoints deserve mention.[19] No amount of legal documents would ever satisfy the Cooks. Whether everything on record was above board or not, they believed they were cheated. The assumption on their part was since Wellington and Gloria's half-brother ended up with much of the property, and Wellington was the young girl's guardian, that there must be some ethical problem.

There are two footnotes to the Cook case. To the chagrin of some of the ranchers and the little town of Canton, the Bureau of Reclamation and Corps of Engineers enlarged the dam on the Missouri at Canyon Ferry just after World War II. The resulting lake inundated the town of Canton and land along the Missouri's banks. Homes, barns, equipment and other valuable assets, were moved from the property when possible.

The Cook Ranch and the Avalanche Ranch were partially covered by the lake, which reached its current level in the mid-1950s. The A. B. Cook home is now a bed and breakfast a few miles north of Townsend.

The ranch would see more death in later years. Early on November 21, 1970, Hervey Cook, then 70 years of age, was murdered by three young thugs who were apprehended the next day. The men had run Cook over with a car and this brutality was in conjunction with the nearly fatal beating of a hired hand.

Rankin's early successes with ranch ownership inspired him to buy more land for investment. Stories, perhaps branching from the Cook estate saga,[20] suggested he obtained property by questionable tactics. One such anecdote centered in Townsend, where the improbable narrative was repeated from barstools and casual corners so often that it was assumed to be fact.

The story went something like this: A local rancher, in a fit of temper, knocked a man down in a bar. The man's head struck a bar stool, or rail, and he died. The rancher was sure that he was going to get a life sentence or maybe even the death penalty, and he went to Rankin, the best defender around.

Rankin agreed to represent him, and when the rancher asked him, "What'll it cost me?" Rankin said, "Well, you've got a ranch there. If I get you off, it'll just cost you your ranch." According to the story, the man agreed. "If you can get me off, keep me from being hung or going to the penitentiary for life, you will have my ranch," he said.

Rankin got an acquittal for him. Greatly relieved the man went out to his ranch, packed his suitcase, walked into Townsend (the geographical site varied), and left, never to be heard from again.

This and similar legends–with vague dates and no names–were told and retold with different locations and characters. Other stories suggested that Rankin obtained ranches by paying a small down payment and then manipulating the contract so that he didn't have to pay the balance. These are mainly fabrications.

One rumor suggests that Rankin bought the Thomas Ranch in Broadwater County under suspicious circumstances. Differing versions of his supposed unethical behavior circulated, but more than one witness exonerated Rankin. A present-day Broadwater County banker is the granddaughter of the ranch's former owner. She, her mother, and her brother say their family received a fair price for the property. "Of course, I heard all the stories," she said. "I don't know of one place in this county where he received land for legal services or took advantage of anyone."[21]

Rankin was, in the words of a friend, "shrewd and gruesome," and he knew how to make a deal. Helen Johnson worked for the U.S. Department of Agriculture in the Federal Loan Agency during the Great Depression. She remembered a client who paid a lot of money for some property and could not make the subsequent payments. The client was about to lose his down payment and ranch when he went to Rankin for help. The contract on the property was unbreakable, so Rankin gave him $50,000–the amount of the original down payment–and assumed the contract. Later Rankin sold the ranch for a profit. Some assumed, wrongly, that he had acquired the property in an illegitimate manner.[22]

He purchased the Manuel Ranch in the same area in 1941. Here

Rankin made a trade. As part of the buyout, he offered to "take care" of Clarence Manuel for the rest of his life. According to Paul Ringling, who lived nearby, you didn't have to be a doctor to see that Manuel, "a heavy drinker and obviously in poor health," wouldn't live very long. Manuel lived until 1945.[23]

A later purchase was the Peg O'Connor Ranch in Meagher County, which Rankin bought when no one else made an offer. He received an interest in some oil leases as part of the bargain.

Rankin had the money to buy land when the opportunity presented itself. Moreover, he saw the value of raw land and undeveloped terrain or abandoned property before others did. He took advantage of the market, buying much of his acreage during times that were not good for small ranchers in Montana. Drought, bitterly cold winters, and depression had carried with them great losses and fear.

Railroad land locators and a few good wet years with bumper crops had enticed thousands of homesteaders, called "honyonkers," to the prairies and foothills of Montana in the 1910s and early 1920s. Railroad magnate James J. Hill encouraged many to take his railroad to the "promised land."

At a gathering in Havre in 1912, Hill predicted that in time there would be a farm family upon every 160 or 320 acres in Montana. He was not far off. During the next ten years more than 90 million acres were homesteaded. Unfortunately, more than eighty percent of the homestead land was unfit for agriculture in normal years. The best land, such as that in the Gallatin Valley and along river bottoms and streams, had been taken by the time of the massive migration. When the weather returned to its normal condition, crops languished. In the 1920s, blizzards with sub-zero temperatures made life miserable. Summer storms with dust penetrated the food, water, cabins, and lungs of the long-suffering pioneers. Lightning and hail destroyed their meager crops and hordes of insects ate what was left. Rain had not followed the plow.

After World War I many homesteaders turned their backs on their dreams and moved into town or went back to Missouri or Kansas or from wherever they had come. Some of the larger ranches weren't able to make a profit in the dry years either. The owners or their heirs, disillusioned by killing winter blizzards and many other hazards of the plains, were more than happy to unload them.

The tragedies that befell many of the impoverished dry land farmers were windfalls to someone like Wellington Rankin. He had the money and leverage to buy land when others were selling at desperate rates. In the sparsely populated state of Montana, there was so much land available that everyone thought they might get some someday. As one rancher put it, "Sure, land was cheap, but we weren't about to gamble on it; most of us didn't have the money anyway."[24]

Rankin was alert as he watched, waited, and maneuvered large and small deals. With patience he was able to buy many smaller ranches from families, individuals, or estates that were no longer profitable. Some of these places were contiguous to his earlier purchases and expanded them; others weren't.

A partial list of property that Rankin bought in Broadwater County, over many years, gives a perspective on how extensive his purchases were: the Avalanche Ranch, part of the Cook Ranch, the Thomas Ranch, the Sandy Allen Ranch, the Clarence Bruce homestead, the Lanson Bruce property, the Wilbert I. Thompson property, the Beatty Ranch, the Ed O. Brown property, the Alice L. Fisher property, John H. Nolan land, Charles Nolan land, Northern Pacific Railroad land, the Schock place, the Snedaker place, the Todd place, and the Welch homestead. The purchase price was sometimes as little as one dollar an acre and sometimes as much as ten. For example, the Noble Ranch, a one-thousand-acre parcel fifteen miles north of Townsend, was bought from Royal and Florence Noble of Bellflower, California, in 1945 for $10,000. Rankin paid $2,000 down and settled the remainder in annual payments of $1,000 at five percent interest.[25]

Rankin purchased larger ranches by financing the deals through insurance companies. In this way, in 1944, he bought the Birch Creek, Catlin, and Moss Agate ranches in a large purchase that combined these plats in Meagher County. This property had been among the holdings of John Ringling, of Ringling Brothers circus fame.

John Ringling was once listed as the twelfth richest man in the world. Early in the twentieth century, he controlled large tracts of land in Montana, including more than 100,000 acres in Meagher County, purchased in 1907. An alert businessman, Ringling looked for financial opportunities everywhere he went. He was said to love money more than anything.

One of Ringling's hobbies was to build short-line railroads. Since he had traveled with the circus by rail, he knew the railroad systems in the United States well. Among the several short-lines he built was the twenty-mile line from White Sulphur Springs, Montana, to Broken Jaw (Ringling), Montana, known officially as the White Sulphur Springs and Yellowstone Park Railway. Ringling's company created a brochure depicting the beautiful Smith River Valley to lure potential land buyers–and railroad business–to the area. The flyer promised prosperity in "the great Northwest." The brochure stated:

> Here are thousands of prosperous men and women…Whole communities of them…. They own the land they live on, with its comfortable home, its orchard and truck garden, its grass, flowers and shrubbery. They work in the open air and the sunshine…. Montana is the healthiest state in the union with a death rate of only 7

per 1,000.... The new tract will supply homes for upwards of twenty thousand people.... Many people imagine that the Northwest is a cold and cheerless region in winter. Low temperatures are not frequent and when they do come they are of short duration.... Prosperity follows the plow. They [Ringling's company] own ... over 100,000 acres of the best agricultural land in this wonderful valley.... Go and see the land first if you want to. It is good business to do so. But go prepared to make a purchase.... Ringling and White will build all or any buildings.... charging only actual cost.... Livestock and equipment will also be furnished at reduced prices.[26]

In a final and poetic touch, the brochure quoted "Adventures in Contentment," by David Grayson.

How sweet an emotion is possession! What a foundation for sanity ... that art of the deep earth is his with all the water upon it, all birds or insects that fly in the air above it, all trees, shrubs, flowers and grass that grow upon it, all houses, barns and fences—all his. As I strode along...I fed upon possession. I rolled the sweet morsel of ownership under my tongue, I can understand why the miser enjoys the very physical contact of his gold. Every sense I possessed, sight, smell, touch, fed upon the new joy.[27]

P.T. Barnum's adage, "There's a sucker born every minute," might very well have applied here. The land was nothing like the brochure that Ringling wrote. Author Ivan Doig, who lived on a section of the Moss Agate as a child, remembered it as "Not exactly a ranch, even less a farm. Moss Agate flapped on the map as a loose end....Sagebrushy, high, dry, windy; except for fingernail-sized shards of cloudy agate, the place's only natural resource was railroad tracks."[28]

Not enough of the "suckers" lasted in Meagher County. Although the town of Broken Jaw was renamed Ringling by grateful citizens who expected great things, it never fully materialized. Today, few people live in this high, harsh part of Montana, and those who do command large cattle ranches.

Ringling still owned much of Meagher County at his death, and his acreage remained in probate for a long time. Much of the large area of land owned by Ringling had been used by neighbors as if it were their own. They ran cattle on the open fields and may have even planted crops there on occasion. This was one reason that Rankin's purchase of the land inspired local resentment—it was no longer free range. Some neighbors disliked losing access, especially to a rich and powerful attorney from Helena.[29]

Rankin abandoned some of his Smith River water rights to settle disputes surrounding the land. However, as one person pointed out, this was no great sacrifice since he owned the Drumheller Well, an oil drill hole that issued a substantial flow of artisian water.[30]

In 1954, the 74,025-acre 71 Ranch, near Martinsdale, came under Rankin's control. It was formerly known as the Smith Brothers Ranch, and was located on the South Fork of the Musselshell River. It had the largest acreage of contiguous deeded land of any ranch in Montana. John M. Smith had developed it in 1873, shortly after he built the first white man's cabin on the Musselshell.[31]

In 1954 Rankin bought the 30,000-acre Lingshire Ranch on the lower Smith River and the smaller 1,280-acre Wieglow Ranch, near Lennep and Martinsdale. The latter was acquired as a place to hold Rankin cattle between the upper and lower properties. Eventually Rankin owned twenty percent of the private land in Meagher County, with six large ranches.

Rankin knew how to assemble and hold property, and made his largest one-time purchase when he bought the famed Miller Ranch in October 1958. This made him the biggest landholder in Montana–and one of the largest in the nation.

The Miller Brothers owned a gigantic property in Blaine County, near Chinook. It represented the culmination of years of expansion by the Miller family. Henry and Chris Miller had begun their careers in 1892 as teenage boys helping their father, Peter Miller, who had bought the original land and sixteen hundred head of sheep. Progressively and with an eye to the future, the family developed this huge dominion, taking up homesteads and buying out adjacent ranches. They reportedly accumulated more property from men (known locally as "Squaw men") who had moved with their Indian wives to the Fort Belknap Reservation. The final result incorporated at least a dozen individual ranches and their stock. At one time the Millers may have had over 300,000 head of sheep.[32]

At the time of Rankin's purchase, the Miller Ranch had 470 miles of outside fence enclosing 130,256 acres of deeded land and 190,000 of leased land. It stretched from the foothills of the Bear's Paw Mountains to the Canadian border, as far as the eye could see.[33]

This purchase, like some of his others, was not entirely welcomed by his family. "We were always cash poor," Louise Rankin said, admitting they sometimes had difficulty making the payments. In 1958, at the time Rankin bought the Miller Ranch, Louise attempted to dissuade him from buying it on the basis of a shortage of cash. He said to her, "Anytime you can buy land for $10 an acre, you can turn around within two or three years and get $20 an acre." Rankin believed that land was the safest investment–there's only so much of it in the world. He said, "You can't go wrong on land."[34]

Wellington Rankin

Gallatin Valley rancher Harry Brainard remembers Rankin's advice to him about land investment:

> He used to call me up sometimes at 4:30 in the morning about some deal. I knew him well and did business with him. He craved land but he had no pride in it. He had a lot of cattle and I bought cattle from him for years. He was a poor operator—he lost a lot of cattle in hard winters. But he told me all you gotta do … get a hold of it (land) and set on it for 10 or 15 years and you'll come out. He'd tell me, "Harry, you're too damned conservative."[35]

Tom Lane, a statewide landholder and cattle trader, purchased cattle from Rankin in the fifties and sixties. To a degree he had patterned his own ranching empire after the attorney's. He says, "I don't think I'd be here if it hadn't been for him." Rankin told him, "I'm going to give you a word of caution…you better hold on to your land; don't hold onto your livestock [if you need money] because they can come along if things get a little tough." The cattle market "went to hell in 1963" and he told Lane, "You gotta be very careful how you structure your load." When financial ruin threatened, Rankin helped Lane restructure his debt and, "he helped us out of a hell of a hole and I'll never forget it." Later, however, when Tom Lane owned a good sized ranch and several hundred head of cattle and "thought I was just going great guns," Rankin said to him, "When are you going to get off that peanut stand and do something."[36]

Henry Wertheimer, a Utica, Montana, rancher whose father did business with Rankin, said that when he was a young man he drove Rankin from Malta to White Sulphur Springs. During the trip Rankin said to him, "Land is so cheap here that if I could get the financing I'd buy the whole damned state." Then, in an apparent reflective mood, he continued, "People are down on me for the way I treat my property. I board up the houses, cut the telephone and power out, and forget about keeping the fences or beautifying the place. I don't give a damn what they think. I'm only interested in the value of the land."[37]

It appears Rankin viewed his kingdom solely for its pecuniary value. As a busy attorney and political power, he rarely visited the holdings, sending law partner Arthur Acher in his place when a personal visit was required. An absentee owner, he maintained control of the ranch empire by hiring foremen and keeping direct telephone lines to them open. Louise Rankin Galt also was involved in the ranch management after she joined the firm. But she says, "The ranch had always had only one manager, and that was Wellington, and he did about ninety-eight percent of it by telephone."[38]

Rankin's style of management was controversial. One young man who worked for him in 1959 remembers that Rankin thought nothing of paying $250,000 for hay because "they (Rankin and Acker) didn't put up any hay." But once, he said, "I bought a shovel or something that I thought we needed and I told him about it. Rankin said to me, 'Well, thanks a lot, that's nice of you.'" He made no offer of compensation; the employee paid for the tool himself.[39] When the same young man suggested that an investment of Prestone antifreeze for the ranch vehicles might be helpful during the long, severe winters, Rankin said pointedly, "If I had a goddamned peanut stand to run like you have, well, I'd have time to think about that."[40]

Pete Poirier, Rankin's foreman for thirty-four years, was hired in 1950. At the age of 79 his small, less-than-agile frame, crippled by years in the saddle and exposure to the inclement weather, recalled, "In 1950 we had Birch Creek, Lingshire, O'Connor, Moss Agate, and Catlin, (ranches) and he bought later the 71 Ranch and I run all of them, more or less."[41]

Of all the memories people have about Wellington Rankin, this aspect of his life–his way of managing his livestock and property–remain the most distasteful. His ranch holdings did not hurt his legal business, though. A former Meagher County official said, "He was the kind of guy everybody cursed because they didn't like the way he ran his operations, but when they got into trouble he was the first one they went to see."[42]

By most accounts from those who knew, Rankin seems to have bought plenty of feed. The problem was, as one neighbor put it, that with numerous cows scattered over hundreds of thousands of acres he couldn't get his cattle together with the feed, nor the feed together with the cattle. Running such huge numbers of cattle and land was an expensive task. No doubt keeping cash available was difficult. Wellington Rankin spent thousands of dollars each year on hay for his stock. Feed bills, unlike utility companies, could not be ignored.

Rankin's operation was sometimes in debt to Teslow and Company. Cory Dogterom, a retired Teslow executive, remembers the trouble they had in collecting from Rankin. Shortly after he joined the firm in the early fifties, he and Walter Teslow paid a visit to Rankin's law office to collect some outstanding bills. He says that they were treated cordially and were paid. After he paid the money, Rankin said, "Teslow, if you think you've got troubles look at this." And then he withdrew from his desk drawer a worthless check for $30,000.00 signed by a prominent cattle dealer in Gallatin County.

In view of the history of sluggish collections, the Teslow Company refused further credit to Rankin. Years later, after he acquired the huge Miller Ranch in northern Montana, his ranch manager ordered five or six truckloads of compressed cottonseed cake as a supplemental cattle feed. The manager agreed that it would be paid for on delivery. As Dogterom recalls, when the trucks arrived the manager said that Rankin wanted credit. As ordered the driver refused to unload the feed, demanded cash and prepared to haul the load back. After exchanging telephone calls with Helena, the manager was finally authorized to pay for the order and the feed was delivered.[43]

Rankin's stock were not confined where they could be cared for. His fences were inadequate, his poorly paid hands were irresponsible, and most winters were severe. Cold was exceedingly hard on exposed livestock, and Rankin had large death losses. One nearby rancher and his wife counted more than one hundred dead cows near the road during the winter of 1955 on one of Rankin's ranches in Meagher County.

Montana stock growers are not strangers to bad winters and can expect some losses. Disastrous cold and blizzard conditions have killed livestock often in the state's history. One of the worst times was the winter of 1886-1887 when more than sixty percent of Montana's range cattle died of starvation and cold. Watching cattle die and facing a spring with the stench of rotting carcasses scattered over the prairie caused pioneer cattleman Granville Stuart to say, "I never wanted to own again an animal that I could not feed and shelter."[44]

Newspaper editors aimed bitter criticism at the stockmen who turned animals out on the land to fend for themselves; their condemnations were aimed primarily at absentee owners who left stock to graze and returned only to round up and collect their profits. Some of these same criticisms were aimed at Rankin.

But Pete Poirier disagreed forcefully with rumors that Rankin neglected his stock:

> He didn't let cattle starve if that's what you're talking about; he bought a lot of hay and Mr. Acher, he was a partner, and he'd come out here and buy hay and we always had feed for the cattle. But as far as his operation, he didn't upkeep on his ranches, it was nil, what I mean, he didn't believe in putting a lot of money back into them, and not even fences—we repaired fences, but we never built very much of any new ones or anything and that's just the way she was.[45]

And, Poirier added, "the neighbors' fences were none too good, either."

But Rankin was a range cattleman. In spite of—or perhaps because of—owning inordinate amounts of land, Rankin ranched as if there was still open range. Bill Williams, a former Rankin employee, said, "He had good, strong cattle, because they'd survive just about everything ... survival of the fittest." He estimates that in the terrible winter of 1959-1960 Rankin lost five hundred head on the 71 Ranch and three or four hundred in Broadwater County.[46]

Although grazing permits on government land came with the Meagher County purchases, Forest Service employees say that Rankin stock often trespassed on government range. He was such a dominating political and legal figure he "tended to intimidate" Forest Service workers and would ignore their requests to remove his animals. The government followed procedure and "several times had to round up Rankin's stock and remove them from the national forest." This meant hiring riders, and took several days. Rankin had to pay roundup costs and grazing fees to redeem his livestock. When he refused to pay, his livestock were sold at public auction.

Over a period of years from 1957-1963, Vern Hamre, Supervisor of the Helena National Forest, which included the Townsend, Canyon Ferry, Helena and Lincoln Ranger districts, says that Rankin's cattle and horses often trespassed on government land. This worked a hardship on permitees who were paying for the grass and the grazing privilege. He says that Rankin or his ranch hands didn't appear to "even try to keep stock from trespassing and damaging public pastures." According to him, some of the Forest Service land is still damaged and won't return to normal for many years. The worst damage, he says, was done to the Dry Range.[47]

Forest service employee, Cloycie Mann, during the early to mid-1960s attempted on two occasions to round up Rankin's "wild horses" that were constantly—"year around"—on the Dry Range, a large plateau on the high rolling hills west of the Smith River. The horses had "grazed it to the dirt," he said. This pasture was leased by the Doggett family's sheep operation. Cloycie, Bill and Jeff Doggett, and several other riders were only able to round up fifteen horses once, and nine during a second attempt. The animals were wild and the studs were so rank and cantankerous that both riders and their horses were in danger. Cloycie carried a revolver but fortunately never had to use it on an aggressive stud. He said that at least seventy-five head of horses were left on the range that they weren't able to catch. During the same period, so many of Rankin's cattle from the Avalanche ranch trespassed that for three summers the Forest Service hired one man full-time to try to herd them back on Rankin's unfenced property.[48]

Because Rankin's stock continually trespassed on the National Forest, Hamre decided to seek an injunction in Federal Court against further trespass. The Forest Service's regional attorney, Morris Hankins of Missoula, prepared the case. It was presented to the court by the U.S. Attorney whose appointment appeared to Hamre to have been "influenced by Mr. Rankin." In Hamre's opinion the U. S. Attorney made such a feeble presentation that the Federal Judge dismissed the case stating that "this appeared to be just a dispute between neighbors that should be settled on the ground and not in Federal Court."[49]

The regulations at the time favored the trespasser. The government was required to give fifteen days notice, then count the animals daily for fifteen more days and then notify the offending rancher again. Sometimes the grazing season was over before the government could legally remove the offending stock. If the trespasser, in this case Wellington Rankin, wasn't informed and given fifteen days of grace, the court wouldn't uphold any fine or penalty. Cloycie Mann remembers one day in the Butte court when Rankin convinced the judge that he was being treated "unfairly." That his horses had been removed by the Forest Service without his knowledge that they were even loose, even though according to Cloycie, "he didn't even have his own property fenced. There wasn't anything we could say, because we hadn't given him fifteen days notice."[50]

Supervisor Vern Hamre said,

> "He beat us many times on the trespass. But we outlived him. He contested one of the round-ups of his trespassing stock that we made because we could not prove that each individual cow was 'the' cow we had given him notice on beforehand, and he won the point. The way the regulation was written we would've had to prove that each cow was the one we saw on Government land."[51]

The Department of Agriculture after pressure from permitees and rangers finally changed the regulation and made it less complicated to prove trespass. Today only one notice is required and if the animals are not removed within fifteen days the government has the right to impound them.

After all those years of conflict, Hamre says:

> "In my opinion, Rankin was a completely amoral man. He was obsessed with power and with acquiring ranch lands. He was a brilliant criminal attorney. As he would acquire the ranches, he reputedly would staff them with some of the felons he had defended, supposedly after they got out of jail or getting them off so they didn't have to go to jail. I believe that his ranch hands were not particularly concerned with running a ranch, some apparently only concerned with putting in their time to work off their legal bill with Rankin. If it is true that some of the men he hired were those he had defended, they would not be motivated to do a good job. That could result in a lot of trespass on national forest lands, which there was. I can recall driving through his ranch on Birch Creek one spring and seeing many dead cattle, apparently dying from starvation."[52]

Rankin's relationship to the Forest Service was so antagonistic that it inspired jokes. Someone said that when Rankin's cattle were confiscated by the government for trespass, and were introduced to good pasture, a few head adapted right away to the lush feed. But the older ones preferred to eat as they had previously–on their callused knees with their necks stretched through the fence.

At the pinnacle of Rankin's ranching operations he owned almost 27,000 head of cattle. At the time of his death he had 20,000. The cattle had to be moved often to adequate pastures, prompting one of his hired hands to comment when the subject of outer space exploration came up in conversation, "I hope they don't find any grass up there or the Old Man will have us movin' cattle again."

Rankin's ill use of his ranch holdings was partly due to his reliance on seasonal help and long-distance communication. According to one man:

> We were working with them [Rankin hands] all the time, because he was the biggest rancher in the state and we had started this riding deal and returned a lot of cattle. The first year that Huckins and I worked Rankin's cattle, we returned over 1,200 head to rightful owners that we got out of his cattle. Rankin would never fix a fence or build fence; he said, "I don't care how much of their cattle run on me, but I'm not going to build any fences, they don't want my cattle on their land, they're going to have to fence them out." He told us that. Oh yes, he used to tell us that he didn't want anybody's cattle. He said, "I've got way too many of my own, as you know, but I don't want anyone else taking mine either." That's something that I could never understand. All he was interested in was having a lot of land and a lot of livestock.
>
> The man was a good man in a lot of ways but he was truly a businessman. The first winter that I was up there I saw heifers with calves stuck in them dead. They were so doggoned thin and weak, by God, they couldn't get up. We'd be riding, working these cattle for strays, riding through them on the range, down along the creek bottoms, along the Canyon Ferry Lake on that Thomas place. We saw the men working for him on horseback ride right by a heifer laying there with a calf half stuck out of her. If they'd got off and pulled it out, they'd probably saved the calf and the heifer both. They'd ride right on by … wouldn't even stop to pull the calf and save both of them.[53]

Locals often reported the absentee-owner look of Rankin's places. Some were frustrated by the situation, such as neighboring Meagher

County rancher Alberta Bair, who contacted her attorney in White Sulphur Springs to get Rankin to pick up some hay he had purchased. Some tried to help the situation, especially neighboring stockowners that found animals in need. Bella Dregson of Hogeland wrote to Rankin in his Helena office:

> Just thought I would drop you a line [and] tell you about a cow of yours is down. She had a calf—calf is dead. She is close to us. We spotted her too late, but we gave her shots of pendeccella [penicillin] and took water and hay to her. She was very dry…. We are doing all we can for her. If we had some range cake for her maybe her legs would strengthen. We give her creepe feed and rolled barley as that's all we have on hand. Thought I'd let you know as she has to be taken care, of quite a chore for us in our old age, lugging water is the hardest part. Maybe you would send someone out to take care of her….I love cattle and don't want them to supher [suffer] and starve to death, so do hope she snaps out of it.[54]

From Oilmont, W. R. Britt wrote regarding Rankin's oil leases and the public notice of their deterioration:

> A few days ago I was in the local Post Office and over-heard a conversation about your leases on the west side not being attended, and a further conversation that several motors had been taken from the Rim Rock Lease, among other items reported missing. This conversation was partially by a friend of your former pumper… decided to make a trip over and look into the matter, and I found all your doors opened, houses, garage, etc. doors blown off or pried off…the jeep and truck had both batteries and spares, etc. gone, and it is apparent that some of the electrical parts are missing….I will be glad to also watch the other leases, however you should purchase some padlocks and hasps in order that all of these buildings can be locked. I assure you that it would pay off, since this country is now plagued by wandering junk dealers as well as a great many light-fingered pumpers and kids.[55]

Others, with weaker characters, took advantage of Rankin's distance. Harry Brainerd remembered:

> I was on most of his places. He hired convicts and every-

thing. He'd cut off the electricity to the places and buy kerosene lamps. He had a man that delivered groceries. He'd buy case after case of the same damned thing. Cases of peas or corn. That's all they had to eat, just peas. He'd tell them to cut out a cow with lumpy jaw or some-thing and butcher it. The men soon learned to take that one over there in the gulch and get rid of it and then kill another one. All them guys on them ranches ate damned good beef. Course he didn't know that.[56]

Around White Sulphur Springs it was thought by some that Rankin's cows were responsible for some disreputable characters getting into the cattle business in the first place. This caused some local wit to say about one of Rankin's neighbors, "Looks like some of his cows have a calf every day." Since Rankin's herds were by-and-large unsupervised, it was easy to hold some of his wandering stock just at calving time, brand the calves with another brand, and later return the cow–but not the calf–to Rankin property. Pete Poirier smiled wryly when questioned about the rustling of Rankin's cows, saying, "If you want to know the truth, probably the neighbors helped themselves a little bit. I don't want to say that they was keeping them, but they were, they did mix in with their cattle and they would probably calve them out and they'd take the calves off and we'd get the cows back."[57]

A former law enforcement officer in Meagher County was quoted in the *Great Falls Tribune* after Rankin's death:

His cattle grazed on other people's ranches. He didn't care about building good fences. He hired mainly ex-con-victs on parole from Deer Lodge. There were few family men. Even in fall his unbranded calves and yearlings would be wandering around the countryside. This was too much of a temptation for some people. They rustled from him.[58]

Rankin's own "convict" employees were among those charged with cheating him. Some claimed that Rankin had some sort of arrangement with the prison officials for many years, including Warden Floyd Powell and the Board of Pardons. Dolores Munden, who was secretary to the Board at Deer Lodge for several years, says that some inmates were paroled to Wellington Rankin prior to April 1955 when the present Board of Pardons was established.[59] Rankin did hire some parolees from the Montana State Prison at Deer Lodge, and was criticized for it, although the practice was over-exaggerated by those who opposed it. Louise Rankin claimed that after she began work at Rankin's law office in 1951, only two Deer Lodge parolees were hired.[60] Pete Poirier also defended his employer. He was adamant that Rankin did not hire criminals: "There was a few parolees, but mostly alcoholics and some men down on their luck.... They were mostly good men." Rankin would hire them in Helena and send them out by car where Poirier would put them to work.[61]

Louise Rankin added that with about sixty people on the Rankin payroll, it was necessary to hire some "rather rough-looking men" at harvest time, "alcoholics and such." Hands were hard to find, and these men sometimes "haunted the office" in Helena waiting for jobs or to receive their pay.

Many of the down-and-out were cowboys by trade, so Rankin's role in hiring them was not out of line. His large ranch holdings provided a place for transients and uneducated laborers to work when they could find no other employment. The trade was low wages. The men were poorly paid, as were most agricultural workers at the time, and they were often untrained. Rankin paid the price. In many cases, the men neglected his holdings and allowed his property to deteriorate.

Many drifters heard about Rankin ranches and potential employment in hobo jungles across the country. A prison circuit also seemed to spread the story. Rankin got letters from prisoners as far away as Steilacoom, Washington, asking for hire.

L. C. Johnson spent a lot of his time on Rankin ranches in the 1950s. The retired chief livestock inspector said that men who were desperate and possibly in hiding found their way to Montana.

> They'd sign a contract: ninety days for ninety dollars. If they quit on the eighty-ninth day, they couldn't collect a dime. And when they did quit, from out on one of those ranches, the Commissary pick-up could've been there that day and delivered grub to them and go right back to Helena, but they weren't allowed to haul them to Helena. Those men, when they got their ninety days in, had to hitchhike into the Helena office to collect their money.[62]

To some of these employees–or other observant folk–Rankin's unsupervised ranches inspired theft. L. C. Johnson and his partner Ben Huckins knew the Rankin property well. In 1957, after many complaints about Rankin's management practices, Chief Livestock Inspector Bill Chaney sent the two men to try to "straighten things out." Johnson remembers that he and Chaney met in Rankin's office, where the attorney welcomed their help and offered the full cooperation of his employees. For several years, Johnson and Huckins rode and patrolled the Rankin ranches and adjacent property in Meagher County. During this time, several rustlers were caught and punished.

Johnson referred to the Rankin hands he knew as "winos and dingbats," saying,

> This one fella, I'll never forget him: big, tall, slim, gangly kind of guy, claimed that he had escaped from the Georgia chain gang. Now whether he did this or not, I don't know, but by looks of the guy, we believed him. He'd showed us the scars on his hands and his ankles where they'd had him in chains.[63]

In some cases, Rankin's hands helped people steal cattle from their employer, or sold stock for little or nothing. One time a local rancher brought whiskey out to two of Rankin's cowboys, who in exchange helped him load his truck with Rankin calves. In another instance, a Rankin employee wrote from prison asking his mother to pick up his last paycheck:

> Will drop you a few lines to let you know I am in trouble again. While I was working for Rankin, I sold some meat to some people in Winnett. I did it without Mr. Rankin's consent. So the Brand Inspector is the one who filed the charges against me. They call it cattle rustling. Anyway, they gave me seven years here at Deer Lodge. I have a few things that the Sheriff at Winnett is sending to you…I also have two months pay coming from Rankin. I will have you to collect that for me. I know I did wrong but didn't realize how serious it could be. If I was to know they would send you up the road, I wouldn't have taken the chance but it is done, so will have to make the best of it.[64]

In yet another case, a neighboring rancher, Bruce Johnson, was charged on September 17, 1964, for rustling Rankin's cattle on the Miller Ranch, branded with the E-Y brand. Extensive investigations began after he had applied for a reverse B-K brand. This was all too obvious–the Rankin brand could be easily altered to the latter suggestion–and the State Livestock Commission and Blaine County law enforcement caught Johnson stealing 299 head of Rankin's cows and calves.

The situation was made more dramatic when, in the course of the investigation and arrest, brand inspector L. C. Johnson had a face-off with his armed suspect. Fortunately Bruce Johnson was outgunned and elected not to resist. Later, in court, the underside of cattle hides showed the telltale alterations. The old E-Y brand produced a scar that was easily distinguished on the underside of the hide from the more recent searing heat of a straight hot bar used to change the "written" E to a reverse or backward B and an additional straight mark that changed the Y to a somewhat deformed K. Eighteen hides were presented as evidence.

The rustler's trial attracted capacity crowds to the town of Chinook.

Historically, Blaine County was no stranger to lawlessness. The nearby Little Rockies were the home and headquarters of notorious outlaws such as Butch Cassidy and Kid Curry. Timer Moses, a prominent lawyer from Billings, was the prosecutor; John McCarville, now a circuit judge, was defending Johnson.

Wellington Rankin himself was called as a witness, and with a lawyer's grandstanding manners, took liberties that aren't usually allowed in court. He chastised and lectured the accused and his attorney during his testimony. McCarville, rightfully objected often, but Judge Elwell ignored him until finally the judge said, "Mr. McCarville, I know you want to object again. The next thing you know, you'll be wanting to object to how I look." This remark sparked a great deal of laughter in the court because the judge was afflicted with a deformed neck that fixed his head far to one side so that he had to lean way back to see forward.

The trial had other theatrics, too. Later in the trial, Timer Moses borrowed L. C. Johnson's coat, several sizes too small, and in his summation pointed out to the jury that this coat fit him better than the accused's story fitted the circumstances of the theft. Bruce Johnson was convicted and spent time in the penitentiary, but was released after a short time for medical reasons.[65]

Rankin received public attention in 1964 for his sale of an extremely large herd of wild horses on the 150,000-acre Savage Ranch near Sumatra and Ingomar in Rosebud County. Rankin had purchased the ranch in the early 1950s.[66]

From 1962, Rankin had used the Savage range to hold his rapidly increasing numbers of wild horses. Domestic horses that had turned wild had always been a part of Montana ranches. Most of Rankin's were in Meagher County, where they had wreaked havoc on neighbors' fences. In addition, the studs lured away neighbors' mares and killed geldings.

In the early 1960s, L. C. Johnson and Ben Huckins worked 1,300 head of horses–heading, heeling, branding them, and castrating the studs–from Rankin's Meagher County land. Many of these horses were shipped to the Savage Ranch at Ingomar, and in February 1964 were sold to a group of livestock men interested in obtaining bucking horses for a contest and sale in Bozeman. These included Mike Quinn of Boulder, Montana; Bish Jenkins of Idaho Falls, Idaho; and Bob Ellerd and Clark Taylor who operated the Bozeman Livestock Auction Company.

The sale made news. The *Great Falls Tribune* alerted the public with the heading, "RANKIN SELLS LARGEST HORSE HERD IN STATE WITHOUT COUNTING ANIMALS." Rankin confirmed that he had sold all the horses on the Savage Ranch near Ingomar and Sumatra, and was quoted as saying, "I don't know the exact number. It is the largest herd in Montana and certainly one of the largest in the nation."[67]

The horses were not collected until late spring of 1964, due to terrible weather. Blizzards, below-zero temperatures, wind, and heavy snows plagued the countryside. The Savage Ranch was held hostage, as was the rest of Eastern Montana. Ingomar, a commerce center in the early days, is surrounded by red dirt land known as the Gumbo Flats. Freight wagons were caught and stuck there for days when it rained. The land there is barren. Sagebrush dominates, with a thin crust of red topsoil and sparse, tough shortgrass and cactus. The horizontal terrain is relieved by outcrops of sandstone sculptured by wind, blowing sand, gravel, and snow. This is a land where everything is weather-related, where the wind at times, according to local myth, is so fierce that it can straighten out a log chain. As some unknown wag said, "the damned wind can blow four ways at once here."

It was not until late April of that dismal spring when the horse buyers could get to Ingomar. A crew of cowboys, photographers, sidekicks, and hangers-on gathered for what was to be the last real wild horse roundup. The men involved included the best horsemen in the state. L. C. Johnson and Ben Huckins were there as state brand inspectors and also to help sort and select the best rodeo stock. The cowboys included rodeo performers Walt Secrest and Carl Holt. Both were well-known in rodeo circles and often worked as pick-up men.[68]

The sale and rodeo in Bozeman were scheduled for May 16-17, 1964, so there was a sense of urgency.[69] Hampered by weather, thick gumbo, and lack of knowledge of the terrain, the roundup progressed slowly. Feelings of defeat permeated the crew, and only the sustenance afforded by the nearby Jersey Lilly Bar and Grill bolstered their flagging spirits.

Neighbors watching the project "volunteered" to help. Albert Newman, his sons Walter, Rodney, and Howard, and his nephew Dean Newman offered to get the horses for a thousand dollars. With their experience as stockmen and knowledge of the territory, they soon had several hundred corralled. The captured herd was trailed overland to Sumatra. From there, two hundred of the best and healthiest animals were sent to Bozeman by truck. The rest went to Canada to be canned. The sale and bucking horse contest was held as scheduled, and some of the horses gained stardom on the circuit.[70]

The horse sale hadn't included all of the wild horses on Rankin's various properties. Several hundred more grazed on the Lingshire Ranch northwest of White Sulphur Springs competing for forage with cattle. Since these had no commercial value another roundup was planned. The previous spring, cowboys had only been able to rope three of these cayuses, but in belly-deep snow with "cowboys" riding snowmobiles, it was a different story. The *Great Falls Tribune* covered the event, showing photographs of exhausted animals crowded into corrals, land mares and colts goaded to move through drifted snow.

The publicity proved embarrassing. One "authority" described the stock as "a bunch of hammer-heads and as spooky as a horse can get."

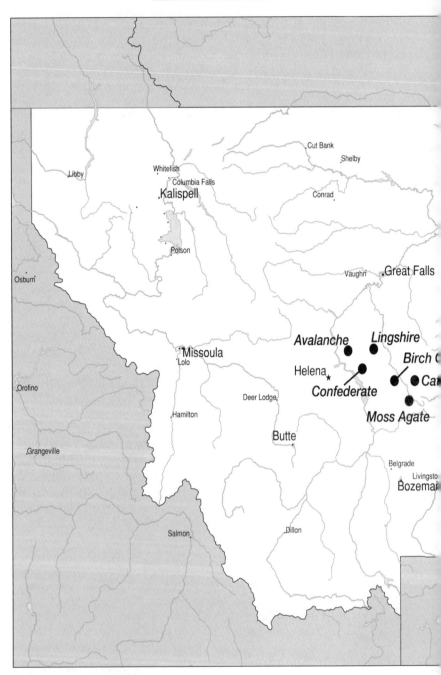

Wellington Rankin's ranch holdings.

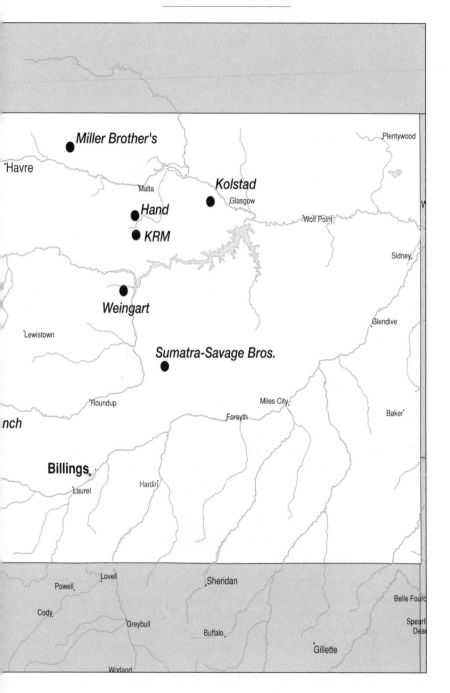

A ranch-hand added, "What's the use of killing a $300 saddle horse to catch a $35 mustang?" The neglected, abandoned, inbred, feral horses were certainly not mustangs. To the embarrassment of many Montanans, True West magazine featured the event. Some state residents responded to the scene. One letter to the editor of the *Great Falls Tribune* went as follows:

> A part of the old West has been lost. These cowboys couldn't capture the wild horse by horseback in a sporting sort of a way, so they waited until the horses were defenseless—with all the grandeur of a Grande Prix. What is the difference of running these horses down by snowmobile, or running down wildlife—which is against the law? Are there no laws to protect the few wild horses that are remaining in our country?[71]

After inspiring newsprint with the Sumatra wild horse sale, Rankin received more public attention the very next month, in May 1964, when he sold the gigantic Miller Ranch. He hadn't changed his ranching practices while holding the title of Montana's biggest rancher.

Even members of the Miller family were concerned about Rankin's treatment of the property they had worked on and cherished for so many years. In 1962, four years after Rankin bought the ranch, Chris Miller wrote to try to explain how he ran the haying operations, using twenty-five tractors, six balers, and many additional rakes, trucks, and wagons:

> Now, I was out to the ranch and checked on your haying equipment ….So far, the machinery working is 3 tractors and mowers, 2 side delivery rakes, and 3 balers—if working. Idle and not working were 2 tractors and mowers. Two tractors they were fixing and one side delivery they hauled in which Pete had bought second-hand. Saw only 2 pickups and one car. So I think you had better be doing something about it.
>
> There are 4000 to 5000 acres to cut over, and there are 4000 to 5000 tons of hay if you can harvest it….You have no equipment left on the ranch and furthermore you have no men that will do a days work, no boss to lead them and get the full time and get something done….
>
> You have done no fencing since you had the ranch, and the winter pasture fields all need going over if you are going to winter any stock as you will have to keep them

separate in the different fields, otherwise they will get into a field and feed it out and starve.

Mr. Rankin, I wish you would take a day off and come to the ranch and look things over for yourself. Erwin and I have done lots of work to save 1,000 head of cattle for you, and you haven't paid Erwin and Jack DePriest yet from my last report. I wish you would take care of them.[72]

Rankin's sale of the Miller Ranch was an immense transaction that required millions of dollars, three grazing associations, and twenty-two additional individuals to buy it. It was parceled out in increments to a total of eighty families. Generally considered a boon to the area, the sale was celebrated on May 2, 1964, at the Chinook Fairgrounds, with a ceremony that included speeches, barbecue, authentic American Indian dances, and a rodeo. Five thousand people attended. John Baker, the assistant secretary of agriculture; Tim Babcock, Montana's governor; and other dignitaries spoke on the occasion.

The cooperative purchase was a pioneer event in the United States. Two years previously Congress had passed legislation, sponsored by Senator Mike Mansfield and Congressman Lee Metcalf, to help organize and finance ventures of that type. Grazing units were encouraged to help the family farms and keep many of the smaller outfits from leaving. The agreement in general was to help the economy of rural areas such as Blaine County.[73]

In spite of the outcome, locals still slandered Rankin's management. Wilma Poirier, Pete Poirier's wife, overheard a conversation at the celebration that "raised her hackles." One woman talking to another said that she had heard that Rankin's hands on the Miller Ranch had trashed the house and even let cattle roam through it. Wilma, a solidly built woman, approached the lady and said, "I lived there and there were never any cows in my living room."[74]

Rankin didn't sell his cattle with the Miller Ranch, he had 9,000 of them to move. Two thousand nine hundred head were trailed to the Fort Belknap Indian Reservation and the rest were trucked to other ranches. The weather was uncooperative as Rankin's bunch moved the cows. His reputation was further tarnished with another livestock catastrophe caused by the rough Montana environment. Edwin Miller recalls:

In 1964 when Rankin moved, sold a ranch and he moved cattle to his ranch in Malta there [the 25,500-acre KRM ranch, twenty miles southwest of Malta, which he purchased in 1960], we had high humidity and about 35 below and the backs froze on them and they couldn't walk. That's the first time I ever heard of cattle having their

> backs froze. I thought when he [Rankin] said they could-
> n't walk their feet froze. I've seen frozen feet but I've
> never seen frozen backs; they were just paralyzed.[75]

Pete Poirier was moving Rankin's cattle when the intense cold front moved in. While the herd was out in the open, the livestock began to freeze. He was finally able to drive them into the brush along the banks of a creek. The brush offered enough protection to save most of them. Many died, but it could have been much worse.

The survivors were shipped to the Savage Ranch at Ingomar, which was used as summer grazing and for overflow pasture. Not even the expansive Savage range was big enough to hold all the stock. In June 1964 Rankin made his last purchase–the 40,000-acre Osler ranch near Mosby, adjacent to the Savage place–to hold the extra head.

Before the Miller Ranch sale, Rankin's landholdings had included the control of one million acres. Cattle and land sales in 1964 alone amount-ed to $699,031, ranch income varied from $500,000 to $1,000,000 a year. He owned other assets including hotels and oil wells. After the sale, he still controlled 629,118 acres of land, 240,597 of which were leased, with ranches in seven different counties.

Rankin's ranch operations were profitable; he made lots of money and put the earnings into acquiring more land. He is still criticized by some for ill use of land (including public land) and cattle. Whether these abuses were purposeful to cut costs, or whether they resulted from neg-lect that came naturally with absentee ownership, in the end they cast shadows on his reputation.

11

A Last "Hoorah"

It's all mental, riding a horse is mental

When Virginia Ronhovde visited her uncle Wellington Rankin's Avalanche Ranch, he told her, "It's all mental, riding a horse is mental. Riding horses safely is like anything else; it is in the head. If you think you can do it, you can."[1] Rankin put the little girl on a horse named Snake-Eyes, and convinced her she knew how to handle him. Although she was afraid of the horse, she rode him because Uncle Wellington told her she could do it.

Rankin had taken the approach of sheer determination himself, in at least one riding episode and, some might say, in much of his legal and political career. A man near Helena who owned an "outlaw" horse that he claimed had put three men in the hospital let it be known that he would give the horse to anyone who could ride it. Rankin was determined to do it. In his business suit and eastern shoes, he rode the beast and stayed on. He said later that he wasn't afraid until the rancher's wife began to cry and begged him not to mount the critter. "I could never stand to see a woman cry," he said.[2]

Once, when he and cattle buyer Tom Lane wanted to look at some bulls, Rankin asked his hired hand to fetch them by horseback. The only horse saddled and ready to go was a big black gelding that was "snortier than hell." When the hand hesitated, fearful of the animal, Rankin was furious. He grabbed the horse by the cheek strap and kicked him a couple of times in the belly, mounted, and "got the bulls in himself."[3]

In spite of an almost debilitating and very large hernia in his later years, Rankin rode horses whenever it was necessary. Gallatin Valley rancher Harry Brainard says, "He was damned good on a horse, and I don't mean just an easygoing one either. Only two years before he died we had to ride to look at some cows. He would push his rupture way over to one side of the saddle. He didn't complain."[4]

Getting back on the horse had seemed to be Rankin's political theme.

In 1952, he made one last stab at public office. He was nominated by the Republican Party as candidate for the U.S. House of Representatives from the First Congressional District. The race began well, and Rankin–who was then a Republican Party leader–defeated Winfield Page of Missoula in the primary.

Both the Republicans and Democrats had high hopes for winning this seat. The Republicans were relieved that the powerful Democrat, Representative Mike Mansfield, had abandoned the House of Representatives and entered the race for the Senate. As a result, the Republican nominee would not have to face this canny politician. And the Democratic contestant was encouraged because the district had traditionally been Democratic and pro-labor.[5]

In the campaign, Rankin tried to gain the support of labor. He pointed to an impressive list of court decisions he had won for labor unions. He stressed his record against corporations on the part of labor groups. While his resume on behalf of labor was impressive, it didn't capture him enough votes. His court record didn't offset the fact that he was a Republican, or that he was educated at Oxford, or that he was the brother of Jeannette Rankin who had voted against both World Wars.

On his part, Lee Metcalf accused Rankin of a dirty campaign and rubbed old wounds raw. He went back as far as 1920 to malign Rankin's record as attorney general during Prohibition. He said that Rankin's term was one of "inattention and inefficiency." This, of course, was unfair.

Metcalf also hit Rankin in his agricultural belt. He claimed that Rankin represented a group of land-grabbers who would take control of the national forests for grazing, and that these stockmen would be superior "to the hunter and fisherman and camper…" He branded Rankin as with his own iron, and suggested that Rankin naturally appealed to "this privileged class of large landowners–a class to which he belonged."[6] Ironically, during the contest, the State Land Board placed a lien on Rankin's wheat crop for his violation of a grazing lease on state owned land. It was a fact that did not escape the notice of Rankin's opponent.[7]

Metcalf's charges hurt since they were indefensible. During Prohibition when Rankin was attorney general, Prohibition laws were nearly impossible to uphold–especially in the huge territory of the state. Jeannette had voted against the wars, and his ranch connection was not a false one. Rankin the entrepreneur was well on his way toward becoming the largest landowner in the state. Many saw him as a ruthless landlord who defied the usual rules and regulations of government-owned land. Deserved or not, many of Rankin's neighbors criticized him, albeit to his back, for neglect of livestock and property.

Rankin countered that Metcalf had sponsored a school bill in 1937 that "smacked of Hitlerism" since it would have compelled the State Board of Education to require instruction in consumer cooperatives for any student graduating from the eighth grade. He called it "a thought-control bill," appealing to the paranoia of the day.[8]

The Montana Citizens Council, an organization formed by corporate executives in 1946 in an effort to defeat Leif Erickson's bid for the U. S. Senate, conducted a smear campaign against Metcalf. This resurrected group, composed of various directors of the Montana Power Company, Anaconda's subsidiary Fairmont Publishing Company and others, did its best to defeat Lee Metcalf. Pamphlets appeared from the Council that portrayed Metcalf as an active Communist.

Rankin had no part in the smear. When public opinion slowly turned against the Council, he denounced the pamphlet, but was criticized by his opponent for being slow about it. Some analysts believe that the Council's smutty circulars turned many voters toward Metcalf and that it helped his cause.[9]

The 1952 national elections were a turning point in the politics of the United States. There was a Republican landslide and General Dwight D. Eisenhower was elected president. The Republicans took over Congress. Rankin was left at the post even though he had fought a hard battle. He undoubtedly sensed that the 1952 campaign was his last shot at national office. He was sixty-eight and even though he knew Eisenhower personally and claimed that the great retired general had asked Montana voters to vote for him, it didn't help.[10]

The invective charged race ended in a dead heat. Lee Metcalf, the forty-one-year-old liberal with Populist-like views, mastered Rankin by a margin of only 1,500 votes. It was a bitter pill for Rankin to swallow. Metcalf's campaign staff believed that Rankin's abrasive personality, in part, helped them achieve their victory. Judge John Harrison was Metcalf's campaign manager. He analyzed the situation years later by saying:

> If you've got a close election, those Republicans-conservatives who were adamantly opposed to Rankin—were either not voting for Rankin's ticket or voting against it....I think anybody in '52 could have beaten Lee Metcalf but Wellington Rankin. Now that puts it very bluntly, but there were just so many people who were absolutely opposed to Rankin that, well, 1,500 votes...[11]

After the votes were counted, Rankin said he didn't really care whether or not he went to Congress. He recognized his campaign had been lackluster. Jeannette was traveling in India at the time, and he said later, "If I'd called Jeannette to come back and put her on the road, I'd have won that." But his well-traveled sister was in the land of her hero, Mohatmas Gandhi, and, besides, Rankin said he didn't have the same burning desire to be one of 450 Congressmen as he did to become a Senator.[12]

Although Rankin was philosophical about the loss and claimed it didn't matter, the 1952 election was Rankin's last hooray. He received both negative and positive mail. Some letters advised him to "go back to his dollars." Other, more positive letters, expressed sorrow for his loss.

Though he never sought public office again, he didn't leave the political scene entirely. He continued to take part in Montana politics as Republican finance chairman, national committeeman, and chairman of the Western Regional Conference of the Republican Party. In this capacity, his skill at oratory took him to many Republican conclaves not only in Montana but to national meetings as well. Even though he couldn't get elected himself, his political influence would be felt for many years.

At the same time, some Republicans were trying to dislodge him from these positions of power. One Montana politician who served in the state senate said:

> When I was young and I was getting involved in politics, sometime in the fifties, I went to one of the state Republican Conventions and Wellington had been the National Committeeman for years. There were a group of younger people that had decided that they would elect somebody else as National Committeeman. It was interesting to watch Wellington Rankin's organization just steamroller that-those people got the word—"if you're going to have any influence in this party you better know who's in charge."[13]

One of Rankin's most celebrated law cases came soon after his 1952 political loss. It became one of the most sensational trials in the history of Montana. The lawsuit in 1954 involved the defense of an old acquaintance and court ally, Judge George W. Padbury, Jr. The judge, aged sixty-three, had been Lewis and Clark District Judge in Helena for nineteen years. Now he was being tried as a felon himself.[14]

A grand jury had indicted Padbury and several others for scheming to defraud the State Board of Equalization by submitting false claims for Montana gasoline tax refunds. The crimes allegedly had been perpetrated between August 1949 and February 1951. The accusers said that the defendants had rented post office boxes in various towns in order to receive state warrants through the mail, and that they divided the proceeds.

Padbury and ten others were charged. Six were already serving sentences at the time Rankin joined the case. Louise Phillips, whose husband John Phillips was already in prison, and George Padbury were the ninth and tenth people accused. Rankin had long been Padbury's friend. The judge had ruled on many of his cases, and they moved in similar legal circles. It was natural that the judge would choose to be defended by his old acquaintance, who he had seen work miracles for others in court.

The case was met with a great deal of publicity. Jury selection was difficult because, in voir dire, it was determined that many from the venue had already formed an opinion. After examining fifty-three potential jurors, the court selected seven women and five men to serve. The prosecutor and federal district attorney was Krest Cyr, who was assisted by Michael O'Connell of Bozeman and others. The defenders were Lester Loble, former governor John Bonner, and Wellington Rankin. It was made clear to all that the defense team was defending their old friend free of charge.

Cyr, the prosecutor, was an aggressive lawyer with what appeared to be an open-and-shut case. His office had been gathering evidence since 1949 and he was certain of a conviction. Howard Hill was one of the accused and was to be a key witness. He allegedly committed suicide in Boise, Idaho in 1951 while being extradited to Montana while in the custody of a state investigator and the Lewis and Clark County attorney.[15] On the streets of Helena, rumors flew. Many suspected that Hill was murdered to prevent his turning state's evidence.

In the course of the trial, Cyr presented testimony that Padbury had opened post office boxes in Townsend under the name of Robert Turner and at Butte under the name of F. E. Perry in order to receive warrants through the mail. He claimed that handwriting experts would prove that Padbury had written fraudulent warrants. The state had forty-two witnesses in all, and Cyr said, "We will establish Padbury … signed warrants, endorsed and wrote checks in connection with this fraud."

Cyr introduced relevant and expert witnesses. One conspirator, Pat Maloney, was serving his term in the state prison and turned state's witness. Maloney had been a bartender at the Blue Moon Bar in Helena, which had served as a meetinghouse for those involved. He testified that Padbury was present when gasoline tax refund warrants were signed, and that Padbury took him to Butte to sign bank deposit slips for a fictitious character named F. E. Perry. Two handwriting experts, one from the FBI and the other from the San Francisco Postal Department, had determined that the checks were endorsed by Padbury, using his own name, and that entries on the warrants as to dates and amounts were in Padbury's handwriting.

Another convicted felon, Theodore Tomlinson, testified that Padbury had brought a notary public seal to the Blue Moon in a little brown paper sack that was used to certify false applications to the Board of Equalization.

Robert Chamberlain, still in prison at Deer Lodge, was another conspirator and witness for the prosecution. Judge Padbury had sentenced him to five years in prison.

With this bounty of evidence, Cyr was forthright in his presentation and confident that he would win. He also underestimated his opposition.

Lester Loble, later himself a district judge, began the defense by describing to the jury Padbury's life of public service. He noted that Judge Padbury started the investigation that had already led to the conviction of six persons in connection with the swindle. Rankin added to the defense team's efforts by thoroughly cross-examining, in Rankin style, the two handwriting experts. One was asked if the documents he had studied were the original documents or photostatic copies of the alleged forgeries. The witness assured the court that he had only made conclusions on original manuscripts. Then Rankin asked the specialist, as he was wont to do, "Have you ever made a mistake in handwriting?" The witness said, "Not to my knowledge." Then Rankin asked, following his pattern, "Have you ever told a falsehood in your life?" But Cyr objected to this, and the objection was sustained. Rankin then went on to use the corroborative evidence doctrine in his favor, noting that two criminals– i.e., untrustworthy individuals–had testified and that their evidence had not been corroborated.

During the final proceedings, Attorney Loble said to the jury, "You are sitting as jurors in the most sensational case in the history of the courts of this state." He also told them, that "The damage is done and will be done forever." Then Bonner, who had been governor of Montana from 1948 to 1952 said, "It is a death penalty for Judge Padbury if you find him guilty."

Rankin gave the final, spellbinding summation. He quoted Bible scriptures, comparing Judge Padbury's alleged faults to David's infidelity to Bathsheba. He recalled for the jury that God had judged David not just for this one weakness. With feeling, he added, "You judge a man by the totality of his life." Joseph Gary, who as a young lawyer had listened to Rankin's summation, said he himself used the same argument successfully in his own practice many times since.[16]

The jury listened; the public didn't. Rankin and his dream team won the acquittal, but Padbury's reputation was ruined. In Helena it was rumored that at least one jury member's vote had been bought. No specific claims were ever made.

In 1960, Rankin was finally unseated as head of the state Republican Party after eight years and two terms as president. While he was leader of the Montana Republicans, nothing happened in the state that he wasn't aware of. He was, perhaps, too well-connected with members of the opposite political party. As head of the Republicans in Montana, Rankin had urged ex-Senator Burton K. Wheeler, a Democrat, to run as a Republican against Mike Mansfield for the House of Representatives. Wheeler would have to change his affiliation to do so. The suggestion made national news. On April 24, 1958, the syndicated conservative Fulton Lewis, Jr.'s column was headed, "MONTANA GOP SEEKING WHEELER FOR SENATE RACE." It read, in part:

A Last "Hoorah"

Democratic Senator Mike Mansfield is up for reelection in November and the Republicans are looking for somebody to beat him. Mansfield is no pushover. Republican National Committeeman Wellington Rankin could have the nomination if he would take it, but he is a tremendous landowner who has just added more, and he doesn't like to campaign. "What makes you think I could beat Mike?" asked Wheeler. "Copper," said Rankin. The "copper" angle is important. Copper is a major foundation of Montana's economy, and the Anaconda Company is the largest employer in the state... some years back then Senator Wheeler... put through a protective tariff to save the jobs of Montana miners, to the dire displeasure of Anaconda. Mike Mansfield was... instrumental in knocking the tariff down. The result is that unemployment has reached a critical level in Montana.[17]

Longtime friends, Wheeler and Rankin had a great deal in common, including the fact that both were very independent. Wheeler, one of the most powerful politicians of his time, was tempted to take Rankin's offer and run against Mansfield, but reneged partly due to his wife's health. The close friendship between Rankin and Wheeler is best demonstrated by later correspondence between the two. Rankin sent a telegram to Wheeler on his eightieth birthday, which read as follows:

Congratulations for your courageous, invaluable and dedicated service to Montana and the nation for the mature part of your eighty years. No Montanan has added more lustre to the pages of Montana History.[18]

On March 2, 1962, Wheeler responded to the telegram,

Dear Wellington,
...Your friendship has meant a great deal to me. I am going to repeat to you what I have said to you many times—that you ought to have been elected to the U. S. Senate—it has been Montana's loss.[19]

Rankin was criticized for such bi-partisanship and hobnobbing with the Democrats. Dr. Millet F. Keller of Great Falls said that Rankin engaged in a conspiracy with Charles Murray [Senator James Murray's son] and "the Company." Rankin and Senator Murray were miles apart in their political views and had battled each other many times but were friends—with mutual admiration—and enjoyed political intrigues. In 1960, Rankin joined forces with Murray and Murray's son, Charles, both Democrats, to campaign against LeRoy Anderson, another Democrat, who was seeking Murray's position.

Partly as a result of this connection, and partly due to younger elements in the Party, Rankin was removed from Republican Party leadership at last–and replaced by James Murphy, a Kalispell lawyer. Delegates were divided. Voting Rankin out was difficult.[20]

Even after losing his prestigious Party position, Rankin still had sources that kept him informed. While Hugo Aronson was governor, some people, including the governor himself, suspected that Rankin had a "tap" on his office phone. He seemed to anticipate every move made in the chief executive's office.[21]

Although he was removed from official standing in Party politics, Rankin remained a keen political analyst, "without equal" in judging elections. When Governor Donald Nutter ran against Congressman Wesley D'Ewart in the primary election for governor in 1960, Rankin checked with the Associated Press, then called Nutter and said, "Well, congratulations, you're going to be governor."

Nutter said, "Oh no, I'm about to concede."

"Hell," Rankin said, "the High-Line isn't in yet; you're going to win this by two hundred votes." Nutter won by about that margin the next day.[22]

An attorney tells the following story to illustrate Rankin's political perspective:

> One event particularly stands out in my mind. It was many years ago in the summer of the race between Renne and Babcock for governor. Over a holiday, I think Memorial Day, six or seven attorneys gathered in Rankin's office to settle a water dispute which was pending in Meagher County. Settlement was achieved and we had several hours to kill while our various clients traveled to Helena. Sitting in Rankin's office someone asked him how he thought this particular race would go. Rankin was an astute political observer despite the fact that he never won election and for more than an hour he sat at his desk without a note of any kind and told us on a county-by-county basis how and why he thought Babcock would win.[23]

Babcock won. Rankin still had the touch.

Rankin also kept his legal finesse. In the late 1950s, he broke new ground when he defended one client, a Helena physician who clubbed a man nearly to death that had been "stalking" a relative. Rankin won an acquittal by trying the complainant on the stand, or as some said, "try-

Memorial service for Wellington Rankin on February 21, 1967, in the Montana Supreme Court Chambers. Left to right: John Bonner, Lester Loble, Arthur Acher, Ted James (standing). Fourth from left on back row is Louise Rankin. Photo: Montana Historical Society, Helena.

ing the victim," a rarely used tactic then but widely used today. According to Rankin-produced witnesses, the man was an unimpressive, unsavory character.

To impress the party during the trial the prosecution repeatedly referred to the weapon that the doctor used as the "Alley Oop" club, alluding to a popular cartoon of the period. In spite of this, Rankin was successful. This and other cases occurred during a period when John Harrison was the Lewis and Clark county attorney. According to Harrison, now a judge, this was a painful period in his life. It seemed that he was always pitted against the abrasive, abusive, and aggressive Rankin.[24]

Another case that Harrison, the county attorney, lost in the Supreme Court of Montana was that of Dorothy Josephine Baker. The district court had agreed with the young county attorney that she–better known as Big Dorothy–be "enjoined from operating an alleged house of prostitution." Her "rooming house" was locally famous and established at 17½ South Last Chance Gulch in Helena. But Big Dorothy was defended by Wellington Rankin and the Supreme Court of Montana set aside that order of "abatement."[25]

In 1973 after Dorothy's Rooms were awarded a $500 urban renewal grant in an effort to revitalize the downtown area, her establishment was raided and finally closed by the Helena police and the Lewis and

Clark Sheriff's Department. Wellington Rankin was no longer around to defend her.[26]

As one might have suspected, the famous lawyer won even his last case. It was tried in Thompson Falls before a judge and jury; Rankin represented a person injured in an automobile accident against an insurance agency. Again and finally, his gifts of words, charisma, and presence overwhelmed the opposition.

Rankin's fifty-nine years of law practice brought him recognition that might have lessened the pain over his lack of success in the political arena. In November 1965, at the age of eighty-one, he was lavished with honors at a Montana Trial Lawyers banquet in Helena and called the "Dean of Montana Trial Lawyers." Judge Lester Loble, the respected jurist and Rankin's old friend, was master of ceremonies, and Chief Justice James T. Harrison of the Montana Supreme Court addressed the group.

Rankin's health suffered that same year. After many years of pain, at age 81, Rankin decided to seek surgical repair of a large hernia that he had neglected. He had never complained although it was uncomfortable and debilitating. Instead, he may have pondered the words of Christian Science founder Mary Baker Eddy as he waited in hospital:

> Until the advancing age admits the efficacy and supremacy of Mind, it is better for Christian Scientists to leave surgery and the adjustment of broken bones and dislocations to the fingers of a surgeon, while the mental healer confines himself chiefly to mental reconstruction and to the prevention of inflammation.[27]

On May 21, 1966, Rankin thoughtfully prepared his will and left for the Mayo Clinic in Rochester, Minnesota. He was admitted to the hospital on May 23. Following surgery, he died suddenly from a pulmonary embolism on June 4.

Rankin's will was straightforward and clear-cut, with no frills or entangling legalese. Wellington had accumulated millions of dollars in assets. The balance of his massive fortune went to his widow, except for $450,000 divided among his four remaining sisters and his law partner, Arthur Acher. In addition to other assets, his widow Louise received 628,918 acres of land, of which 388,521 acres were deeded. There were more than 20,000 head of cattle scattered over this enormous space, distributed on ranches in seven counties with more than sixty employees.[28]

Following a series of flattering articles about Rankin in the *Great Falls Tribune* in 1966 after his death, Harry L. Burns, former chairman of the Montana Highway Commission and a Chinook attorney, wrote the newspaper a very critical letter about Rankin. Burns objected to the complimentary tone of the report, saying that when it was read by citizens of Blaine and Phillips Counties, it would "certainly destroy whatever confidence there is left in the press and articles published by it." Burns's complaints about Rankin were directed at his neglect of livestock, and at one alleged instance of fee gouging (later proven false).[29]

But Burns was right, to some degree. C. T. Sullivan, the author of the *Great Falls Tribune's* series of articles on Rankin, admired his subject so much that he accentuated the positives and suppressed the negatives. Burns finished his critical letter on this note:

> On the other hand, it would be a very fine project for someone to write a biography of Wellington D. Rankin as a character study. This should be written from an objective viewpoint and not entirely critical but would be to show what a brilliant intellect this man had.... There is no question about that. In addition he was one of the finest trial lawyers Montana ever had. It is sad to think what he might have accomplished for his state and for the Republican Party if his efforts had been used in anything but a selfish way. He had all the mental ability to accomplish most anything. In addition to that he had a most affable personality and it was a pleasure to sit and visit with him. It indeed would be a study in psychology to speculate on why a man of these brilliant attributes should ruin his life by the irresponsibility of ownership that he evidenced wherever he did own livestock, cattle and other property.[30]

Burns's letter reflects the attitude of many others, heard over and over in interviews and attested to by former neighbors. One thing is brazenly clear: Rankin's enemies respected him. After Rankin's death, a member of the bar in Helena was heard to remark, "Who are we going to talk about now that Wellington's gone?" That statement was repeated by many.

A prominent 94-year-old rancher in the Gallatin Valley, a long-time friend of Wellington Rankin's, business associate, and sometime legal client, says about him:

> You know he was about the smartest man that ever lived in Montana. In World War II they had him back there in Washington, to see the president, consulting him about the war—how to fight it and everything. He was well thought of all over and Washington D.C.—he was a big man.[31]

At Rankin's death numerous testimonials surfaced, and his friends-

and enemies—made fluent statements regretting the loss. A few days after his death, the liberal newspaper *the People's Voice* said:

> Mr. Rankin was much more than his millions, his land, or his surface politics. One friend said, "W. D. was a most outrageous man." Rankin would probably have been delighted with this statement because he made no bones about his satisfaction in "outraging" people. His biography will not be written in words like "mild" or "subtle." If anything he became more colorful as he grew older…he was a law unto himself; he had a flare for the dramatic…he made strong political enemies and strong friends and if he made himself a millionaire and landowner Montana history is also going to have to record his fights in the courts for the underdog…history will have to record his early years as counsel for the defense of injured working men.

Burton K. Wheeler expressed his loss in a letter to Louise Rankin by recalling, "Mr. Frank Kerr of the Montana Power Company once said 'We can never beat you as long as Wellington Rankin and Sam Ford quit the Republican party to stand up for you.'"

Attorney Leif Erickson of Helena and Montana's national Democratic committeeman, a longtime political opponent of Rankin's, said, "W. D. was a formidable political and legal foe. He was a one-of-a-kind in both politics and in law. Montana won't be the same."[32]

Rankin's four surviving sisters came for the funeral. Edna came from as far away as Ethiopia, where she had been living for ten years. Jeannette came from California. A few months after Wellington's death, a memorial service was held in the chambers of the Supreme Court of Montana by the justices. This was an exceptional and unique honor.

After the funeral and the ceremony there was silence. Rankin had pulled the curtain—the shroud to his life—and left just like that. He had made no attempt to prolong his presence by diaries, letters, philosophical treatises, recordings, or any other device that powerful people sometimes use. He just stopped.

Rankin's power and prominence during his lifetime prompted one attorney, landowner, former state senator, and rancher, who was considerably younger than Rankin to say:

> Well, when I was a young fellow, if anybody was to do anything in this state that had to do with the law, and had to do with politics and government, or had to do with cattle ranching, one way or another you were going to have to contend with Wellington Rankin. It was just that he just

simply dominated those three cultural areas of our state. He was truly a phenomenon.[33]

The *Great Falls Tribune* hailed his death as "THE END OF AN ERA IN MONTANA." And indeed it was.

FOOTNOTES

Preface

1   Michael McDonald, unpublished paper, 1990, in SC 1232, Montana Historical Society Archives, Helena, Montana.

Introduction

1   Bill Williams, interview with author, Toston, Montana, September 1995.

2   One sister, Phila the second oldest, died in 1891.

3   Ted Carlton Harris, *Jeannette Rankin: Suffragist, First Woman Elected to Congress, and Pacifist*, Dissertation, (Athens, Georgia, University of Georgia: 1972), 23. Olive Pickering Rankin came from a Baptist family, but married John Rankin, a Presbyterian.

4   Wilma Dykeman, *Too Many People, Too Little Love: Edna Rankin McKinnon, Pioneer for Birth Control* (New York: Holt, Rinehart and Winston, 1974)

5   Merrill G. Burlingame and K. Ross Toole, eds., *A History of Montana*, 3 vols. (New York: Lewis Historical Publishing Company, 1957), Vol. 1, pp. 506-07.

6   Wellington D. Rankin taped interview by John Board, University of Wyoming, March 23, 1964.

7   Jim Moore and Ben Berg, attorneys, interviews with author, Bozeman, Montana, June 1993.

8   Judge Henry Loble, personal communication February 1993 and interview with author, Bozeman, Montana, June 1993.

9   *Great Falls Tribune*, July 8, 1966.

10   Memorial Service, Supreme Court, Helena, Montana, February 21, 1967.

11   Gretchen G. Billings, "What Do You Think?", *The People's Voice*, June 10, 1966.

Footnotes

12 *Great Falls Tribune*, February 24, 1970.

13 Detroit Free Press, May 21, 1961, clipping in SC 1232, Wellington D. Rankin papers, Montana Historical Society archives, Helena, Montana.

14 Letter, Gary Cooper to Wellington Rankin, October 9, 1946, in SC 1232, Montana Historical Society archives, Helena, Montana.

15 *Harvard Class of 1905 Twenty-fifth Anniversary Report* (Boston: Harvard University Press, 1930), p. 522.

16 Elliot West, *"Stegner, Storytelling, and Western Identity,"* Wallace Stegner, Man & Writer, Charles E. Rankin, Ed., (Albuquerque: University of New Mexico Press, 1996), pp. 61-71.

Chapter 1 • The Rankins of Montana

1 Winfield Page, taped interview, OH-104-1, University of Montana archives, Missoula, Montana.

2 Harris, pp. 1-19. Burlingame and Toole, Vol. 3, p. 109; Helen Fitzgerald Sanders gives John Rankin's birthdate as 1848 and his Montana arrival as 1863 in *A History of Montana*, Vol. 2 (New York: Lewis Historical Publishing Co., 1913), pp. 1280-1281. Kevin S. Giles, *The Flight of the Dove: The Story of Jeannette Rankin* (Beaverton, Ore.: Touchstone Press, 1980), pp. 11, 20, 26.

3 Ferdinand V. Hayden, *The Great American West* (Bloomington, Ill., 1880), p. 219.

4 John A. Alvin, *Patterns of Montana Towns*, 1860-1920 (Missoula: University of Montana, in partial fulfillment of requirements for the degree of Master of Arts, 1972) p. 12 and pp. 18-23. William J. Trimble, "The Mining Advance into the Inland Empire," Bulletin of the University of Wisconsin, No. 638, History Series, Vol. III, No. 2 (Madison: University of Wisconsin, 1914), p. 7. Merrill G. Burlingame, *The Montana Frontier*, (Bozeman, Montana, Montana State University: Big Sky Books, 1942 and 1980), pp. 139-41. Michael P. Malone, Richard Roeder, and William Lang, *Montana: A History of Two Centuries* (Revised edition, Seattle: University of Washington Press, 1991), pp. 72-78. William Kittredge, and Annick Smith, Editors, *The Last Best Place*, "Miners and Travelers' Guide" by John Mullan, pp. 219-22.

5 Aubrey L. Haines, "A Voyage to Montana, Part 1," Montana, *The Magazine of Western History*, Vol. 49, No. 4, Winter 1999, p. 16. The other commercial way to travel to Montana was by rail and stage coach. This is the route young Olive Pickering would take nine years later. In 1869, a passenger could go by train on the just completed Union Pacific-Central Pacific transcontinental railroad. The end of the line was the little Mormon town of Corinne, Utah. From Corinne, by Wells Fargo and Company's stage, it was a sixty-six hour trip to Helena, Montana Territory.

6 Haines, p. 16. This was the route the Henry Dana Washburn family traveled in 1869.

7   Harris, p. 3, and quoted from a Jeannette Rankin Interview, March 31, 1970, p. 1, and John Board interview, Burlingame, The Montana Frontier.... pp. 66-67. During the fur trade the keel boat was the most popular. This type of boat was from sixty to seventy feet long. It was pulled upstream. The steamboat revolutionized travel on the shallow river. It required fifty inches of water when loaded. It had no hold and carried its cargo on the deck.

8   Haines. It has been estimated that a Missouri River steamboat consumed twenty-five cords of hardwood or thirty cords of cottonwood each twenty-four hours of steaming.

9   Haines.

10 Haines. A boat sometimes needed to be wenched against a strong current. If no tree was available to tie to, a "deadman" (a log buried crosswise) on the bank would serve as well.

11 Burlingame, *The Montana Frontier*, pp. 219-26. Malone et al., pp. 117-23. Military reprisals against the Indians were planned by the military, and the retaliation culminated in the tragic "Baker massacre" on the banks of the Marias River north of Fort Benton. On the cold morning of January 23, 1870, a drunken Major Eugene M. Baker and his troops from Fort Ellis slaughtered 173 Blackfeet men, women and children, all members of Chief Heavy Runner's innocent tribe, surprised in their beds and already suffering from starvation, freezing temperatures and smallpox. This essentially spelled the end of any further Blackfeet "disturbance."

12 John Board Interview.

13 John Board Interview. Wellington's middle name is Duncan.

14 Paula Petrik, *No Step Backward, Women and Family on the Rocky Mountain Mining Frontier*, Helena, Montana 1865-1900, (Helena: Montana Historical Society Press, 1987) p. 5.

15 Malone et al., p.172-78. Working hurriedly from the East and West, Northern Pacific railroad crews would bring the rails together at Gold Creek, about fifty miles east of Missoula on September 8, 1883. Checkerboard sections along each side of the right-of-way amounted to forty-four million acres in Montana Territory alone. This industry would become Montana's largest landowner. See also Michael P. Malone, *James J. Hill, Empire Builder of the Northwest* (Norman and London: University of Oklahoma Press, 1996), p. 76.

16 Lenora Koelbel, *Missoula the Way It Was*, "*A Portrait of an Early Western Town.*" (Published by Lenora Koelbel, 1972. Library of Congress Card No. 72-92413) pp. 31-41. Alwin, p. 13.

17 U. S. Census, 1870: Territory of Montana, Montana Historical Society Library, Helena. This first census counted 20,595 people.

18 H. G. Merriam, *The Golden Valley: Missoula to 1883* (Missoula: Mountain Press Publishing Company, 1997), pp. 12 and 19.

Footnotes

19 Merriam, pp. 1-2. Excerpt from her poem, "Paradise."

20 Rankin Papers, University of Montana archives, Missoula, Montana.

21 Koelbel, p. 41. See also, Carroll Van West, *A Traveler's Companion to Montana History*, (Helena: Montana Historical Society Press, 1986), p. 135-47.

22 Lumber for the construction of this bridge came from John Rankin's mill at Grant Creek. "Grant Creek Has Colorful Past," *MSLN* April 17, 1980.

23 Rankin Papers, University of Montana archives, Missoula, Montana.

24 Grant had married a Flathead Indian woman; their daughter married into the prominent Higgins family of Missoula.

25 It is not clear from the material available if this was the first sawmill in Missoula, nor is it possible to tell if he built the mill at Grant Creek himself or if he purchased it after someone else constructed it. Whatever, John was a lumberman and he made the enterprise profitable.

26 "The Flight of the Nez Perce," US Department of Agriculture, Washington, DC, *Bulletin* R1-95-79.

27 Helen Addison Howard and Dan L. McGrath, *War Chief Joseph* (Caldwell, Idaho: The Caxton Printers, Ltd., 1941), pp. 197-204. Merrill D. Beal, *"I Will Fight No More Forever,"* (Seattle and London: University of Washington Press, 1963), 90-104.

28 Michael A. Leeson, *History of Montana 1739-1885* (Chicago: Warner, Beers, & Co., 1885), p. 864.

29 Howard and McGrath. Harris, pp. 24-25.

30 Leeson, pp. 137-41. Malone et al., pp. 134-39.

31 Beal, pp. 244-246. General O. O. Howard estimated that his command marched one thousand three hundred and twenty-one miles in pursuit of the Nez Perces. The total casualties, Indian, civilian and military were 328 killed and 235 wounded. This epic and melancholy tale of the bloody, fighting retreat of the Nez Perce across hundreds of miles of Montana, finally ended in defeat at the foot of the Bear's Paw mountains near the present town of Chinook. The conquerer, Colonel Nelson A. Miles, assured Joseph that he and the 430 other captured Nez Perce would be returned to the Idaho reservation in the spring. Instead, as prisoners of war, they spent the winter at Fort Keogh and then Fort Leavenworth, and were finally exiled to the Indian Territory of Oklahoma. As prisoners they suffered from malnutrition and malaria and many died from these conditions. Several years later the survivors were allowed to return to the Pacific Northwest. Chief Joseph was never to live in his homeland again. He lived out his days at Fort Colville in the state of Washington where he died in 1904. By 1880 almost all of the Indian tribes of the West were subjugated and confined to reservations.

32 Harris, pp. 1-19.

33 Jules Karlin, *Joseph M. Dixon of Montana* (Missoula: University of Montana Publications in History, 1974). (N.p.: n.d.).

34 The Rankins, like all Scots, were a close-knit family. Wellington must have known about Dixon's disparaging remarks to his father; it was a black mark against his colleague-turned-competitor.

35 Rankin Papers, University of Montana archives, Missoula, Montana.

36 Harris, p. 1-19.

37 Harris, p. 24.

38 John Board Interview.

39 Virginia Ronhovde, interviews with author, 1993-1995.

40 Lawrence F. Small, ed., *Religion in Montana, Pathways to the Present*, (Billings, Montana: Rocky Mountain College in cooperation with SkyHouse Publishers, an imprint of Falcon Press Publishing Company, Inc., Helena, Montana, 1992), Vol. 1, pp. 47-76. See also Malone et al., pp. 62-63. In 1841 Father Pierre-Jean DeSmet accompanied by Fathers Gregory Mengarini and Nicholas Point established St. Mary's Mission in the Bitterroot Valley. It was the first school and cultural center of Montana. In 1846, priest, physician and man of many skills, Father Anthony Ravalli, joined the other priests. Largely through his efforts a flour and sawmill were built. Already wheat, potatoes, and oats were being grown in the basin. However, there were many troubles and St. Mary's was closed a short time later. It did not reopen until Father Ravalli, accompanied by Fr. Joseph Gioda, returned in 1866. Ravalli's broad expertise was considered a godsend by many, and especially for the local white people. Ravalli's influence extended throughout the region and he cared for many sick, Native American and white. He was selfless and always willing to go the distance to help someone in need. He died in 1884.

41. Harris, pp. 5-8. John Board interview. It seems unlikely that Olive was the second teacher to come to Missoula since the town was twenty years old when Olive arrived.

42 Harris, pp. 1-6 with quotes from the Elizabeth Huber Interview, September 12, 1971, p. 3, and *The Daily Missoulian*, May 4, 1904.

43 Wellington described his great uncle William Berry as, "A very popular man—always elected to county offices. They never could beat him. He died in a county office there, but drank quite a lot—a big man." John Board interview. Sheriff William Berry performed the first "legal" hanging in Missoula on August 16, 1883. Ah Yung, a member of the Chinese population killed a man during an attempted robbery. Although he denied it to three clergymen that visited with him and said over and over, "Me no kill him," he was condemned. The hanging took place before 100 invited guests. The Sheriff asked the witnesses to remove their hats and had Reverend George Fisher say a

prayer. Then he pulled the lever. Koelbel, p. 60.

44 Virginia Ronhovde, interviews with author, June 1993 and August 1993. According to Virginia Ronhovde, William Berry had traveled on a sailing ship from New England around Cape Horn to the West Coast, and from there returned by land over the mountains.

45 Norma Smith, *Fighting Pacifist, Jeannette Rankin and Her Times* (Unpublished and quoted with permission), p. 11.

46 Julie Roy Jeffrey, *Frontier Women* (New York: Hill and Wang, a division of Farrar, Straus and Giroux, 1979 and 1998), pp. 47-49.

47 Carlos A. Schwantes, "The Steamboat and Stagecoach Era in Montana and the Northern West," Montana, *The Magazine of Western History*, Vol 49, No. 4, Winter 1999, pp. 1-15.

48 Harris, pp. 1-19.

49 Ibid.

50 Smith, p. 11.

51 Koelbel, p. 31. In 1871, Dickinson was attacked by Sioux near Fort Peck. He was shot in the chest but escaped and survived. He fatally wounded one of the Sioux and later scalped him. Dickinson's head scar may have been from some other injury and the story embellished to impress the young teacher.

52 Harris, pp. 1-19.

53 Smith, p. 13.

54 Jeffrey, pp. 98-130.

55 Koelbel, p. 34. In 1870 Marshall Wheeler took a census of Missoula County.

56 Rankin Papers, University of Montana archives, Missoula, Montana.

57 Ronhovde interviews.

58 Smith, p. 11, and 19.

59 In 1953, Wellington purchased one of forty-seven carillon bells in Old Main Hall at his alma mater, the University of Montana, for $1,000. The text read "PRESENTED by WELLINGTON D. RANKIN '03 in memory of his mother, OLIVE PICKERING RANKIN, 1854-1947, PIONEER SCHOOLTEACHER OF MONTANA." He cared for her financially until she died.

60 John Board interview.

61 Ibid.

62 Giles, pp. 27-28. Virginia Ronhovde interviews.

63 Jean M. Emery, "Jeannette Rankin, Ahead of Her Time," *Montanan* (Winter 1993).

64 Giles, p. 19.

65 Harris, pp. 14–15.

66 John Board interview.

67 Smith, pp. 28–30.

68 Giles, pp. 24–25.

69 Emery.

70 Smith, p. 41.

71 Smith, p. 46.

72 Smith, p. 40.

73 Phil Rostad, *Still Going Strong: The Lady From Montana* (N.p., n.d.).

74 Smith, pp. 67–70. See also Harris, pp. 39–66.

75 Walter Lord, *The Good Years* (New York: Harper Bros., 1960), pp. 272.

76 Morrison, John and Catherine Wright Morrison, *Mavericks: The Lives and Battles of Montana's Political Legends* (Moscow, Idaho: University of Idaho Press, 1997), p. 132–33.

77 Harris, Chapter 3.

78 Lord, p. 272.

79 Giles, p. 17.

80 Smith, p. 4.

81 Smith, pp. 101–104.

82 Virginia Ronhovde interviews.

83 John Board Interview.

84 Virginia Ronhovde interviews.

85 Sanders, Vol. 2, p. 1280.

86 Giles, p. 52.

87 Dykeman, p. 24.

88 Mary Melcher, "Women's Matters," Montana, *The Magazine of Western History* (Spring 1991) pp. 42–56

89 Dykeman, p. 96.

90 Melcher.

91 Dykeman.

92 Dykeman, p. 49.

93 Rankin files, MHS, Helena, Montana: Letter to Rankin. As late as 1962 Rankin was still receiving acrimonious letters accusing him of being responsible for his sister's pursuits. One letter from Mrs. Edna Peterson of Anaconda in February of 1962, accuses his sister of "100 percent socialist,"

Footnotes

"100 percent pacifist," and an "admirer of India's Nehru." Admittedly much of this type of correspondence was of a "crank" variety, but it substantiates the persistence of negative beliefs about Jeannette in the minds of some Montanans.

94 Melcher.

95 Letter from Edna Rankin McKinnon to WDR, August 3, n.d., in Wellington D. Rankin papers, AC 85-17, Montana Historical Society archives, Helena, Montana.

96 Dykeman, p. 276.

97 Dykeman, p. 275.

98 Letter from Edna Rankin McKinnon to Hattie, Wellington and Mary, November 22, 1963, in Wellington D. Rankin papers, AC 85-17, Montana Historical Society archives, Helena, Montana.

99 Letter from Edna Rankin McKinnon to WDR, November 22, 1963, in Wellington D. Rankin papers, AC 85-17, Montana Historical Society archives, Helena, Montana.

100 Edna was working in Ethiopia when notified of Wellington's death in June 1966. She came home. That same year her colleagues and fellow workers in the field, Margaret Sanger and Dr. Clarence Gamble died. All three of these close associates, with different motives, guided her into a productive, far-reaching service.

101 John Board interview.

102 Winfield Page, taped interview, OH-104-1, University of Montana archives, Missoula, Montana.

Chapter 2 • Education

1 Elliott West, *Growing Up With the Country: Childhood on the Far Western Frontier* (Albuquerque: University of New Mexico Press, 1989), p. 7.

2 Arthur E. Sutherland, *The Law at Harvard: A History of Ideas and Men*, 1817-1967 (Cambridge: The Belknap Press of Harvard University Press, 1967), p. 222.

3 West, *Growing Up. . .* pp. 246-47.

4 West, *Growing Up. . .* pp. 251-53.

5 Jeffrey, p. 110.

6 The building that was once the Grant Creek school was donated in 1976 to the Historical Museum at Fort Missoula and is used today to show young students what education was like in more primitive times.

7 Martha Williams, "The Grant Creek School," *Montana Journal* (March-April 1993).

8   Wayne E. Fuller, *The Old Country School: The Story of Rural Education in the Middle West* (Chicago: The University of Chicago Press, 1982), pp. 4-5.

9   Fuller.

10 Hubert M. Reid, Bozeman and Jane Huffine, Bozeman, personal communication, April 2000. Isolated Montana communites continued this form of education for many years, and there are still a few one-room schools in the state. The Story Mill School at the northeast border of Bozeman was not closed until 1959. The teacher was Mrs. Erma Larkin Reid. The school was a one-room structure with thirty students from the first to the fourth grade. There was a boys and girls outhouse, and a year-around outdoor water pump.

11 Reid. Mrs. Erma Reid taught the students of the Story Mill School during the last twelve years of her long teaching career. She had taught in several different schools in the valley, and retired along with the Story Mill School in 1959. Erma began teaching in the Gallatin Valley in 1913 at the age of nineteen. She had applied to the school board the year before but was told that she was too young, but to return the next summer. During the interval she studied at her home in Minnesota and was awarded her teaching certificate.

12 Interview with Lois and Jack McGuire, …

13 Fuller.

14 Linda Peavy & Ursula Smith, *Pioneer Women, The Lives of Women on the Frontier,* (New York: Smithmark Publishers, 1996), pp. 138-39.

15 John Board interview.

16 Virginia Ronhovde inteviews. It is most likely that Wellington suffered from a severe concussion that resulted in unconsciousness and amnesia. The term "brain fever" is no longer used.

17 This was just the beginning of a long period of education; in1905 he earned his A..B. at Harvard College and in 1909 an LL.B at the same college.

18 Probably bottled water from a spring in the Yellowstone National Park of the same name.

19 Merriam, pp. 2, 10, 13, and 17.

20 *Missoulian,* June 1, 4, 1902.

21 The Snowcrest Ranch is a large and well-known cattle operation on the Ruby River about ten miles from Alder, Montana. The ranch has changed hands many times in recent years, and is now owned by Turner Enterprises.

22 Ronhovde is the daughter of Hattie Rankin and Oscar Sedman, Ellis's brother.

23 This common tick-borne disease, called the "Black Measles" in frontier times, had a high mortality rate and was most common in the Bitterroot Valley. Now it is known to be a Rickettsial disease transmitted by ticks and treatable, but then it was a mysterious malady that seemingly struck at random

Footnotes

and killed whom it pleased.

24 Norman Beasley, *The Cross and the Crown* (New York and Boston: Duell, Sloan and Pearce, Little Brown and Company, 1953), p. 396.

25 Beasley, pp. 41–42, 46, 107, and 377–78. For further study see, Mary Baker Eddy, *Science and Health with Key to the Scriptures* (Boston: Published by The First Church of Christ, Scientist, copyrighted and renewed numerous times until 1934), and Robert Peel, Mary Baker Eddy (Boston: The Christian Science Publishing Society, 1982). For further study see Eddy.

26 Ronhovde interviews.

27 Later in his life, Rankin often donated to the missionary and philosophical efforts of Maria Soubier, a Christian Science leader in Chicago. Letters from Soubier to Rankin exist in the Wellington D. Rankin papers, AC 85-17, Montana Historical Society archives, Helena, Montana.

28 Smith, pp. 31–33.

29 Ronhovde interviews.

30 Interview with Louise Rankin Galt, 1993.

31 This author by correspondence could find no records of Rankin's activities or achievements while at Oxford.

32 Robert Stevens, Law School, *Legal Education in America from the 1850s to the 1980s* (Chapel Hill and London: The University of North Carolina Press, 1983), pp. 21 and 28.

33 Stevens, p. xiv.

34 Arthur E. Sutherland, *The Law at Harvard: A History of Ideas and Men, 1817-1967* (Cambridge: The Belknap Press of Harvard University Press, 1967), pp. 221–23.

35 Sutherland, p. 220.

36 Sutherland, pp. 206–07.

37 Stevens, p. 52.

38 Stevens, p. 134.

39 Stevens, pp. 132–33.

40 Louise Rankin Galt interviews.

41 Stevens, p. 134.

42 Stevens, p. 59.

43 William Kittredge, *Montana, The Magazine of Western History*, 36 (Winter 1986), pp. 2–11.

44 Sanders, Vol. 2, p. 1280.

Chapter 3 • The Young Attorney

1 Charles H. Cooley, *Social Organization, and Human Nature and the Social Order* (Glencoe, Illinois reprinted from Charles Scribner's Sons, 1902, 1909, 1922: The Free Press, 1956), Social Organization, pp. 278-79, 273-77. Note: Cooley also writes that as free schools, libraries, magazines, newspapers, and cheap travel became available, those of more humble circumstances broke the financial barrier to education.

2 Bob Davis, interview with author, Seattle, Washington, November 18, 1993; Winfield Page, taped interview, OH-104-1, University of Montana archives, Missoula, Montana.

3 "W. D. Rankin More Interesting than Jeannette," *Great Falls Tribune*, July 14, 1991.

4 Karlin.

5 Jerre C. Murphy, *The Comical History of Montana, A Serious Story for Free People* (San Diego, Calif.: E. L. Schofield).

6 Mary Murphy, *"Mining Cultures, Men, Women and Leisure in Butte, 1914-41"* (Urbana and Chicago: University of Illinois Press, 1997), p. 4. Statement by W. A. Clark quoted from several sources.

7 Malone et al, pp. 197-98.

8 Joseph Kinsey Howard, *Montana, High, Wide, and Handsome* (Lincoln and London: University of Nebraska Press, First Bison Book printing, 1983), pp. 58-65.

9 Howard, pp. 55-57.

10 David M. Emmons, *"The Orange and the Green in Montana: A Reconsideration of the Clark-Daly Feuds."* Montana Heritage: An Anthology of Historical Essays (Helena, Mont.: Montana Historical Society Press, 1992), p. 140.

11 Malone et al. Chapter 9. The whole sordid, sometimes humorous and always confusing story of the "Copper Wars" has been told in every way and by observations from every viewpoint. This baffling behavior influenced and continues to affect the State of Montana.

12 Nolan had been offered and refused $100,000 on behalf of Wellcome. As a result Wellcome was disbarred and disappeared from public life, and Clark had resigned his nomination before a vote could be taken.

13 Lord, pp. 180-205.

14 Jere Murphy, *Comical History. . . .* This is an oft-quoted book and one that has influenced historians who followed. It is a story of greed and avarice written by the former editor (1904) of the *Butte Intermountain*, a paper controlled by the corporate forces Murphy opposes. For more information and a critical look at Murphy's scathing hyperbole see Richard Roeder's article

Footnotes

"Who Was Jerre Murphy?" in the *Montana Academy of Sciences Journal,* 26 (1966): 82-86.

15 Richard White, *"It's Your Misfortune and None of My Own" A History of the American West* (Norman and London: University of Oklahoma Press, 1991), pp. 175-77, 186-87.

16 White, pp. 222-27.

17 White, p. 230.

18 An organization formed in 1905 by union leaders, socialists, and radicals. The group was militant and its members came to be known as "Wobblies." The IWW denounced capitalism and favored a worker dominated cooperative commonwealth. John D. Buenker and Edward R. Kantowicz, *Historical Dictionary of the Progressive Era,* 1890-1920 (New York, Westport, Connecticut and London: Greenwood Press), p. 217.

19 David M. Kennedy, Editor, *Progressivism, The Critical Issues* (Boston: Little, Brown and Company, 1971), p. 166. Quoted from Otto J. Graham, Jr., *"Progressivism and the New Deal."*

20 Kennedy, p. 166. Quoted from Otto L. Graham, Jr., *"Progressivism and the New Deal."*

21 K. Ross Toole, *Montana, An Uncommon Land* (Norman: University of Oklahoma Press, 1959), p. 211.

22 Kennedy, p. vii.

23 Charles Greenfield reminiscence, File 876a, Merrill G. Burlingame Special Collections, Montana State University Libraries, Bozeman, Montana.

24 Letter from Mary O'Neill to WDR, November 18, 1917, in Wellington D. Rankin papers, AC 85-17, Montana Historical Society archives, Helena, Montana.

25 Greenfield reminiscence.

26 Loble interview.

27 Ronhovde interviews.

28 Greenfield.

29 Ibid.

30 Torn letter from "Elizabeth" to WDR in Wellington Rankin papers, AC 85-17, Montana Historical Society archives, Helena, Montana.

31 Buenker and Kantowicz, p. 116.

32 Sanders, *A History of Montana,* Vol. 2, pp. 1280-81.

33 Malone et al., pp. 251-52.

Chapter 4 • Jeannette

1   Giles, pp. 24-25.

2   Rostad.

3   Virginia Ronhovde interviews.

4   In 1972 she addressed the combined House and Senate during Montana's Constitutional Convention. At this time the "Lady from Montana" was over ninety and, according to Jim Moore, a state senator who heard her then, she was still powerful. He said, "I had never agreed with her politically but never was I more moved by an oration than I was on that occasion."

5   Harris, Chapter 3. See also, Dave Walter, "Jeannette Rankin Rocks the House," *The Independent Record*, Thursday, January 28, 1999.

6   Harris, Chapter 3.

7   Ibid.

8   Smith, p. 106.

9   Giles, p. 70.

10   Giles, p. 71

11   Harris, p. 84.

12   W.D. Rankin. Interview by John Board taped interview, University of Wyoming, March 23, 1964.

13   Giles, p. 71.

14   Smith, p. 108.

15   Giles, p. 76.

16   *Broadwater Bygones* (Townsend, Mont.: Broadwater County Historical Society, 1977).

17   Giles, p. 86.

18   Giles, pp. 79-80.

19   Board interview.

20   Ibid.

21   Buenker and Kantowicz, pp. 406-07.

22   Dave Walter," Rebel With a Cause," *Montana* (November-December 1991).

23   Walter, "Rebel. . . "

24   Board interview.

25   Ibid.

26   Smith, p. 124.

27   Giles, p. 95.

Footnotes

28 Ibid.

29 Harris, pp. 120.

30 Board interview.

31 Malone et al., pp.268-70.

32 Morrison et al., pp. 142-44. See also Smith, pp. 132-38.

33 Richard Brown Roeder, *Montana in the Early Years of the Progressive Period*, (A Dissertation in The Department of History, University of Pennsylvania, in Partial Fulfillment of the Requirements for the Degree of Doctor of Philosophy, 1971), p. 99. When Lanstrum died in 1928 he was characterized by a local newspaper as follows," No man in Montana enjoyed politics better than did 'Doc' Lanstrum, and he played it with a zest and finesse exhibited by few Republicans. He delighted in political forays or ambuscades, the grand assault, the landslide or the coup d'etat thrilled him with boyish ardor." Quoted from Raymer, op. Cit., III, 555.

34 Morrison et al., pp. 144-46.

35 Ibid.

36 Malone et al., pp. 280-292. See also, Buencker and Kantowicz, pp. 503-504.

37 Board interview.

Chapter 5 • The Young Lawyer

1 Charles Greenfield reminiscence.

2 Anonymous reminiscence in Rankin Papers, Merrill Burlingame Special Collections, Montana State University Library, Bozeman, Montana.

3 *Townsend Star*, November 4, 1911.

4 *Townsend Star*, November 4, 1911.

5 *Great Falls Tribune*, July 14,1991. This story was still making the rounds in 1959. Ed. Note.

6 Loble interview.

7 *Helena Independent*, September 19, September 20, and October 2, 1917.

8 *Helena Independent*, July 31, 1917.

9 *Helena Independent*, September 19, 22, and 30, 1917; October 2, 1917.

10 Loble interview.

11 *Helena Independent*, May 7, 1920.

12 State ex rel. Rankin v. District Court of First Judician Dist. In and for Lewis and Clark County et al., No. 4641, Supreme Court of Montana, July 9, 1920. According to the record, here is what happened. In May of 1920 Rankin was defending Dr. D. E. Rainville against a charge of murder resulting from an

alleged criminal operation. The trial was in District Judge R. Lee Ward's court. Sometime during the trial the Judge reprimanded Rankin and claimed that in open court before those present that three times the court had to admonish counsel (W. D. Rankin) that the question covered by his question had already been ruled upon by the court.... "and that he (Judge Ward) was interrupted by counsel," and also that Rankin had been, "insulting and impudent." Because of this the court found that counsel (W. D. Rankin) was in contempt. Therefore the Judge stopped the trial and said, "Stand up, Wellington D. Rankin. The court finds you guilty of contempt, and it is.... the sentence of this court that you be confined for 48 hours in the jail.... and that you pay a fine of $250..." With this Rankin was escorted to the Lewis and Clark Jail by the sheriff. Less than two months later the Montana Supreme Court annulled the order. The annullment was based on the following: "An attorney, before being adjudged in contempt should be accorded an opportunity to explain or excuse his contempt and thus purge himself or show that no contempt was intended."

13 *Montana Reports* 58 (1920), p. 283.

14 *Townsend Star*, September 1, 1960.

15 Malone et al, p. 265. Montana officially went "Dry" at the end of 1918. In 1920 prohibition became the "law of the land" nationwide.

16 Helen Johnson, personal communication to author, Bozeman, Montana, 1993.

17 Michael P. Malone, *The Battle for Butte, Mining & Politics on the Northern Frontier* (Helena: Montana Historical Society Press, reprinted 1995), p. 213.

18 See Chapter two. Only three years out of Harvard Law School, in 1912, Rankin presented himself as Montana's Bull Moose candidate for Congress. At the time he was head of the county Progressive committee and a Theodore Roosevelt devotee. Running for the office of U.S. Representative in the first election held by popular vote in the State of Montana. He was defeated soundly. Of a possible 80,000 votes, Rankin received only 6,600.

19 Morrison et al., pp. 59-87.

20 Roeder, p. 1.

21 Morrison et al., p. 76, and pp. 59-87.

22 Buenker and Kantowicz, pp. 116-117.

23 Burlingame, p. 274. Two years later Wheeler won a seat in the U.S. Senate. He managed to continue as Montana's Senator from 1923-1947. During the early part of his political life, Wheeler was known throughout the state as "Bolshevik Burt"; but by 1937–now Senator Wheeler–he led anti-New Deal and pacifist forces against the administration of President Delano Roosevelt and shed the integuments of a "liberal. See also, et al., pp. 161-95.

24 Morrison et al., p. 174.

Footnotes

25 Burton K. Wheeler and Paul F. Healy, *Yankee from the West* (Garden City, New York: Doubleday & Co., Inc, 1962), p. 17.

26 Buenker and Kantowicz, pp. 335-36. The Nonpartisan League was a farmer's organization that began in 1915 in North Dakota. It spread to many western farm states. It called for reform and demanded grain inspection laws and state-owned elevators, mills, and meat packing plants. During World War I the league came under attack as its many Scandinavian and German members were charged with disloyalty and Bolshevism. By the 1920s it was absorbed by the major parties.

27 Arnon Gutfield, *Montana's Agony: Years of War and Hysteria* Gainsville: University of Florida Press, 1979, p. 61. For more information on the Citizen's Council see, Nancy Rice Fritz, *The Montana Council of Defense*, Thesis, Master of Arts, University of Montana, 1966 and Malone et al., pp. 275-79.

28 *Helena Independent*, October 17, 1917.

29 Gutfield, pp. 60-63.

30 Fritz.

31 Gutfield, pp. 40-41.

32 Gutfield, p. 38.

33 Roscoe Pound, *The Formative Era of American Law* (Boston: Little, Brown and Company, 1938), p. 119.

34 Pound, pp. 10-11.

35 Gutfield, p. 38.

36 Morrison et al, p. 175.

37 Wheeler and Healy, p. 188.

38 John Board Interview.

39 Morrison et al., pp. 59-87.

40 Burlingame, *The Montana Frontier*, p. 265. Sam Ford, elected governor in 1940, was the only governor since 1900 to take office without the reported backing of the ACMC. See also, Howard, pp. 244-50.

41 *Missoula Sentinel*, August 10, 1921.

42 Patrick F. Hooks, personal communication to author, June 18, 1993.

43 Hooks.

44 Sanders, pp. 343-44.

45 Karlin.

46 Karlin.

47 Karlin.

48 Karlin.

49 Karlin, Vol I, pp. 106–17.

50 Toole, pp. 265–66.

51 Karlin.

52 Murphy, pp. 1–35.

53 *The Billings Gazette*, "Scourge of the 'rummers'," by Lorna Thackeray, Monday, June 1.

54 Mary Murphy, p. 48.

55 Mary Murphy, pp. 42–64. This chapter called "Habits of Drink" is a comprehensive and important contribution to frontier drinking habits and the prohibition era.

56 Mary Murphy, p. 55.

57 Mary Murphy, p. 56.

58 Letter from Mary E. O'Neill to WDR, January 8, 1921, in Wellington D. Rankin papers, AC 85-17, Montana Historical Society archives, Helena, Montana.

59 *Helena Independent*, January 22, 1921.

60 *Missoula Sentinel*, August 25, 1922.

61 Howard, pp. 194–95.

62 *Helena Independent*, September 28 and 30, 1921; October 1, 1921.

63 *Helena Independent*, January 25, 1922.

64 *Helena Independent*, June 12, 1921.

65 *Helena Independent*, January 9, 1922.

66 *Great Falls Tribune*, February 29 and March 1, 1924.

67 Ibid.

68 Ibid.

69 *Anaconda Standard*, March 30, 1924.

70 Dennis Williams unpublished papers, private collection, Townsend, Montana.

71 Elizabeth Wheeler Colman, *Mrs. Wheeler Goes to Washington* (Helena, Mont.: Falcon Press Publishing Company, Inc., 1989).

72 Colman.

73 Daniel N. Vichorek, *The Hi-Line; Profiles of a Montana Land* (Helena, Mont.: American and World Geographic Publishing, 1993), pp. 103.

74 Vichorek.

75 Ibid.

Chapter 6 • Higher Ambitions

1   Maverick: When Samuel A. Maverick, the pioneer cattleman, refused to brand his calves in 1870, his name became synonymous with the un-marked, or motherless critters roaming the range. This western cattleman's term has come to mean an independent individual that refuses to conform to his group. John Morrison and Catherine Wright Morrison published their book, *Mavericks, The Lives and Battles of Montana's Political Legends* in 1997 and listed as "Mavericks": Joseph K. Toole, Ella Knowles, Joseph M. Dixon, Thomas Walsh, Jeannette Rankin, Burton K. Wheeler, James E. Murray, Mike Mansfield, and Lee Metcalf.

2   C. Wright Mills, *The Power Elite* (New York: Oxford University Press, 1956), 269-361.

3   Morrison et al., pp. 161-95.

4   Ellis Waldron, *An Atlas of Montana Politics since 1864* (Missoula: Montana State University Press, 1958, p. 153. Jeannette won this race with 22,549 votes and George W. Farr came in second with 15,469. She and Farr then faced Democrats John M. Evans and Harry B. Mitchell.

5   Sherry L. Smith, "After the Trail Dust Settled: Reimagining Montana's Indians in the Early 20th Century," Bozeman Trail Conference, July 30, 1999, Bozeman, Montana. See also, Harold G. Merriam, "Sign-Talker With Straight Tongue: Frank Bird Linderman, *Montana, The Magazine of Western History*, Vol. 12, No. 3, p. 2. July 1962; Burlingame and Toole, Vol. I, p. 185, 269-271, and Vol. II, p. 271. Among some of Linderman's best known works are Indian Why Stories 1915, How It Came About Stories 1921, American 1930 (the life of Crow Chief Plenty Coups), and Red Mother 1932 (a biography of the Crow woman Pretty Shield).

6   Charles D. Greenfield, "Letter about Linderman," *Montana, The Magazine of Western History*, Vol. 12, No 4, October 1962, p. 77, and p. 2. According to Charles D. Greenfield of Scratch Gravel, Montana, Dr. O. M. Lanstrum, a leading Republican and newspaper publisher, and Linderman were very close friends. Linderman was not able to get any of his writing published. But Lanstrum through contacts in New York was instrumental in getting Scribners to publish the Indian Why Stories.

7   Morrison et al., 89-122.

8   Burlingame and Toole eds., *A History of Montana* "Progressive Politics in Montana," by Jules Alexander Karlin, 269.

9   *Great Falls Tribune*, July 6, 1966. This statement is from the sixth article in a series by C. T. Sullivan, staff writer for the newspaper, about Rankin's life.

10 Gutfield, p. 51.

11 It is said that he was named after his family doctor.

12 *Great Falls Tribune*, August 31, 1924.

13 Louise Rankin Galt, interview with author, 1995.

14 See Chapter five.

15 *Great Falls Tribune*, December 23, 1925.

16 Ibid.

17 See Chapter five.

18 Tom Stout, "The Montana Governorship," *Great Falls Tribune*, October 15, 1928, p. 4.

19 *Great Falls Tribune*, November 2, 1928.

20 Michael Malone and Richard Roeder, *The Montana Past; An Anthology* (Missoula: University of Montana Press, 1988), p. 288.

21 Ibid. Malone and Roeder.

22 *Helena Independent*, March 24 and 25, 1924.

23 Malone et al., pp. 367-68.

24 *Great Falls Tribune*, September 28, 1928.

25 *Great Falls Tribune*, October 15, 1928.

26 Malone et al.

27 Malone et al. Richard T. Ruetten, "Anaconda Journalism: The End of an Era," *Journalism Quarterly* (Winter 1960). "The Company's" control of the press didn't end until 1959 when they sold their newspapers to Lee Enterprises. By 1929 "the Company" in the state that was called by some "America's largest feudal empire" had acquired eight newspapers with a total circulation greater than all the other dailies in the state, combined.

28 *Great Falls Tribune*, November 2, 1928.

29 Ibid. *Great Falls Tribune*.

30 *Great Falls Tribune*, October 13, 1928; October 28, 1928.

31 Letter from A. B. Cook to WDR, November 1, 1928, in Wellington D. Rankin papers, AC 85-17, Montana Historical Society archives, Helena, Montana.

32 *Great Falls Tribune*, November 8, 1928.

33 Bill Williams, interview with author, Toston, Montana, October 16, 1995.

Chapter 7 • Montana Trial Lawyer

1 White, pp. 464-95. See also Malone et al., pp. 280-13.

2 Dewey Street, banker, Bozeman, Montana, personal interview with author, circa 1972.

3 Howard, pp. 210-24 and 225-35.

Footnotes

4   White, pp. 472-73.

5   Mary Murphy, pp. 200-25.

6   Patrick F. Hooks, personal correspondence with author, June 18, 1993.

7   Wellington D. Rankin papers, AC 85-17, Montana Historical Society archives, Helena, Montana.

8   C. T. Sullivan series of articles on Rankin, Great Falls Tribune, June-July, 1966. Also, Louise Rankin, April 1997 letter. "We were never the sole occupants..." Other businesses rented the first floor.

9   Joseph Gary, interview with author, Bozeman, Montana, October 27, 1993.

10   Louise R. Galt, letter to author, April 1997. The name of the elevator operator was Abdo Kateeb. He was from Lebanon. According to Mrs. Galt the story related here about Abdo and Lester Loble allegedly occurred during the Arab-Israel war, but "it was never substantiated..." Abdo worked for Rankin until he retired about 1965. Also, Judge John Harrison, interview with author, Helena, Montana, 1995.

11   Jack and Lois McGuire, interview with author, White Sulphur Springs, Montana, 1993.

12   Sullivan articles.

13   Harry Brainard, interview with author, Bozeman, Montana, January 29, 1994.

14   *Great Falls Tribune*, June 5, 1966.

15   *Independent Record*, January 4, 1935; State Bar of Montana, Montana Reports, Vol. 98, p. 456.

16   Much of the information about Rankin's most colorful cases comes from a series of articles by C. T. Sullivan that appeared in the *Great Falls Tribune*, June-July 1966.

17   Benjamin Berg, interview with author, Bozeman, Montana, 1995.

18   Louise Galt letter of May 13, 1997. Mrs. Galt writes, "I do not know what Wellington's arrangements were with the companies, but about once a year or so, more or less, the Helena heads of the Telephone Company, or the Power company would phone for an appointment. These men were not collectors, but top officials. They were never kept waiting..."

19   Louise Galt letter of April 1997. Mrs. Galt says that she doubts this story, "...he never had a house in Helena, nor a basement anywhere..."

20   Harrison interview.

21   Berg interview.

22   Rumors say that Acher had a serious problem with alcohol, at times disabling. If true, this was one of his few weaknesses.

23 Berg interview.

24 Wheeler, p. 109.

25 Berg interview.

26 Berg interview.

27 Louise Rankin Galt interview.

28 *Great Falls Tribune*, July 5, 1966, "Rankin Worked Hard, Long on Intriguing Cases," by C. T. Sullivan.

29 L. C. Johnson, interview with author, Billings, Montana, March 29, 1993.

30 Henry Loble, interview with author, Helena, Montana, February 22, 1993.

31 Loble interview.

32 C. T. Sullivan in Great Falls Tribune, June 1966.

33 C. T. Sullivan.

34 Helen Johnson, interview with author, Bozeman, Montana, 1993.

35 Mary Leffingwell, *Diamonds in the Snow* (N.p.: n.d.); Mary Leffingwell, interview with author, July 28, 1994.

36 Leffingwell.

37 Ibid.

38 Ibid.

39 Ibid.

40 Ibid.

41 Howard, pp. 251-74.

42 Howard. Few of the present generation realize the importance of the "Broadwater-Missouri case." The outcome of that court case has affected water use and conservation throughout the United States to the present. A few facts about the great Missouri River system listed by Howard are of interest in understanding the significance of these disagreements. The Missouri River is the fifth longest in the world. The agricultural acreage served by its water is huge; 500,000 square miles. Although its flow can be torrential there are times when it can drop precipitously. And this is what happened in 1937 that resulted in lawsuits. Joseph Kinsey Howard covers the subject succinctly and lucidly.

43 Harry Brainard, interview with author, Bozeman, Montana, January 29, 1994.

44 Montana Supreme Court proceedings, State, v. Simpson, October 1939.

45 Darwin Lehfeldt, interview with author, 1994.

46 Montana Supreme Court proceedings, State v. Simpson, October 1939.

Footnotes

47   Gordon, Lehfeldt, and Morsanny, *Dawn in Golden Valley* (N.p.: 1971), pp. 362-64.

48   C. T. Sullivan in *Great Falls Tribune*, June-July 1966; Supreme Court proceedings, March 5, 1940.

49   *Great Falls Tribune*, June-July, 1966.

50   *Townsend Star*, September 1, 1960.

51   *Townsend Star*, January 18, 1940.

52   *Townsend Star*, January 25, 1940.

53   Dan Sullivan, interview with author, Townsend, Montana, 1993.

54   Montana Supreme Court proceedings, 1939.

55   Bob Davis, interview with author, Seattle, Washington, November 18, 1993.

56   Ibid. Bob Davis.

Chapter 8 • Against War, Against Washington

1   Malone et al., p. 389.

2   *Missoula County Times*, October 22, 1940.

3   *Great Falls Tribune*, September 4, 1940.

4   *Townsend Star*, October 5, 1939.

5   Harris, p. 280.

6   Giles, p. 176.

7   Giles, p. 177.

8   Giles.

9   Ibid. Giles

10 Walter, "Rebel With a Cause."

11 Tape in University of Montana Archives, OH 104-1, Missoula, Montana.

12 Mike Mansfield, personal correspondence with author, May 8, 1995. Senator Mansfield includes in his letter about Jeannette, "...she was one of the great ladies of our country...no one could doubt her integrity....She was an outstanding leader....I think Montana, in Statuary Hall in the Capitol, has in the persons of Jeannette Rankin and Charlie Russell...two of the great characters of our State."

13 Virginia Ronhovde, speech given at the dedication of the Jeannette Rankin statue, Capitol rotunda, Washington, DC, May 1, 1985. Jeannette's peace efforts continued long past her final stint in Congress. She outlived Wellington and died in 1973 at the age of 92. Allegedly when she was asked in her old age what she might do differently, she said, "I'd be meaner."

14 Virginia Ronhovde, interview with author, 1983.

15   Donald E. Spritzer, *Senator James E. Murray and the Limits of Post-war Liberalism* (New York and London: Garland Publishing, Inc., 1985), pp. 56-79.

16   *Great Falls Tribune*, November 2, 1942.

17   *Great Falls Tribune*, November 2, 1942.

18   During the early part of his career he was deemed so liberal that he was labled a Communist.

19   He earned this nickname when after a speech in Dillon when he escaped from his enemies by hiding in a boxcar. This after one of his supporters stabbed another man.

20   Letter, Burton K. Wheeler to Barclay Craighead, October 19, 1942. Barkley Craighead Papers, MC 182, Box 7, Folder 3-5, Montana Historical Society Archives, Helena, Montana.

21   Barkley Craighead papers, MC 182, Montana Historical Society Archives. Both Wheeler and Craighead were sorely chastised by a Helena Caucus of Democrats for supporting Republican Rankin and for his open antagonism to Franklin Roosevelt. A letter written to them in early March 1943 began, "Many of your former supporters," then berated him for sabotaging the Democratic Party and for hostility toward the administration.

22   Loble. Also, Louise R. Galt, letter of April 1997. Quote, "The Pittsburgh Block was never condemned." As previously noted it was taken down along with other buildings for Urban Renewal.

23   Louise R. Galt, letter of April 1997.

24   Letter from Rankin law office, November 27, 1942, in Wellington D. Rankin Papers, AC 85-17, Montana Historical Society archives, Helena, Montana.

Chapter 9 • Labor and Politics

1   Verle Rademacher, interview with author, White Sulphur Springs, Montana, October 1995.

2   *Montana Reports*, Butte Miner's Union No. 1 v Anaconda Copper Mining Company (1942), 113 Mont 406.

3   Louise R. Galt, April, 1997 letter.

4   *Great Falls Tribune*, June 9, 1948.

5   Copied from "A Manuscript History of Montana: Letter, Emmet Glore to Prescott Cookingham," Portland, Oregon, October 1947. The letter was published in a paper called "The Collision of Interests, Politics in the 20th Century." Glore describes Montana's traditional complex of ideological beliefs, interests, and factional loyalties as a tangled network. Probably his attitude is applicable to Montana politics during most of the century.

6   Spritzer, p. 78.

Footnotes

7   John Harrison, interview with author, Helena, Montana, June 1995.

8   Ibid. John Harrison.

9   Letter from Howard C. Gee to Rita Shields, Lewistown, Montana, June 16, 1948, in Wellington D. Rankin papers, AC 85-17, Montana Historical Society archives, Helena. "...after all, in a primary campaign, the voter usually marks his "X" for the candidate that he met during the campaign, and so the candidate that makes the most favorable impression with the majority of voters will be nominated, of course, there are exceptions like the members of Masonic Lodges that vote for Klan candidates and persons, and in this particular election, Mr. Davis apparently has the support of this part of the Masonic Club as well as the active support of the personal enemies, political and otherwise, of Judge Rankin.

10   Ibid.

11   Jules Karlin in Merrill G. Burlingame and K. Ross Toole, A History of Montana (New York: Lewis Publishing Co., n.d.), p. 277.

12   Charles Murray, taped interview with Don Spritzer, University of Montana archives, Missoula, Montana.

13   Ken Byerly, "Daily News Publisher a 'Carpetbagger from Wyoming' Wellington D. Rankin Charges," Lewistown Daily News, clipping, n.d. [1949] in Wellington D. Rankin papers, AC 85-17, Montana Historical Society archives, Helena, Montana.

14   WDR to Associated Press, letter, November 28, 1949, in Wellington D. Rankin papers, AC 85-17, Montana Historical Society archives, Helena, Montana.

15   Ibid. Montana Historical Society archives, Helena, Montana.

16   Joseph Gary, interview with author, Bozeman, Montana, October 27, 1993.

17   Ibid. Joseph Gary

18   John Harrison, interview with author, Helena, Montana, 1995.

19   Gary interview.

20   Louise Replogle Rankin Galt, interview with author, Helena, Montana, March 1993.

21   Lewistown Democrat-News, October 11, 1947; a series of articles in the Great Falls Tribune, June-July 1966, by C. T. Sullivan, deals with Rankin; State vs Joyland, No. 8962, Montana Reports, June 1950; Great Falls Tribune, December 31, 1989; also, assorted copies of undated newspaper articles about Louise Replogle Rankin Galt in her possession.

22   Galt interviews.

23   Helen Johnson, interview with author, Bozeman, Montana, March 1993.

24   See letters from "Marjorie" to WDR in Wellington D. Rankin papers, AC 85-17, Montana Historical Society archives, Helena, Montana.

25 Edna Rankin McKinnon, letter dated December 3, 1957, in posession of author; Louise Rankin Galt, personal correspondence with author, December 4, 1995.

Chapter 10 • Investment Rancher

1 L. C. Johnson of Billings, Montana, personal communication with author, March 29, 1993.

2 Burlingame and Toole, pp. 582-583.

3 Charles Greenfield reminiscenses.

4 Louise R. Galt, letter of April 1997.

5 Greenfield. Also, Louise R. Galt, April 1997 letter. "Floweree Jr., actually died in Helena in 1918. Wellington purchased the ranch from A. T. Hibbard and a Mr. Loeb who held the mortgage on it. Wellington purchased the property in 1927.

6 Greenfield.

7 Virginia Ronhovde, interviews with author, Missoula, Montana, March and June 1993; September 1993. On November 7, 1976, the ranch was declared a National Historic Landmark in a ceremony honoring the memory of Jeannette Rankin. The ten-room ranch house and eighty acres were set aside for the memorial.

8 B. C. (Bud) Snidow, "A. B. Cook, An Unsung Achiever," *Hereford Journal* (July 1987); Robert J. Weitz, unpublished paper, "The Highlights of A. B. Cook, His Ranch, and The Dispersion Sale as Narrated by Axel Holmstrom," Montana State College, February 5, 1953, in A. B. Cook papers, Montana Historical Society, Helena, Montana.

9 Art H. Watson, *Devil Man With a Gun*, 2nd. ed. (White Sulphur Springs, Mont.: Meagher County News, 1967), pp. 80-82. The Dunlavy brothers were long-time bachelors, but late in life Anthony married a woman of his own age—about 70 years old. Legend has it that the fairly well-off bridegroom offered to buy a gift for his bride. When this elderly partner chose a house in Townsend, Anthony reportedly said to her, "My, my, woman, Townsend is no place to raise a family."

10 Weitz.

11 Snidow; Weitz. Also, Will of Andrew B. Cook dated August 2, 1921, and filed December 3, 1928. Helena Abstract and Title Co., Helena, Montana. It is also noted that this will was written, dated, and signed in Andrew B. Cook's own handwriting.

12 Will of Mary A. Cook dated December 20, 1928 and filed February 11, 1929. Helena Abstract and Title Company, Helena, Montana. In addition, Mary A. Cook's will designated that it was her desire that Hervey Cook and Gloria

Cook give Mary Agnes what they think she needs–(furthermore) after the age of thirty-five years of age in case the said Mary Agnes Patenaude is separated, divorced from the said Edward Patenaude–Hervey Cook and Gloria Cook should give Mary Agnes the sum of one hundred dollars a month. She further stipulated that Frank H. Cook is not to marry or have anything to do with Mrs. Pauline Ely.

13   Resignation of Guardian, filed November 2, 1931, Helena Abstract and Title Company, Helena, Montana.

14   Broadwater Historical Museum; Gloria Cook Walker, interview with Grace Averill Hollaway, Townsend, Montana, March 20, 1971. In a letter dated May 24, 1975, to Holloway, Gloria says "Just for the record–I was twelve, not fourteen, when Mother and Daddy died & (Rankin) took over. I had him removed as my guardian when I was fifteen with the help of M. S. Gunn. By then it was too late–all the damage had been done. [He was] a Rasputin if ever there was another. Poor weak Hervey believed in him."

15   District Court of the First Judicial District of the State of Montana in and for the county of Lewis and Clark, Probate Case No. 3186 and the Decree of Final Distribution, # 32310.

16   Louise Galt letter, dated May 13, 1997. Her threatened suit was settled and secured by a first mortgage on the Newlan Creek Ranch that was already mortgaged for $38,142.13.

17   Lena Cook Last Will and Testament, dated March 14, 1933 and filed August 9, 1933. Helena Abstract and Title Company, Helena, Montana.

18   Quit Claim Deed, Document no. 35047 Broadwater County Abstract Company, Townsend, Montana.

19   Broadwater Historical Museum; Gloria Cook Walker, interview with Grace Averill Hollaway, Townsend, Montana, March 20, 1971. In a letter dated July 26, 1993 to the author, Gloria Cook Walker says, "Mr. Rankin acquired the Dunlavy Place, our home and known then as the Home Ranch, for Cook Stock Farms from some deal worked out with my half-brother Frank Hervey Cook. I have no idea how it all came about." A letter to the author from Gloria Cook Walker's daughter, Carol Austin of Hawaii, dated September 9, 1995, delivers a different tone. Austin says that in the memory of her mother, "I am ready to help . . . nail him . . . for what he did to mother . . . a defenseless orphaned child." She believes Rankin's behavior was "dreadful, evil, unethical." Austin's letter is lengthy and vitriolic, especially toward her uncle Hervey, whom she feels was overpowered by Rankin.

20   *Helena Independent*, February 25, 1930. When Rankin was being re-appointed as United States Attorney for the State of Montana, Senator Walsh admitted that he had received a letter of protest complaining of Rankin's actions as attorney for the "Cook estate" and that an early disposition of the protest

was indicated.

21 Mary Alice Upton, interview with the author, Townsend, Montana, August 2, 1993.

22 Helen Johnson, interview with author, Bozeman, Montana, March 29, 1993.

23 Paul Ringling, interview with author, Bozeman, Montana, September 1995. Also, Clarence G. Manuel Estate, The District Court of the First Judicial District of the State of Montana, Estate No. 5195, filed March 24, 1947.

24 Lois and Jack McGuire, interview with author, White Sulphur Springs, Montana, 1993.

25 Louise Rankin Galt provided lists of Rankin holdings in Broadwater County.

26 Ringling & White brochure circa 1925, published by Ringling & White, Inc., 17 East 42nd Street, New York City, in author's files.

27 Ibid.

28 Ivan Doig, *Heart Earth: A Memoir* (New York: Atheneum, 1993).

29 Louise Rankin Galt, interview with author, Helena, Montana, 1993.

30 Ben Berg, Bozeman, Montana, personal communication to author, 1995.

31 Louise R. Galt, April 1997 letter. Concerning this ranch, "...The Smith brothers were John M. Smith and William A. Smith. They incorporated as Smith Bros. in 1890. William A. Smith died in 1897, leaving 3 small children, one of which was William J. Smith."

32 Burlingame and Toole, pp. 308–309; *Great Falls Tribune*, October 17 and December 7, 1958. A story circulated about one of the Miller brothers, who moved to town after the sale of the ranch to Rankin. He and his wife settled quietly into a modest neighborhood, and one morning after a snow, dressed in old coveralls, heavy overshoes, and an old gray cap with earflaps, the way he had dressed on the ranch, he was shoveling snow from the walk in front of his new house. A neighbor lady approached him and asked him if he would shovel her walk, too. The wealthy old rancher said, "Sure." Then she asked, thinking him to be an itinerant handyman, "How much does this lady pay you?" Miller thought for a minute, then said, "Well, she lets me sleep with her."

33 *Great Falls Tribune*.

34 Louise Rankin Galt interview; See letter, Hall and Hall, Inc., Billings, Mont., to WDR, November 26, 1963, in Wellington D. Rankin papers, AC 85-17, Montana Historical Society archives, Helena, Montana.

35 Harry Brainard, interview with author, Bozeman, Montana, January 1994.

36 Tom Lane, interview with author, Livingston, Montana, 1995.

37 Henry Wertheimer, Jr., interview with author, October 1995.

38 Louise Rankin Galt, letter to author, December 4, 1995.

Footnotes

39   Bill Williams, interview with author, Toston, Montana, October 1995.

40   Ibid. Williams now (1996) owns two ranches in Broadwater County.

41   Pete Poirier, interview with author, Townsend, Montana, September 1993.

42   *Great Falls Tribune,* February 24, 1970.

43   C. A. (Cory) Dogterom, Bozeman, personal interview with the author, May 19, 1998.

44   Malone et al., p. 165.

45   Pete Poirier, interview with author, Townsend, Montana, September 1993.

46   Bill Williams interview.

47   Vern Hamre, interview with author, Bozeman, Montana, November 1993 and May 13, 1998. Vern Hamre says that because Rankin's horses were trespassing on Forest Service land it became necessary under regulation T-12 to corral the animals and sell them at public auction. Cloycie Mann, a Forest Technician was in charge of these operations and hired other ranchers from White Sulphur Springs to assist him.

48   Cloyzie Mann, interview with author, Helena, Montana, May 20, 1998.

49   Hamre.

50   Mann

51   Hamre.

52   Ibid.

53   L. C. Johnson, interview with author, Billings, Montana, March 1993.

54   Letter from Bella Dregson, Hogeland, Montana, to WDR, June 12, 1963, in Wellington D. Rankin Papers, AC 85-17, Montana Historical Society archives, Helena.

55   Letter, W. R. Britt, Oilmont, Montana, to WDR, December 12, 1962, in Wellington D. Rankin papers, AC 85-17, Montana Historical Society archives, Helena.

56   Brainard interview.

57   Pete Poirier interview.

58   *Great Falls Tribune,* February 24, 1970.

59   Dolores Munden, personal correspondence with author, July 1995. She said, "I recall inmates being paroled to jobs on the Wellington Rankin ranch…The people involved in the parole system at that time are all deceased…All I can tell you is–yes inmates were paroled there–nothing more.

60   Galt, April 14, 1997 letter. Mrs. Galt says concerning the two parolees, "I am sure no Warden ever contacted us. The parole officers who were assigned the task of finding jobs for them, called personally at the office, and said

they were successful in finding jobs for them, but the jobs would not be open for a few days, and one for 2 or 3 weeks, after their parole date, and could we take them in the meantime...We did so as an accommodation to these young officers..."

61 Pete Poirer interview.

62 L. C. Johnson interview.

63 Ibid.

64 Letter from "Gordon" to "Mom," August 12, 1961, in Wellington D. Rankin papers, AC 85-17, Montana Historical Society archives, Helena.

65 According to local rumor Johnson was only one of a group of rustlers, but the only one prosecuted. He suffered from severe asthma and was released from prison with the aid of friends and relatives.

66 L. C. Johnson interview. The Savage family had come to Montana from Utah in 1942. Their Brahma cattle were said not able to tolerate cold and were wiped out by the winter of 1948-1949. Brand inspector L. C. Johnson rode the ranch after that record-breaking winter and claimed to have seen skeletons of cattle bunched together standing upright; they had died on their feet.

67 *Great Falls Tribune*, February 19, 1964.

68 L. C. Johnson interview; Bob Ellerd, personal communication with author, 1993.

69 *Bozeman Daily Chronicle*, May 15, 1964.

70 Personal interview with Albert Neuman at his ranch near Ingomar, and Dean Neuman by telephone, 1993.

71 *Great Falls Tribune*, February 6, 1968.

72 Letter, Chris D. Miller to WDR, July 12, 1962, in Wellington D. Rankin papers, AC 85-17, Montana Historical Society archives, Helena.

73 *Great Falls Tribune*, October 17, 1958, April 16, 1964, April 17, 1964, April 22, 1964, May 3, 1964, May 9, 1964, May 10, 1964, and October 16, 1964; *Helena Independent Record*, April 30, 1964.

74 Pete Poirier interview.

75 Edwin Miller, interview with Jeff Safford, in Montana Historical Society archives, Helena, Montana.

Chapter 11 • A Last "Hoorah"

1 Virginia Ronhovde, interviews with author, 1993.

2 Ibid.

3 Lane interview.

Footnotes

4   Harry Brainard, interview with author, Bozeman, Montana, 1994.

5   David Dean Everett, "The 1952 Montana Elections: Politics as Usual." A thesis submitted in partial fulfillment of the requirements for the degree of Master of Arts in History, Montana State University, Bozeman, Montana, December, 1976, pp. 49-50.

6   *Great Falls Tribune*, October 9 and October 10, 1952.

7   Everett, pp. 54-55.

8   Ibid.

9   Everett, pp. 52-54.

10 Everett, p. 57.

11 John Harrison, interview with author, Helena, Montana, June 1995.

12 Louise Rankin Galt, interview with author, Helena, Montana, 1993.

13 Jim Moore, interview with author, Bozeman, Montana, 1993.

14 Much of this information comes from the near-daily coverage of the trial throughout June and July 1954 in both the *Independent Record* and the *Great Falls Tribune*.

15 *Independent Record*, July 26, 1951.

16 Joseph Gary, interview with author, Bozeman, Montana, 1993.

17 Fulton Lewis, Jr., in the *Los Angeles Examiner*, April 24, 1958.

18 Correspondence in the personal files of Louise Rankin Galt.

19 Ibid.

20 Mackey interview, Roscoe, Montana, January 1995.

21 Ibid.

22 Louise Rankin Galt interview.

23 Ben Berg, interview with author, Bozeman, Montana, 1993.

24 John Harrison, interview with author, Helena, Montana, 1995.

25 *Great Falls Tribune*, May 29, 1959; *Independent Record*, May 29, 1959.

26 *Great Falls Tribune*, April 18, 1973.

27 Mary Baker Eddy, p. 401.

28 C. T. Sullivan series of articles re: Rankin in the *Great Falls Tribune*, June-July 1966.

29 Sullivan series, *Great Falls Tribune*.

30 Ibid.

31 Harry Brainard, interview with author, Bozeman, Montana, 1994.

32 Ibid.

BIBLIOGRAPHY

Alvin, John A. *Patterns of Montana Towns, 1860–1920* (Missoula: University of Montana, in partial fulfillment of requirements for the degree of Master of Arts, 1972).

Beasley, Norman. *The Cross and the Crown* (New York and Boston: Duell, Sloan and Pearce, Little Brown and Company, 1953).

Bill Williams, interview with author, Toston, Montana, October 16, 1995.

Billings, Gretchen G. "What Do You Think?" *The People's Voice*, June 10, 1966.

Broadwater Bygones (Townsend, Mont.: Broadwater County Historical Society, 1977).

Buenker, John D. and Edward R. Kantowicz. *Historical Dictionary of the Progressive Era, 1890-1920* (New York, Westport, Connecticut and London: Greenwood Press).

Burlingame, Merrill G. and K. Ross Toole, eds. *A History of Montana*, 3 vols. (New York: Lewis Historical Publishing Company, 1957), Vol. 1, pp. 506–507.

Burlingame, Merrill G. *The Montana Frontier*, (Bozeman, Montana, Montana State University: Big Sky Books, 1942 and 1980).

C. T. Sullivan series of articles on Rankin, *Great Falls Tribune*, June–July, 1966.

Colman, Elizabeth Wheeler. *Mrs. Wheeler goes to Washington* (Helena, Mont.: Falcon Press Publishing Company, Inc., 1989).

Cooley, Charles H. *Social Organization, and Human Nature and the Social Order* (Glencoe, Illinois reprinted from Charles Scribner's Sons, 1902, 1909, 1922: The Free Press, 1956).

Dennis Williams unpublished papers, private collection, Townsend, Montana.

Detroit Free Press, May 21, 1961, clipping in SC 1232, Wellington D. Rankin papers, Montana Historical Society archives, Helena, Montana.

Doig, Ivan. *Heart Earth: A Memoir* (New York: Atheneum, 1993).

Dykeman,Wilma. *Too Many People, Too Little Love: Edna Rankin McKinnon, Pioneer for Birth Control* (New York: Holt, Rinehart and Winston, 1974).

Bibliography

Eddy, Mary Baker. *Science and Health with Key to the Scriptures* (Boston: Published by The First Church of Christ, Scientist, Copyrighted and renewed numerous times until 1934).

Emery, Jean M. "Jeannette Rankin, Ahead of Her Time," *Montanan* (Winter 1993).

Emmons, David M. "The Orange and the Green in Montana: A Reconsideration of the Clark–Daly Feuds." *Montana Heritage: An Anthology of Historical Essays* (Helena, Mont.: Montana Historical Society Press, 1992).

Everett, David Dean "The 1952 Montana Elections: Politics as Usual." A thesis submitted in partial fulfillment of the requirements for the degree of Master of Arts in History, Montana State University, Bozeman, Montana, December, 1976.

Fritz, Nancy Rice. *The Montana Council of Defense*, Thesis, Master of Arts, University of Montana, 1966.

Fuller, Wayne E. *The Old Country School: The Story of Rural Education in the Middle West* (Chicago: The University of Chicago Press, 1982).

Giles, Kevin S. *The Flight of the Dove: The Story of Jeannette Rankin* (Beaverton, Ore.: Touchstone Press, 1980).

Gordon, Lehfeldt, and Morsanny. *Dawn in Golden Valley* (N.p.: 1971). March 5, 1940.

Greenfield, Charles. Reminiscence, File 876a, Merrill G. Burlingame Special Collections, Montana State University Libraries, Bozeman, Montana.

Greenfield, Charles D. "Letter about Linderman," *Montana, The Magazine of Western History*, Vol. 12, No 4, October 1962.

Gutfield, Arnon. *Montana's Agony: Years of War and Hysteria* (Gainsville: University of Florida Press, 1979).

Harris, Ted Carlton. *Jeannette Rankin: Suffragist, First Woman Elected to Congress, and Pacifist*, Dissertation, (Athens, Georgia, University of Georgia: 1972).

Harvard Class of 1905 Twenty-Fifth Anniversary Report (Boston: Harvard University Press, 1930).

Hayden, Ferdinand V. *The Great American West* (Bloomington, Ill., 1880), p. 219.

Haines, Aubrey L. "A Voyage to Montana, Part 1," *Montana, The Magazine of Western History*, Vol. 49, No. 4, Winter 1999, p. 16.

Howard, Helen Addison and Dan L. McGrath. *War Chief Joseph* (Caldwell, Idaho: The Caxton Printers, Ltd., 1941), pp. 197–204. Merrill D. Beal, *"I Will Fight No More Forever,"* (Seattle and London: University of Washington

Press, 1963).

Howard, Joseph Kinsey Montana, High, Wide, and Handsome (Lincoln and London: University of Nebraska Press, First Bison Book printing, 1983).

Jeffrey, Julie Roy. *Frontier Women* (New York: Hill and Wang, A division of Farrar, Straus and Giroux, 1979 and 1998).

Karlin, Jules. *Joseph M. Dixon of Montana* (Missoula: University of Montana Publications in History, 1974). (N.p., n.d.).

Kennedy, David M. Editor, *Progressivism, The Critical Issues* (Boston: Little, Brown and Company, 1971).

Kittredge, William. *Montana, The Magazine of Western History*, 36 (Winter 1986).

Kittredge, William, and Annick Smith, Editors. *The Last Best Place*, "Miners and Travelers' Guide" by John Mullan, pp. 219-222.

Koelbel, Lenora. *Missoula the Way It Was, "A Portrait of an Early Western Town."* (Published by Lenora Koelbel, 1972. Library of Congress Card No. 72-92413).

Leeson, Michael A. *History of Montana 1739-1885* (Chicago: Warner, Beers, & Co., 1885).

Leffingwell, Mary. *Diamonds in the Snow* (N.p.: n.d.); Mary Leffingwell, interview with author, July 28, 1994.

Letter, Gary Cooper to Wellington Rankin, October 9, 1946, in SC 1232, Montana Historical Society archives, Helena, Montana.

Lord, Walter. *The Good Years* (New York: Harper Bros., 1960), p. 272.

Malone, Michael P. *The Battle for Butte, Mining & Politics on the Northern Frontier* (Helena: Montana Historical Society Press, reprinted 1995).

Malone, Michael P., Richard Roeder, and William Lang. *Montana: A History of Two Centuries* (Revised edition, Seattle: University of Washington Press, 1991).

Malone, Michael P. *James J. Hill, Empire Builder of the Northwest* (Norman and London: University of Oklahoma Press, 1996).

Malone, Michael and Richard Roeder. *The Montana Past; An Anthology* (Missoula: University of Montana Press, 1988).

McDonald, Michael. Unpublished paper, 1990, in SC 1232, Montana Historical Society Archives, Helena, Montana.

Melcher, Mary. "Women's Matters," Montana, *The Magazine of Western History* (Spring 1991).

Memorial Service, Supreme Court, Helena, Montana, February 21, 1967.

Bibliography

Merriam, H. G. The Golden Valley: Missoula to 1883 (Missoula: Mountain Press Publishing Company, 1997).

Merriam, Harold G. "Sign-Talker With Straight Tongue: Frank Bird Linderman," *Montana, The Magazine of Western History*, Vol. 12, No. 3, p. 2. July 1962

Mills, C. Wright. *The Power Elite* (New York: Oxford University Press, 1956).

Montana Reports, Butte Miner's Union No. 1 v. Anaconda Copper Mining Company (1942), 113 Mont 406.

Montana Supreme Court proceedings, State, v. Simpson, October 1939.

Morrison, John and Catherine Wright Morrison, *Mavericks: The Lives and Battles of Montana's Political Legends* (Moscow, Idaho: University of Idaho Press, 1997).

Murphy, Jerre C. *The Comical History of Montana, A Serious Story for Free People* (San Diego, Calif.: E. L. Schofield).

Murphy, Mary. *Mining Cultures, Men, Women and Leisure in Butte, 1914-41* (Urbana and Chicago: University of Illinois Press, 1997).

Peavy, Linda & Ursula Smith. *Pioneer Women, The Lives of Women on the Frontier*, (New York: Smithmark Publishers, 1996).

Peel, Robert. *Mary Baker Eddy* (Boston: The Christian Science Publishing Society, 1982).

Petrik, Paula. *No Step Backward, Women and Family on the Rocky Mountain Mining Frontier*, Helena, Montana 1865-1900, (Helena: Montana Historical Society Press, 1987).

Pound, Roscoe. *The Formative Era of American Law* (Boston: Little, Brown and Company, 1938).

Rademacher, Verle. Interview with author, White Sulphur Springs, Montana, October 1995.

Ringling & White brochure circa 1925, published by Ringling & White, Inc., 17 East 42nd Street, New York City, in author's files.

Roeder, Richard. "Who Was Jerre Murphy?" in the *Montana Academy of Sciences Journal*, 26 (1966):82-86.

Roeder, Richard Brown. *Montana in the Early Years of the Progressive Period*, (A Dissertation in The Department of History, University of Pennsylvania, in Partial Fulfillment of the Requirements for the Degree of Doctor of Philosophy, 1971)

Ronhovde, Virginia. Speech given at the dedication of the Jeannette Rankin statue, Capitol rotunda, Washington, DC, May 1, 1985.

Rostad, Phil. *Still Going Strong: The Lady From Montana* (N.p., n.d.).

Ruetten, Richard T. "Anaconda Journalism: The End of an Era," *Journalism Quarterly* (Winter 1960).

Sanders, Helen Fitzgerald. *A History of Montana*, 3 vols. (New York: Lewis Historical Publishing Co., 1913.

Schwantes, Carlos A. "The Steamboat and Stagecoach Era in Montana and the Northern West," Montana, *The Magazine of Western History*, Vol. 49, No. 4, Winter 1999.

Small, Lawrence F., Ed. Religion in Montana, Pathways to the Present, (Billings, Montana: Rocky Mountain College in cooperation with SkyHouse Publishers, an imprint of Falcon Press Publishing Company, Inc., Helena, Montana, 1992), 2 Vols.

Smith, Norma. *Fighting Pacifist, Jeannette Rankin and Her Times* (Unpublished and quoted with permission), p. 11.

Smith, Sherry L. "After the Trail Dust Settled: Reimagining Montana's Indians in the Early 20th Century," Bozeman Trail Conference, July 30, 1999, Bozeman, Montana.

Snidow, B. C. (Bud). "A. B. Cook, An Unsung Achiever," *Hereford Journal* (July 1987).

Spritzer, Donald E. *Senator James E. Murray and the Limits of Post-war Liberalism* (New York and London: Garland Publishing, Inc., 1985).

State ex rel. Rankin v. District Court of First Judician Dist. in and for Lewis and Clark County et al., No. 4641, Supreme Court of Montana, July 9, 1920.

Stevens, Robert. *Law School, Legal Education in America from the 1850s to the 1980s* (Chapel Hill and London: The University of North Carolina Press, 1983).

Stout, Tom. "The Montana Governorship," *Great Falls Tribune*, October 15, 1928

Sutherland, Arthur E. *The Law at Harvard: A History of Ideas and Men, 1817-1967* (Cambridge: The Belknap Press of Harvard University Press, 1967).

Sutherland, Arthur E. *The Law at Harvard: A History of Ideas and Men, 1817-1967* (Cambridge: The Belknap Press of Harvard University Press, 1967).

The Billings Gazette, "Scourge of the 'rummers'," by Lorna Thackeray, Monday, June 12, 1995, Section B.

"The Flight of the Nez Perce," US Depatment of Agriculture, Washington, DC, *Bulletin* R1-95-79.

Toole, K. Ross. *Montana, An Uncommon Land* (Norman: University of Oklahoma Press, 1959).

Trimble,William J. "The Mining Advance into the Inland Empire," Bulletin of the University of Wisconsin, No. 638, History Series, Vol. III, No. 2 (Madison: University of Wisconsin, 1914).

Van West, Carroll. *A Traveler's Companion to Montana History*, (Helena: Montana Historical Society Press, 1986).

Vichorek, Daniel N. *The Hi-Line; Profiles of a Montana Land* (Helena, Mont.: American and World Geographic Publishing, 1993).

"W. D. Rankin More Interesting than Jeannette," *Great Falls Tribune*, July 14, 1991.

Waldron, Ellis. *An Atlas of Montana Politics since 1864* (Missoula: Montana State University Press, 1958).

Walter, Dave. "Rebel With a Cause," *Montana* (November–December 1991).

Walter, Dave. "Jeannette Rankin Rocks the House," *The Independent Record*, Thursday, January 28, 1999.

Watson, Art H. *Devil Man With a Gun, 2nd. ed.* (White Sulphur Springs, Mont.: Meagher County News, 1967).

Weitz, Robert J. Unpublished paper, "The Highlights of A. B. Cook, His Ranch, and The Dispersion Sale as Narrated by Axel Holmstrom," Montana State College, February 5, 1953, in A. B. Cook papers, Montana Historical Society, Helena, Montana.

Wellington D. Rankin papers, AC 85-17, Montana Historical Society archives, Helena, Montana.

West, Elliot. *"Stegner, Storytelling, and Western Identity," Wallace Stegner, Man & Writer*, Charles E. Rankin, Ed., (Albuquerque: University of New Mexico Press, 1996), pp. 61–71.

West, Elliot. *Growing Up With the Country: Childhood on the Far Western Frontier* (Albuquerque: University of New Mexico Press, 1989).

Wheeler, Burton K. and Paul F. Healy. *Yankee from the West* (Garden City, New York: Doubleday & Co., Inc, 1962).

Williams, Martha. "The Grant Creek School," *Montana Journal* (March–April 1993).

White, Richard. *"It's Your Misfortune and None of My Own" A History of the American West* (Norman and London: University of Oklahoma Press, 1991).

INDEX

Index

Index